Praise for

Guerrilla Marketing Goes Green

"In a world filled with shameless sel...
Horowitz and Jay Conrad Levinso...
like the clear, high-content, value-...
integrity they teach in *Guerrilla M*...
I know their ideas can generate hi...

—Bob Bly, master copywriter and ...
  business

"A wonderful combination of gue... ...ing ...ook full of practical
Green marketing tips and firsthand advice from two pros."

—Jacquelyn Ottman, author of *Green Marketing: Opportunity for Innovation*
  (www.greenmarketing.com)

"*Guerrilla Marketing Goes Green* proves marketing and making the world a better place are not mutually exclusive. Jay Conrad Levinson and Shel Horowitz
demonstrate how you can build a better business based on ethical, Green, and
value-centered principles."

—Michael Port, *New York Times* best-selling author of *The Think Big Manifesto*
  (www.MichaelPort.com)

"Green marketing is here for good. This book will show you how to market,
influence others, and resonate with the times. The advice is simple and the
premise is compelling—read this and join the twenty-first century."

—Tim Sanders, author of *Saving the World at Work* and *Love Is the Killer App*
  (www.TimSanders.com)

"One of my Joynerisms goes like this: 'The second best form of marketing
is superb customer service. The first is word of mouth. You don't have one
without the other.' *Guerrilla Marketing Goes Green* shows you step-by-step how
to integrate that kind of thinking into your business. It's not just the *right*
way to do business. It's the *better* way. In retrospect, Jay and Shel should have
named their book *The One and Only Way to Get the Most Profit Possible from
Your Business.*"

—Mark Joyner, #1 best-selling author of *The Irresistible Offer, The Great Formula,* and *Simpleology*

"In Jay Levinson's and Shel Horowitz's world, people do matter. The book
combines the best of marketing and relationship theory with real-world examples and practical advice to create a winning, inspirational package. If we
all adopted their advice to create value for others in everything that we do,
the world would be a better place."

—Melanie Rigney, former editor, *Writer's Digest* magazine/Editorial Director,
  Writer's Digest trade books

"*Guerrilla Marketing Goes Green* is a clear call to action and a magnificent mandate for the rewards of our better nature. Jay Conrad Levinson and Shel Horowitz enlighten you with a bright new world and give you a clear manifesto for feeling good about yourself as you reap bigger profits and create a better, more ethical place in which to live and work. This book will *impact*!"

—Ken McArthur, best-selling author of *Impact: How to Get Noticed, Motivate Millions and Make a Difference in a Noisy World*, and founder of jvAlertLive.com

"As consumers use their own guerrilla techniques to hold companies accountable, *Guerrilla Marketing Goes Green* levels the playing field. It is a playbook for companies that want to succeed in a world where integrity and transparency trump slick slogans. This is a gem that should be required reading—not just for so-called Green marketers, but for any marketer who wants to succeed in today's economy, and tomorrow's."

—Joel Makower, Executive Editor, GreenBiz.com, and author of *Strategies for the Green Economy*

"Jay Levinson and Shel Horowitz have always been known for their nothing-held-back, nontraditional, straight-shooting, and creative solutions to some of the most perplexing problems that plague entrepreneurs today. They're not just authors, they're entrepreneurs, so they know from where they speak!"

—Azriela Jaffe, journalist, college English professor, and author of 15 books

"Creating socially responsible businesses not only is a good thing to do, but it will also give your company a unique competitive advantage. And *Guerrilla Marketing Goes Green* shows you how to do that. This book will give you dozens of new and fresh Green ideas about how to not only market your business' commitment to responsibility."

—David Frey, author of *The Small Business Marketing Bible*, and President, MarketingBestPractices.com

"An exceptional and well-researched book that is totally in line with the way I have done business in the past 35 years. I urge every business owner, every speaker, and every serious student of marketing or psychology to buy it."

—Tom Antion, small business Internet marketing expert

"When I was writing the e-book manifesto, 'The Next Evolution of Business,' I researched the ways that ethical businesses were outearning their greedy competitors: a powerful reason to be the good guy that cannot be ignored. Jay Conrad Levinson and Shel Horowitz are absolutely right to point out how ethical, eco-friendly businesses can actually gain the advantage and create massive ethical success. As an entrepreneurship strategist and speaker, I'm proud to be an ethical business owner who puts people before profits. *Guerrilla Marketing Goes Green* shows you how you can be one, too."

—Stefanie Hartman, "The Entrepreneur's Best Friend" (www.stefaniehartman.com/manifesto)

"This book should be required reading, not only in the hallowed halls of corporate America or in the MBA classes at top universities, but by everyone, everywhere. *Guerrilla Marketing Goes Green* takes us on a journey of responsibility, values, and hope and shows us, in a simple yet profound manner, that we have an unprecedented opportunity and sacred duty to leave this world a much better place than we found it. Future generations will be grateful that Jay Conrad Levinson and Shel Horowitz were courageous enough to share such important information with us."

—John Harricharan, award-winning author of the best seller, *When You Can Walk on Water, Take the Boat*

"In the aftermath of the Enron, Global Crossing, and WorldCom disasters, no message could be more timely than Jay Conrad Levinson and Shel Horowitz's. In the long run, only an ethical approach to marketing works."

—Al Ries, author of several best-selling marketing books

"Jay Levinson and Shel Horowitz have got it right. No business can go it alone today. There's far more to gain by teaming up with competitors than by ignoring their existence or bad-mouthing them. The bigger the competitor you team up with, the greater the chance that you'll end up with some of the business they can't handle. There is a halo effect from hanging around with the best people in your field. Try it!"

—B. L. Ochman, Internet marketing strategist and publisher, What's Next Blog (http://whatnsextblog.com)

"Do you want your ideal prospects seeking you out, willingly listening to your sales presentation, and talking themselves into doing business with you? Or would you rather keep shouting into the noisy bedlam that today's world of conventional marketing has become?

Shel Horowitz has teamed up with Jay Conrad Levinson to create a masterpiece. *Guerrilla Marketing Goes Green* is a guidebook on ethical marketing, from two experts with the highest standards and values in the industry.

To many business owners, values, trust, morals, integrity, and ethics are little more than buzzwords. Shel and Jay show how they can become cornerstones holding up your business—and ensuring survival in tough times.

The Golden Rule was never better illustrated than in this exquisite guide on value and ethics in business today. And learning about the Magic Triangle of quality, integrity, and honesty will completely revamp and revolutionize the way you think about business success.

Today, value addition involves tapping into a global trend toward embracing Green practices that preserve natural resources. Discover how to marry 'Green' to 'marketing' in this interesting, insightful, and intensely thought-provoking book.

In the end, this is not merely a book about business tactics, but one that's about mind-set change and adopting a philosophy of abundance, generosity, and compassion toward your audience—creating a business that fulfills needs and adds value."

—Dr. Mani Sivasubramanian, author of *Think, Write & Retire* (www.ThinkWriteRetire.com)

"This book is a remarkable breath of fresh air on how to perfect the better way. It offers a practical method for building profitable relationships in an often noisy, confused world.

Repeatedly and in different ways throughout, this book actually demonstrates, with a generous mix of insight and proven examples, how dog-eat-dog marketing simply isn't necessary; how ethical marketing is not only easier to implement but far more effective; how honesty, integrity, trust, and quality are natural partners that are more likely to lead to long-term growth, with minimal effort and less waste; how by applying Green thinking and treading more lightly on the Earth we can bring unexpected and richer rewards; and more, much more!

That's why, without doubt, *Guerrilla Marketing Goes Green: Winning Strategies to Improve Your Profits and Your Planet*, by Jay Conrad Levinson and Shel Horowitz, gets my highest recommendation. It's an excellent desktop reference resource that can help keep you grounded and focused in the right direction, especially in times of doubt, turmoil, and massive change."

—Brian Austin, MISTC (www.InternetTIPS.com)

"The tools that wire the social web are perfect for driving interest and action around sustainability. Jay Levinson and Shel Horowitz have a clever blend of ideas, recipes, and thoughts for the future. Their ideas might just become your blueprint, if you want to see the successful greening of the world."

—Chris Brogan, co-author of *Trust Agents* (www.chrisbrogan.com)

"Combining a strong emphasis on environmental responsibility with a powerful grounding in business ethics, Levinson and Horowitz provide an amazingly useful and powerful success toolkit for turning your values into business value. As Jay and Shel emphasize all along in their brilliant book, always remember that you help the world best when you're helping others to change. And the way you do that is by basing your business on a solid foundation of three principles: quality, integrity, and honesty:

Quality: Provide the best value you can.

Integrity: Run your business in alignment with your core values; don't try to be something you're not.

Honesty: Value the truth and be eager to share it with your prospects and customers.

As the founder of the International Network of Social Entrepreneurs (INSE), the world's largest online community of socially and environmentally conscious entrepreneurs, with 8,800+ members on five continents, I will eagerly recommend it."

—Christophe Poizat, founder/president and CEO of International Network of Social Entrepreneurs, Inc. (http://newentrepreneurship.com)

"Must you be ruthless in your quest for profits to be a successful business owner? Shel Horowitz and Jay Conrad Levinson explain, through examples, personal experience, and great advice, how to be highly successful and still sleep at night. *Guerrilla Marketing Goes Green* is a jewel of a book."

—Lorilyn Bailey, CEO, NewsBuzz.com

"When it comes to finding your voice online or offline, it takes much more than transparency and authenticity. It takes connectivity and inspiration. Jay and Shel are no strangers to helping brands and entrepreneurs build creative and effective channels to reach and attract customers. Now they're helping businesses increase profitability through Green and eco-friendly strategies and services that also benefit our environment. Go Green or go home!"

—Brian Solis, authority on emerging media, blogger at PR 2.0, and co-author of *Putting the Public Back in Public Relations* and *Now Is Gone*

"You are the way you are for a reason. Ever wondered why you're in the business you're in? Why you're interested in the things you do? It's because you have a unique place in the world—one that nobody else can take, not even your closest competitor!

Jay Levinson and Shel Horowitz have a knack for giving the reader useful tools and comprehensive understanding. They write about what they know, and what they know—firsthand, from their own passions and everyday practice—is how to market goods, services, ideas, and perspectives. Their marketing is always lean but not mean, face to face without being in your face, and more memorable than that of the competitor, who spends too much casting wasted seed on unprepared soil. The marketeer who wants to succeed without losing identity and integrity will learn a lot from what Shel Horowitz and Jay Conrad Levinson have to share."

—Ira Bryck, Director, University of Massachusetts Family Business Center

"As a marketing consultant, copywriter, and merchandiser, I know firsthand (1) that a profitable long-term business hinges on strong customer relationships and repeat business, and (2) how much harder it is to develop a new customer than to please an existing one. Jay Conrad Levinson and Shel Horowitz's innovative new book, *Guerrilla Marketing Goes Green*, takes this concept well beyond customer satisfaction. Jay and Shel show you *how* to build mutually beneficial and profitable relationships not only with customers, but with employees, suppliers, and even competitors. This partnership approach is both powerful and profitable. A terrific and long-overdue book."

—Eric Gelb, MBA, CPA, author of *Book Promotion Made Easy* and editor of *Publishing Gold* e-zine

"Very wise words from very wise men. Shel and Jay are seasoned marketing pros who not only talk the talk, but walk the walk of principled profit. Their brilliance shines through and their methods will not only help you to make lots of money, but to feel great while doing so. And that, in essence, is free enterprise—that the money you make is directly proportional to how many people you serve and how well you serve them.

Follow the advice of *Guerrilla Marketing Goes Green*. Your current customers, your new customers, and your bank account will be richer for it."

—Bob Burg, author of *Endless Referrals* and co-author of *The Go-Giver*

"*Guerrilla Marketing Goes Green* is a course in marketing for mensches. Stop wallowing in the sleazy world of big business and learn how doing the right thing will actually improve your bottom line! *Guerrilla Marketing Goes Green* is the wave of the future. Books on ethical marketing, like this one, are sorely needed in today's world. Jay Conrad Levinson and Shel Horowitz's *Guerrilla Marketing Goes Green* is a winner—and one of the best books on the topic of ethical marketing that I've seen. Buy it for your CEO."

—Fern Reiss, Director, AssociationofWriters.com

"The essential key to marketing is making friends and creating relationships. Shel Horowitz is my friend (as well as my competitor). I wish him and Jay well. This book is a must-read for anyone who wants to understand the new way of doing business and doing it well."

—John Kremer, author of *1001 Ways to Market Your Books*

"*Guerrilla Marketing Goes Green* dismisses quick-buck marketing strategies and presents the real secret for succeeding in today's increasingly cynical marketplace: establishing long-term client and customer relationships built on trust, integrity, and reciprocity."

—Steven Van Yoder, author of *Get Slightly Famous*

"Jay Conrad Levinson and Shel Horowitz's marketing savvy—encapsulated within the confines of this content-rich book—is the entrepreneur's best friend and companion when it comes to taking action steps to fame."

—Marisa D'Vari, President, Deg.Com Communications, and author of *Building Buzz*

"PR Leads grew to a six-figure company in less than 12 months by following ethical marketing practices, working with competitors, and following the other valuable concepts outlined in this indispensable book—and you can, too!"

—Dan Janal, founder, PR Leads

"The kings of frugal bootstrap marketing have made the case for putting people first. Which people? Clients. Prospects. The people you do business with.

Business in this cyber-age, when computers talk to databases, 'bots' make lots of decisions, and 'intelligent' machines are supposedly taking the place of thinking people, Jay Levinson and Shel Horowitz remind us that it's all about people. All about relationships. All about people dealing with people.

But that's just the beginning. Conventional marketing wisdom (how's that for an oxymoron?) says that critical mass requires seven impressions within anything from 18 months to just two weeks (depending on your product). But Shel and Jay place that hoary old shibboleth in its place—every single marketing impression can be the one that motivates the prospect to reach for that checkbook!

But that's not all—far from it. For example, forget about zero-sum marketing—you can win *and* your competitor can win. In fact, Shel and Jay show you how, if you do it right, you can even turn your competitors into allies. Talk about radical!

And in example after example, radical notion after radical notion, Jay and Shel don't just make the assertion about something that challenges everything we thought we knew about marketing—they give readers chapter-and-verse examples that make the case for one simple concept after another that . . . well, could just revolutionize everything.

As a longtime reader of both Jay Conrad Levinson's and Shel Horowitz's previous books, I have to keep wondering why I'm surprised to see such a remarkable collection of wisdom-busting innovative ideas, all in one place. The answer is simple: Their slap-on-the-side-of-the-head ideas are so at odds with what you learned in marketing school (or in the marketing school of hard knocks) that they always surprise, always reward. They always give you more than you paid for, more than you expected . . . *but never* more than you really need to know in order to succeed."

—Ned Barnett, APR, CEO, Barnett Marketing Communications, and author of
   nine books on PR, advertising, and marketing

"In today's climate of corporate scandal and public cynicism, Jay Conrad Levinson and Shel Horowitz provide a deep breath of fresh air. They show, on every page, that not only is it possible to succeed by appealing to the good side of human nature, but the resulting success is easier to achieve and more satisfying, far outdistancing the outcome of take-the-money-and-run approaches. People need to know that doing the right thing not only feels good, it works. This book communicates that message without preaching it.

Levinson and Horowitz's well-documented real-life examples provide a framework for ethical, successful marketing. The book is well written, so it's easy to read, not something that can be said of many such books. *Guerrilla Marketing Goes Green* should be required reading in every marketing class."

—Mary Westheimer, Founding President, Bookzone.com

"It's about time someone wrote a book about the way things *really* work at the values and ethics level in the marketplace. Yes, there are scandals and scoundrels in business. But they're truly in the minority. Because the people who last . . . the people with whom others most want to do business . . . the people who set the pace for the rest . . . are quietly and consistently principled individuals operating in a basically decent way. This book spells out what those people are doing and why it's to your advantage to follow their lead."

—David Garfinkel, publisher, World Copywriting Blog,
   www.worldcopyblog.com

"Do you believe that marketing means doing anything to get the sale and do in your competition? Shel Horowitz and Jay Conrad Levinson disagree, and in this book they show how putting people first can make you a marketing success.

Guerrilla Marketing Goes Green says that nice guys don't finish last. Honesty, integrity, and quality are keys to building a successful business with repeat customers. According to Shel and Jay, 'Too many businesses see marketing as a weapon of war. They think that to succeed, they have to climb over their competitors, fool their customers, and herd their employees into constricted conformity. We think that's just plain wrong.'

Form partnerships with customers, employees, suppliers, and even your competitors. They will become a marketing force for you. Take on customers you can serve well, network and form alliances with complementary companies and competitors, be honest in your copywriting and advertising, and treat those you deal with the way you would like to be treated.

Jay Conrad Levinson and Shel Horowitz are highly respected copywriters and marketing experts, and both the how-to and the philosophy in this book make it clear why."

—Cathy Stucker, IdeaLady.com

"This quotation particularly caught my eye: 'Create value for others in everything you do. . . . You help yourself best when you're helping others.'

That captures so succinctly my hopes for Gifts from the Heart. I wanted to create a book that had something new to say, and help fund-raisers help themselves while we met our own objectives for the cancer society and while helping readers create a more caring holiday.

I think our vision, which you sum up so beautifully, is the real reason that we have been able to sell 17,000 copies without a distributor or marketing budget. One of the unanticipated joys of this project, however, has been meeting customers who have become friends. I have pen pals all over North America, who forward news clippings and articles about people contributing in positive ways. I never expected that at all!

You are absolutely right when you tell readers to develop good customer relations. And not just because you or I want to sell them something, but because we are increasingly in need of that connection in what seems to be a less friendly world."

—Virginia Brucker (www.webelieve.ca)

"This is a refreshing, wonderful, and practical book. Jay Conrad Levinson and Shel Horowitz tell you that integrity is not naïveté and that you can stand up for what you believe in and still make a profit. I'd like to thank the authors. Bravo!"

—Jeffrey Eisenberg, *New York Times* best-selling co-author of *Waiting for Your Cat to Bark*, *Call to Action*, and other books

"Each page of *Guerrilla Marketing Goes Green* draws you toward the next. Jay Conrad Levinson and Shel Horowitz masterfully blend conversational style with logical flow and unparalleled research. Their ethical, people-first message is the new paradigm in marketing. I'll be referring to this book for years to come. Highly recommended."

—Lee Godden, author of *ZenWise Selling* (www.DrivenToSell.com)

"True win-win marketing is the ideal everyone in business should strive for. Jay Conrad Levinson and Shel Horowitz's *Guerrilla Marketing Goes Green* is the definitive book on the art and practice of win-win marketing. They show you not only how to create marketing that helps your own business, but how helping another business simply passes around success that enhances every business or situation it touches.

Levinson and Horowitz not only practice what they preach, they live it. With true examples, they show how the system works for just about every business situation imaginable. They show that even helping your competition can help you help your own business.

Practicing these principles bodes well for business, as well as in our personal lives. What a wonderful world this could be!

Well recommended for anyone, not just businesspeople, looking to make a positive mark in this world."

—Kitty Werner, author, *The Savvy Woman's Guide to Owning a Home* and *How to Care For, Maintain and Improve Your Home*

"Jay Conrad Levinson and Shel Horowitz are both the Johnny Appleseed and the Thomas Paine of ethical marketing. Their book, *Guerrilla Marketing Goes Green*, is the *Common Sense* for the twenty-first century for those of us trying to make a better world for ourselves, our families, our communities, and indeed the world. They show, step-by-step, how I can help myself and my business by helping every customer, client, and contact around me."

—TJ Walker, Media Training Worldwide (www.mediatrainingworldwide.com)

"I like not only what Shel and Jay have to write, but also how they write as well, and can recommend this book wholeheartedly. Judging from the testimonials—including many from well-known people—everyone likes this book. This is more than a 'be nice' or 'feel good' book (although it did make me feel good about being nice). It contains practical business advice."

—Ted Demopoulos, co-author, *Blogging for Business* (www.demop.com)

"This is *the* book for folks who think they hate sleazy marketing, but need sales. You'll learn how to make more sales, do good for the environment and the world, and feel good about yourself and your efforts all at the same time. It gives specific, practical examples of people and organizations that are doing the things discussed, and talks about ways to adapt the techniques to a variety of situations.

Don't sabotage your company or your career by avoiding marketing. Buy this book and follow its advice. Not only will you feel terrific about what you're doing, but you'll also help the world, your customers, your company, and yourself. I've been using Shel's techniques, with great results, since his earlier book, *Principled Profit*. And if it works for me, it will work for anyone!"

—Marion Gropen, CEO, Gropen Associates, Inc., and moderator of two publishing-industry discussion lists

"I'm impressed with this thoughtful approach to marketing. Every entrepreneur and marketer should read Jay and Shel's book *Guerrilla Marketing Goes Green*."

—Patrick Byers, CEO, Outsource Marketing, Seattle/Responsible Marketing blog (http://responsiblemarketing.com)

"This is *the* book for those of us looking for hard data to support our intuition. In case after case, Jay and Shel remind readers that yes, there is a better way to do business. Yes, it really works. And yes, each of us can make a difference."

—Susan Tull, Vice President of Marketing, BlueHornet.com

"*Guerrilla Marketing Goes Green* not only backs up everything it says with well-established facts and figures so you finish the book thoroughly convinced Jay and Shel are telling you the absolute truth, it also opens your mind to endless possibilities around marketing your business. Even for the most veteran of marketers, Jay and Shel's collaboration will put more money in your pocket and a new spin on your business while making the world a better place."

—Jan Janzen, author of *Devil with a Briefcase: 101 Success Secrets for the Spiritual Entrepreneur and Getting Off the Merry-Go-Round: How to Create the Life You Want Without the Fear, Doubt and Guilt*, www.janjanzen.com

"As a marketing consultant, copywriter and merchandiser, I know firsthand, (1) that a profitable long-term business hinges on strong customer relationships and repeat business, and (2) how much harder it is to develop a new customer than to please an existing one. Jay Conrad Levinson and Shel Horowitz's innovative new book, *Guerrilla Marketing Goes Green*, takes this concept well beyond customer satisfaction. Jay and Shel show you HOW to build mutually beneficial and profitable relationships not only with customers, but with employees, suppliers, and even competitors. This partnership approach is both powerful and profitable. A terrific and long-overdue book."

—Eric Gelb, MBA & CPA, author, *Book Promotion Made Easy* and editor, Publishing Gold E-zine

"Jay Levinson and Shel Horowitz have always been known for their nothing held back, non-traditional, straight-shooting, and creative solutions to some of the most perplexing problems that plague entrepreneurs today. They're not just authors; they're entrepreneurs, so they know from where they speak!"

—Azriela Jaffe, journalist, college English professor, and author of fifteen books

"Why are mailboxes and e-mail boxes full of unwanted sales pitches? Packaging needs to be less wasteful-why are landfills full of old packaging? Why is it necessary to damage the environment in order to make energy-inefficient products that will break and be disposed of in a year or two? This book is the first to really tackle green marketing head on, and it's more than high time. I wholeheartedly recommend it as bedtime reading for every executive, marketer, and consumer. We're all part of the green marketing solution if we choose to be!"

—Alex Hiam, author, *Marketing For Dummies, 3rd Edition*, http://www.insightsformarketing.com

---

Please visit http://www.guerrillamarketinggoesgreen.com to read the rest of the endorsements for this life-changing book. Space did not permit printing all of them here.

GUERRILLA MARKETING GOES GREEN

Winning Strategies to Improve Your Profits and Your Planet

JAY CONRAD LEVINSON
and SHEL HOROWITZ

WILEY

John Wiley & Sons, Inc.

ISBN 978-0-470-40951-0

Printed in the United States of America.

10   9   8   7   6   5   4   3   2   1

I dedicate this book to Al Gore, who has put his heart where his mind is.

—JAY CONRAD LEVINSON

To those of my generation but not of my household: Helen Horowitz and Joe Clayman, Jeanne Horowitz, Michael Friedman and Susan Hasti, Daniel Friedman

—SHEL HOROWITZ

Contents

PART III HANDS-ON WITH COOPERATIVE, PEOPLE-CENTERED MARKETING

Foreword by
Stephen M. R. Covey

It's been my privilege to spend the last several years focusing on the issues and opportunities of trust, both in business and in life. As a result of this exploration, I have come to this simple conclusion: Trust is a two-part equation. If you want the benefit of high trust relationships, you need to inspire confidence that you're a person or business grounded in integrity, that you always want to do the right thing (*character*). But you also need to inspire confidence that you have the skill to make it happen (*competence*). Both halves of this trust equation are essential to business success.

That's why I'm so delighted to lend my endorsement to this wonderful book.

Since the ethics scandals of the early 2000s, many business schools have started to incorporate ethics into their curricula. While this is a good trend, too often, they're only looking at doing the right thing from the moral—or character—point of view.

But the practical—or competence—part is often missing. Yes, you want to build trust through your integrity, but you also want to build profits. The reality is this: when trust goes up, speed will go up (things can be done faster) and costs will come down (things will cost you less). This is the dividend of high trust. But you can't earn that dividend without competence as well as character.

So in today's world, you want your business to be as eco-friendly as possible. Part of the 21st century ethical code is the commitment to Green practices, which demonstrates the principle of contribution that helps build societal trust. You also want to use your eco-friendliness to create swarms of eager customers, all excited to do business with you. As you develop the character and competence to create that excitement, your customers reciprocate that trust, and you both reap the rewards: business is faster, easier and costs less. You accomplish more. *And* your customers refer more business to you!

Guerrilla Marketing Goes Green shows you how to make it happen. This tremendous book is thoroughly grounded in both character and competence. It demonstrates how to build trust based on the commitment to Green practices and also on the specific, doable actions that fulfill that commitment. It will powerfully teach you how to replace old-style intrusive marketing tools with creative and ethical strategies to engage not only your customers but other stakeholders, even your competitors... to convert Green initiatives from expenses into savings or even revenue streams... to create effective win-win partnering relationships with charities whose missions align with yours... and most importantly, to be proud of the person you see in the mirror.

But this book will not only instruct you; it will also delight you. It will be such a relief to you to find proof that "nice guys" of either gender finish first, not last; that the values you hold dear are also of value in the business world; and that not only can you champion earth-centered eco-friendly business practices, but that you can profit handsomely by doing so.

It's an exciting journey, and I'm thrilled to hold the gate open for you as you start down this Green and ethical road, with the Sherpa-like wisdom of Jay and Shel as your guide.

—STEPHEN M.R. COVEY, author of the *New York Times* and #1 Wall Street *Journal* bestseller *The Speed of Trust: The One Thing That Changes Everything*

Preface
Tastes Great *and* Good
for You

It's hard to imagine now, as you start with a fresh organic mesclun salad, savor your beautiful healthy entrée, lick your lips to get the last crumb of that amazing vegan brownie, and wash it all down with a few sips of all-natural premium beer that a few decades ago, if you wanted to dine out, you were told you had to choose between healthy and tasty. Either your plate was full of unappetizing piles of healthy mush, or with something delicious but deadly. But now, the world knows that great food can also be healthy.

Similarly, in marketing, we've been told most of our lives that we had to choose between *value* and *values*. But like the choice between healthy and scrumptious, that's a false choice. It turns out that when we create companies based in core values of Green awareness and high standards of ethics, cooperation, and service, *our marketing actually works better—and costs much less.*

This book is designed to redefine what the business world thinks of as possible, and to show through hundreds of powerful examples that not only can we succeed by basing our business practices in our values but also see that the path of success is noticeably easier.

—SHEL HOROWITZ

Acknowledgments

I owe acknowledgments to many enlightened souls, the most important of whom is co-author Shel Horowitz, who braved the battles of
apathy and ignorance in causing this book to rise from the ashes
and alight in your consciousness and indeed, the consciousness of all
citizens of planet earth, our home sweet home.

—JAY CONRAD LEVINSON

I want to thank (in alphabetical order within each category)...

➤ Those sources who kindly gave permission for me to quote or
reprint large chunks of their material: Eric Anderson, Kare Ander-
son, Stefan Apse and Susan Witt of the E. F. Schumacher Society,
Bill Baue of CSRWire, Christopher Bauer, Mary Boyle of Common
Cause, Bob Burg, Patrick Byers, Melissa Chungfat of Ecopreneurist,
Beth Craig of Webcom, Seth Godin, Hazel Henderson, John Kre-
mer, Wendy Kurtz, Amory Lovins, Perry Marshall, Myelita Melton,
Robert Middleton, B. L. Ochman, Jacquelyn Ottman, Jode Roberts
of Ecojustice, John Todd, Al Vital of Fidlar-Doubleday, Barbara
Waugh, and David Wood

➤ Tom Antion, Jeff Eisenberg, and all the people I follow on
Twitter, who pointed me toward additional research relevant to
some of my examples

➤ The more than 50 environmentalists, entrepreneurs, authors,
social media strategists, and modern-day geniuses who lent and
will lend their endorsements to this world-changing book (you're
listed at GuerrillaMarketingGoesGreen.com)

➤ Mark Joyner, for providing the introduction to Matt Holt at
John Wiley & Sons, Inc. that led to this book

➤ Stephen M.R. Covey, for not only graciously agreeing to write the wonderful Foreword, but also being an enthusiastic champion of the book.

➤ Matt Holt, Linda Indig, Shannon Vargo, and Beth Zipko at John Wiley & Sons, Inc., for bringing this project to reality

➤ Randy Bernard, Stacey Kannenberg, and Terry Mollner, for doing their best to hook us up with key influencers

➤ Becca Rhodes, whose research greatly facilitated the resources section (online at GuerrillaMarketingGoesGreen.com)

➤ The many smart and creative people who have added so much to the world's understanding of Green principles, people-centered marketing strategies, and social media in the years since I wrote *Principled Profit*

➤ Jay Conrad Levinson, for being an enthusiastic supporter and a delight to deal with since I first approached him about partnering on this book

➤ Robin MacRostie, for the chart on page 52.

➤ Members of the SmallPub-Civil discussion list on Yahoo-groups, and especially Barbara DesChamps, for helping to resolve a thorny issue with the cover copy.

➤ My wife, novelist D. Dina Friedman, for 30 years of encouragement, constructive criticism, and love

—SHEL HOROWITZ

If You've Already Read
Principled Profit: Marketing That Puts People First

Even though *Guerrilla Marketing Goes Green* is based heavily on Shel's earlier book *Principled Profit: Marketing That Puts People First*, there's a great deal of new material here. In almost every chapter, new examples, new research, and in quite a number of cases, whole sections have been added. The entire Marketing Green chapter is completely new, as are the sections on trust building, social media, reputation management, and so forth. We expect that you will receive substantial value from this book, even though some of it will be familiar.

Introduction: Green Marketing Is a Mandate from Nature

I've believed from the start that marketing is part of evolution. It helps the world go round and is part of mass communications, so it greases the skids of progress inside and outside the mind.

Imagine my delight when I teamed up with Shel and was able to generate the Green ideas that will help evolution, which does not exclude the generating of more greenbacks for your paperless bank account. In fact, that's the whole purpose of this book: to prove that successful Green guerrilla marketing can contribute to your financial well-being *and* the well-being of our entire planet, now and in the future.

There is no choice between Green guerrilla marketing and standard guerrilla marketing. The reality is that the two go hand in hand in a mutual effort toward making the best of both worlds while making each world the best it can be.

When I wrote the first Guerrilla Marketing book in 1984, this was an alien concept. But life has changed since that date. Finally, civilization has caught on to the idea that we can do something about the deteriorating state of the environment and about beautifying our planet. Amazingly, at the same time, you can do your part to beautify your own bottom line.

What we say in this book is not theory. It is a call to action. It is a mandate from nature.

—JAY CONRAD LEVINSON

Part

I

The Way of the Golden Rule

Chapter 1

Because People Matter

People *do* matter. This book shows you how to be a successful marketer while acting ethically. It's about the idea that you don't have to be crooked or mean-spirited to succeed in business. It's about the idea that the success strategies of a business formed in an attitude of abundance and grounded in ethics and cooperation are powerful and long-lasting. They also help you feel good about yourself even while bringing in profits.

Your parents and teachers probably taught you to treat others the way you want to be treated, play fair, and cooperate. This book is about the idea that you can use those principles as a cornerstone of your business and that you can design marketing that not only follows this precept but harnesses its incredible power to bring success and abundance into your life.

Too many businesses see marketing as a weapon of war. They think that to succeed they have to climb over their competitors, fool their customers, and herd their employees into constricted conformity. We think that's just plain wrong.

Marketing is a series of partnerships—of courtships, really. Businesses that succeed with this model understand that they have to woo their customers, just as a suitor woos for the chance to marry. And just as a successful marriage is built on years of mutual communication and meeting each other's needs, successful marketing looks for a deep and long-lasting relationship based on meeting the needs and wants of everyone involved. That means your customers, your employees, your suppliers, and, yes, even your competitors. You can knock someone's socks off on the first date, but if you betray that trust afterward, you become your own biggest obstacle on the road to success.

And just as in a courtship, you want to go as fast as possible but as slow as necessary. The singles scene is littered with the carcasses of relationships that never went anywhere because on the first contact, one person came on too heavy, too fast, or too self-involved. Many business failures result when companies spend too much time crowing about how great they are and forget to listen to their prospects.

Always remember that successful marketing is about how you can add value for the other person. And the most effective way to add value is by developing a long-term positive relationship with a customer, just as it is with romance.

So stay out of marketing divorce court; be trustworthy and add value for the long term. It takes work to achieve a successful, long-lasting marriage, but the rewards are worth it. Similarly, you have to work at a successful long-term relationship with all the other interest groups that interact with your business. It's got to succeed for everybody involved.

Remember, too, that in our Internet era, scandals and problems never go away. In 2009 as we write this, you can still find thousands of articles about business scandals of the past, including a juicy little *Forbes* magazine chart that details the 22 worst U.S. business scandals of 2000 to September 2002.[1]

Just as a romance that's based on false promises and miscommunication is doomed to failure, so business relationships based on greed and backed by false promises aren't going to work over time. But the good news is that if you treat others well, they will become your best marketers. The better you treat others, the more they will want not just to do business with you but to *bring business to you.*

You make your own success by helping others succeed—you succeed without selling your soul. Think about this style of business as a practical, day-to-day expression of the old Golden Rule: Do unto others as you would like others to do unto you—a precept found in every major religion.[2]

Although we believe very strongly in the Golden Rule, this is not a religious book. Rather, it's a book based on a code of ethics. Your ethics might or might not be religiously based; the important thing is that you have an ethical basis for your professional or business behavior.

The modern business world doesn't usually assume that business should be based on ethics. But we do. We'll assume that you're reading this book because you really want to do what's right. But perhaps you've been told for many years that Nice Guys Finish Last, and you aren't sure it's really possible to succeed, thrive, and be profitable while doing the right thing.

We're here to tell you that you *can* succeed and still have a clear conscience. In this book, you'll encounter many success stories that put a practical handle on this philosophy. You'll see that others are doing very well by doing good and that you can, too.

Spend an hour or two with this book, and you may find that you don't have to live in a dog-eat-dog world—and that in fact, when the dogs learn to work together, they can accomplish much more than any of them could on their own. Think of the incredible weight a team of sled dogs can comfortably pull across the snow; no single dog could accomplish that. Thus, when you join forces with others—even those you've been trained to think of as your competitors—truly amazing things can happen.

This is an opinionated and personal book; we make no pretense otherwise. It is based on our combined 80+ years in marketing. We've built thriving decades-old businesses using the principles in this book. And we want you to do at least as well.

■ LESSONS AND ACTIONS

➤ Marketing is like a romance: subtlety works better.

➤ The Golden Rule actually works in business.

➤ Success is not only compatible with ethics, it's easier.

Chapter 2

Basic Concepts

■ THE ROAD TO YOUR SUCCESS: PROVIDING VALUE TO OTHERS

In the business world, we hear a lot about cutthroat competition and gaining advantage over the enemy. In some circles, it seems to be a game to see how best to cheat customers.

These are the concepts of win–lose marketing, and we believe this kind of thinking is a dinosaur. It will not survive.

This book is about Marketing That Puts People First. Most of the time, everyone can win—nobody has to lose. Not only can you succeed in business by doing the right thing with every person and business that interacts with you, but often it's the only way to succeed.

Don't take our word for it. Listen to some experts.

➤ Consumers Avoid Buying from—and Will Put Pressure on—Companies They Perceive to Be Unethical

Long before the current awareness around issues like climate change and fair trade, a study commissioned in 1998 by the UK-based Cooperative Wholesale Services found that 60 percent of retail food customers, even in the absence of an organized boycott, avoided a shop or product they associated with unethical behavior. A 1999 survey of consumers in 23 countries by Environics International, in cooperation with The Prince of Wales Business Leaders Forum and The Conference Board, found that 40 percent of consumers had considered punishing a company based on its social actions, and nearly 20 percent had actually avoided a company's products because of its social actions.[1]

Well beyond the impact of individuals acting alone, trends of shareholder activism and widely publicized boycotts force companies to negotiate from a position of perceived weakness. These have built momentum since the 1950s, when the Montgomery, Alabama, bus boycott organized by Dr. Martin Luther King Jr. and others struck a powerful blow against racial segregation. In 2008 alone, Green America documented 334 social or environmental activist shareholder resolutions on issues ranging from CEO pay to climate change to sustainability reporting. Of these, 139 were negotiated ahead of the vote and withdrawn, in most cases because the companies had agreed to make significant progress.[2]

In one case, a UK-based insurance association and ExxonMobil shareholder actually sent out a press release opposing the reappointment of CEO Lee Raymond on environmental grounds.[3]

If groups like Corporate Accountability International (formerly known as INFACT), the Interfaith Center on Corporate Responsibility, or major labor unions organize shareholder actions or call a boycott, it is not only very bad for the targeted business, but can even bring down governments (e.g., the apartheid regime in South Africa or communism in Poland).

Here is a more recent example:

>...the investor advocacy network launched [in August 2008] to promote an end to forced child labor in the cotton fields of Uzbekistan. The move came in response to media accounts and reports that the world's third largest cotton exporter relies heavily on harvesting by kids as young as 10. A group of socially responsible investors (SRIs) and activist NGOs [nongovernmental organizations] banded together to push the Uzbek government to enforce International Labor Organization child labor conventions—a move supported by four retail trade organizations. "It is our experience that collaborative efforts of investors, non-governmental organizations, trade unions, companies and industry associations can make a difference," said [the Reverend] David Schilling of the Interfaith Center on Corporate Responsibility.[4]

Thus, when your business takes a proactive stance in favor of socially, economically, and environmentally responsible behavior (the so-called triple bottom line) and your marketing brings your position into the public consciousness—you can potentially avoid profit-killing shareholder initiatives and consumer boycotts. You can be seen as a leader, not a Johnny-come-lately forced to the table by threats.

➤ **Consumers Prefer to Buy from Companies That Support Their Social Agenda**

When price and quality are equal, 76 percent of consumers would switch brands or retailers to a company associated with a good cause. Criteria frequently cited by consumers as affecting their purchasing decisions include environmental responsibility, community philanthropy, and avoiding the use of "sweatshop" or child labor.[5]

Interestingly, one study found that the best predictor of whether a person will respond to eco-products even if they're more expensive is not income or education, but current or past contributions to environmental groups.[6]

More recent research shows even greater swings toward social consciousness. As an example, a remarkable November 2008 study by the PR superagency Edelman, long an advocate of trust-building, surveyed 6,000 consumers across 10 countries, and found extremely high numbers for social consciousness:

➤ 68 percent of consumers "would remain loyal to a brand during a recession if it supports a good cause."

➤ 71 percent have donated as much or more time and money to good causes despite the economic downturn.

➤ 42 percent would choose a brand with commitment to a social purpose over design, innovation, or brand loyalty, if price and quality are equal.

➤ 52 percent would recommend a brand that supports a good cause over one that doesn't, and 54 percent would actually promote the product to support the cause.

➤ An astonishing 87 percent feel an obligation to contribute to a better society and environment; 83 percent would change their own consumption habits to help create that better world.

➤ 76 percent prefer to buy from brands that give to worthy causes.[7]

Equally fascinating is a *Washington Post* study that ranked 498 major corporations for social responsibility and compared market performance during the 2008–2009 downturn. Performance among the top-rated companies equaled or surpassed the whole market. But even more remarkably,

> *We called the three companies that ranked lowest on the list—Eastman Chemical, Lockheed Martin, and ExxonMobil—to see what they thought about CSR [corporate social responsibility]. You might think they would agree with [free-market economist Milton] Friedman that a company's first duty is to its shareholders, especially during a downturn. But they turned out to be less interested in talking about the limitations of corporate responsibility than explaining what they were doing to achieve it.[8]*

The article goes on to document the companies' claimed CSR efforts.

This social consciousness seems particularly strong in Generation Y—whose members are just beginning their several decades of active adult consumerism. And Green concepts have clearly entered the public consciousness. A Google search for *global warming* (exact match) plus 2002 yields 5,740,000 hits. By 2008, the results multiply almost fivefold, to 25,100,000. Searching for *climate change* shows similar gains, from 8,180,000 for 2002 to 36,100,000 for 2008.[9]

Business school students are also acutely aware of Green concepts. A fascinating article in *Business Week* documents a strong recent trend among students at top-flight b-schools who do not just care about Green and socially conscious values, but are looking to start entrepreneurial ventures in line with those commitments, such as a solar-powered trash compactor manufacturer, or a retailer positioning itself as "the Whole Foods of hardware."[10]

Many consumers also actively support companies that court business from their ethnic or subculture group. African-Americans control $320.6 billion in discretionary spending; Latino-Americans control $261.2 billion; people with disabilities, $176 billion.[11] A different study estimates gay and lesbian purchasing power at $400 billion.[12]

In the online world, male Americans and Western Europeans who embraced the Internet early are being supplanted by users of color, often female, often from non-Western countries. Women are now a majority of Internet users—and of the 29 million new Internet users that are expected to join the online community by 2011, 54 percent will be Hispanic, African-American, or Asian.[13]

Marketers who ignore this massive demographic shift do so at their peril.

These types of loyalties extend beyond mere demographics—into values:

> *Another growing area of company interest is cause-related marketing, in which companies align with charities or causes in a marketing campaign. Such campaigns have become increasingly common as consumers become more accepting of the concept. For many companies, the question no longer is whether they will engage in cause-related marketing, but which cause to embrace.*[14]

Actually, not only have consumers become more accepting of social and environmental responsibility but they have begun to demand it. Companies that refuse to embrace sustainability values will be left to a world of diminishing markets, falling profits, and increasing lawsuits. More than ever before, today's consumer wants to feel a part of solving the world's pressing problems, from global warming to child toy safety, from treatment of farm workers to getting out from under the thumb of foreign oil.

We see this in the enormous growth of Fair Trade and organic products, the Buy Local movement, and the backlash against highly processed foods with their trans fats and unpronounceable ingredients.

And we see it in the vast stream of social and environmental responsibility initiatives from the world's largest companies—General Electric, Siemens, Boeing, Toyota, Wal-Mart, Dow Chemical, and BP, to name a few—that are not only beginning cost-cutting initiatives based on Green principles but are marketing the heck out of these commitments.[15]

We also see it in the rapid and widespread worldwide adoption by more than 450 key financial institutions, managing assets totaling $18 *trillion*, of the UN's Principles for Responsible Investment, which require signers to consider "environmental, social and corporate governance (ESG) issues within their investment decisions and processes."[16]

We even see it in the growing shift among MBA (Master of Business Administration) programs toward including ethics and sustainability in the core curricula, and in the eagerness of such mainstream organizations as the *Wall Street Journal* and the *Financial Times* to rate corporate social responsibility in their evaluations of business schools.[17]

► **Investors Have Shifted 13 Percent of All Investment Dollars into Socially Responsible Companies**

In November 1999, the Social Investment Forum reported that more than $2 trillion was invested in the United States in funds identified as socially responsible, an increase of 82 percent from 1997 levels. This represents roughly 13 percent of the $16.3 trillion under professional management in the US, or one out of every eight dollars.[18]

And that trend continues to grow. While the percentage of socially screened investment dollars remained constant, by 2007 the actual dollars had reached $2.7 trillion.[19] To put that in perspective, the growth in socially responsible investment about equaled the $700 billion bailout of the U.S. financial industry in the fall of 2008.

And on the private investment side, let's take a look at investment funds set up specifically for socially responsible investing (SRI; in other words, not counting the much broader picture of investments in socially responsible companies through more general funds). The market went from 55 SRI funds in 1995 with $12 billion in assets, to 201 funds managing $179 billion just a decade later.[20]

A related trend, microlending, lets investors seed businesses among the poorest of the poor in developing countries, where a loan of $50 or $100 can be enough to lift a family out of poverty. These small amounts of money can help borrowers achieve some specific business goal that had been out of reach, and a circle of borrowers creates peer pressure to succeed and repay the loan. Even with no collateral, Bangladesh-based microlending pioneer Grameen Bank achieves 99 percent repayment. Popularized by Grameen founder Dr. Muhammad Yunus, the concept has spread to dozens of organizations, such as Kiva.org, Acción, Finca, and many others.[21] Meanwhile, Dr. Yunus, who was awarded the 2006 Nobel Peace Prize for his work, has stated a goal of eliminating poverty by 2030.[22]

It's not at all surprising that socially responsible investing is growing so rapidly. Here's a little secret: Well-managed SRI funds often outperform the market.

► *Socially responsible investment funds continue to demonstrate their ability to match or outperform their full market diversified counterparts. For example, the Domini 400 has outperformed the S&P 500, with 11.75 percent and 11.21 percent annualized returns from socially responsible investments respectively.*

➤ *In* Corporate Knights *magazine's three year survey, 75 percent of the 54 Canadian socially responsible funds outperformed their 3,800 unscreened counterparts.*[23]

More evidence, this time from the very mainstream consulting firm Booz Allen Hamilton, in partnership with the Aspen Institute:

Among financial leaders—public companies that outperform their industry averages—98 percent include ethical behavior/integrity in their values statements, compared with 88 percent for other public companies. Far more of these financial leaders include commitment to employees (88 percent vs. 68 percent), honesty/openness (85 percent vs. 47 percent) and drive to succeed (68 percent vs. 29 percent). Forty-two percent of the financial leaders emphasize adaptability in their values statements, compared with a mere 9 percent for other public companies.[24]

Individual companies with a commitment to social and environmental responsibility also outperform the overall market, even during a recession. A. T. Kearney tracked the market from May to November 2008 (a period of drastic decline), and found:

In 16 of the 18 industries examined, companies recognized as sustainability-focused outperformed their industry peers over both a three- and six-month period, and were well protected from value erosion. Over three months, the performance differential across the 99 companies in this analysis worked out to 10 percent; over six months, the differential was 15 percent.... This performance differential translates to an average $650 million in market capitalization per company.[25]

In other words, not only can you have both values *and* profits, it's actually easier with both.

➤ Customers, Investors, *and* Workers Like This Approach

Not only does the socially and environmentally responsible approach win friends among customers and investors, current and potential employees love it, too. In fact, studies that compare stock market performance of ethics-oriented and/or socially and environmentally conscious companies consistently report higher performance than the overall market. As examples, both the Domini 400 Social Index and informal indexes of firms named in *Business Ethics (*now renamed

The CRO) magazine's Top 100 routinely outperform the S&P 500, both short- and long-term.[26]

Social Venture Network (www.svn.org) is a national membership organization committed to business as an instrument of social justice and environmental improvement—and many of its member companies hire and actively nurture employees who share these core values. In general, they stay profitable, enjoy enormous employee loyalty with minimal attrition, and often find that their employees do their recruiting when they need to fill positions.

And many of these companies approach the employer–employee relationship with the idea that employees have a lot more to contribute than just their labor on the job:

➤ Clif Bar funds employee community service projects during regular working hours, up to the equivalent of one full-time employee's entire year's work (2,080 hours).[27]

➤ While Ben & Jerry's was still operated by Ben Cohen and Jerry Greenfield, CEO pay never exceeded seven times the compensation of the lowest-paid full-time worker in the company.[28]

➤ The consulting firm Mal Warwick and Associates saw its profits rise more than 400 percent once it instituted a profit-sharing plan; the company also has a charity matching initiative.[29]

➤ Greyston Bakery not only located in a depressed area in Yonkers, New York, so that its success could lift the community, but it also uses an open hiring system for entry-level jobs, providing employment—and the training and support employees need to turn their lives around—to people often seen as unemployable, such as those with disabilities or criminal records.[30]

Today's employees are happier working for firms that share their values—but tomorrow's employees demand it. The *International Business Times* reports on a November 2008 survey conducted by Top Employers Ltd. of more than 1,000 students at Britain's prestigious Oxford University and Cambridge University.[31] Just three factors were cited by more than 70 percent of respondents: Life Balance (74 percent), Ethical Business Practices (72 percent), and Variety of Work (72 percent). Public service was tied (with media) for the top choice of industry to work in. Issues like salary and opportunity to advance were much lower on the list.

Interestingly, the study notes that recruitment spending by Britain's top companies has increased. They're having to work harder to recruit these talented grads, and social screens will probably be an ever-growing factor.

Yet companies ignore these trends and essentially force the best and brightest to go elsewhere. A 2007 survey of 1,943 students at 15 business schools in the United States, Canada, and England by the Aspen Institute Center for Business Education found that only 50 percent of the students felt a candidate's personal integrity was important to recruiters, and a mere 7 percent believed their grasp of sociopolitical issues mattered to recruiters.[32]

In the United States, *MarketWatch* referred to the current crop of MBA students as "the Zen class of 2010: They are seeking more social, environmental, and economic perspectives built into their education." And 79 percent would choose a job at an environmentally aware company over a conventional one.[33]

Going even further, Harvard Business School professors Rakesh Khurana and Nitin Nohria call for businesses to take a "Green Hippocratic Oath": first do no harm—to the environment.[34]

In his book *The Company We Keep: Reinventing Small Business for People, Community, and Place* (Chelsea Green, 2006), John Abrams describes his decision to create a values-based construction firm and then eventually turn ownership over to his workers:

> *The idea was to spread that control widely, so the voices of all the owners had meaning. You can't steal second without taking your foot off first, and we came to agree that the only protection needed [for Abrams and his wife, who lived on premises] was veto power over issues directly related to the property.* (p. 33)

■ LESSONS AND ACTIONS

➤ Social responsibility attracts better employees and customers

➤ As problems with the old model continue to surface, capital is shifting toward companies that can be trusted to do the right thing

➤ Social and environmental responsibility minimizes disruption and conflict and allows you to put resources toward your business goals

*Cha**3**ter*

Advantages of Doing the Right Thing

Running an ethical business is actually pretty simple. In fact, Frank C. Bucaro, author of *Trust Me! Insights into Ethical Leadership* and *Taking the High Road: How to Succeed Ethically When Others Bend the Rules*, boils it down to saying yes to just two questions:

Does the action meet company's objectives?

Is it the right thing for the customer?[1]

And when you look at any number of performance indexes—customer loyalty, stock performance, employee retention, and more—ethical behavior turns out to be very good for the companies that embrace it.

■ WHY RESPONSIBLE COMPANIES PERFORM BETTER

It makes total sense that socially responsible investments do better. Consider these factors:

➤ Clean-hands companies don't have to pay expensive lawsuit settlements around pollution, safety violations, or discrimination.

➤ When customers fall in love with the way a company does business, they start recruiting other customers. They actually become that firm's unpaid sales force, and that leads to greater profits through reduced marketing expenditures. (We'll talk more about this later.)

➤ Ethical and eco-friendly companies are much more likely to build a lasting business, and build it more easily.

17

➤ When customers believe that you have their best interests at heart, they come back again and again.

➤ Joint ventures are much easier to organize, because the other partners expect that they'll be treated ethically and respected for what they bring to the table.

➤ The high value of goodwill will be factored into the sale price if the business is sold.

➤ If you tell only the truth, you don't have to worry about being caught in an embarrassing and profit-killing lie.

And the number one reason . . .

➤ You never have to worry about seeing your picture on the front page—with you in handcuffs.

Not surprisingly, socially and environmentally responsible companies perform well in the financial markets, too.

In a report released in the fall of 2008, Merrill Lynch put the value of "values based investing" at over $5 trillion, and noted that "companies that ranked high in responsible economic, environmental, social and corporate governance issues demonstrated lower volatility globally and provided higher dividend yields in the U.S. than those with lower scores."[2] In other words, CSR policies reduce the risk of investment. This leads us to wonder: Would Merrill Lynch have gotten into so much trouble in 2007 and 2008 if the company had itself pushed an agenda of economic, environmental, and social responsibility?

The top-tier consulting company Deloitte wrote an entire white paper on the advantages of strong CSR programs and the disadvantages of environmental liabilities during mergers and acquisitions. Risk assessment and due diligence lead to lower prices for companies whose acquisition could bring in toxic assets that result in lawsuits and negative publicity. On the other hand, companies have increased their worth to a buyer by exercising CSR and environmental leadership, especially if they market these virtues properly. For example,

In one recent deal, a grocery retailer paid a premium for a target company because of its advanced sustainability approach and capabilities in such functions as procurement, store operations, distribution, and community involvement programs.[3]

■ BUILDING TRUST

Trust, says Stephen M. R. Covey in his deservedly best-selling book, *The Speed of Trust*, is a key ingredient in business success. When there's trust—in both your character and your competence—people are much more willing to do business with you, they'll come to the deal faster, and the deal itself may well be bigger and go smoother.

And lack of trust can have serious bottom-line repercussions, including new laws that can require expensive compliance procedures. In the United States, compliance with the Sarbanes-Oxley Act (known colloquially as SOX), passed in the wake of the Enron, WorldCom, and Tyco scandals of the early 2000s, is extremely expensive—and could have been avoided if businesses had acted responsibly.

> *The purpose of SOX . . . was to help reestablish investors' trust in the financial reports issued by public companies. However, SOX has come at a substantial price. For starters, the amount of time it takes to comply with SOX regulations significantly slows the speed of business operations by adding many extra layers of red tape. It also adds considerable cost. A recent study estimated the cost of implementing section 404 alone at $35 billion—28 times greater than the SEC's original estimate.*[4]

And despite all that expensive compliance, SOX has not convinced the public that business is to be trusted—in the United States or elsewhere. Gallup International found in 2005 that 40 percent of people in 60 different countries have no faith in the honesty of business leaders, and a 2006 Harris poll could find only 13 percent who had high confidence in big business.[5]

More recently, consumer trust in the business community has reached a new low, as ranked by the 2009 Edelman Trust Barometer. Overall trust in U.S. corporations is at 38 percent: a stunning 20 percent drop in just one year, and lower even than in the Enron era. For information conveyed by CEOs, it's 29 percent—but just 17 percent among ages 35 to 64. The same study noted that 91 percent of 25- to 64-year-olds worldwide purchased from a trusted company, while 77 percent chose not to do business with a distrusted company.[6]

Perhaps this is why one recent study found that trust-based advertising can outpull advertising that uses sex—at least for a B2B (business-to-business) audience looking for accounting services.[7]

And when you do have that trust, it goes straight into your positive bottom line. The Great Place to Work Institute notes that trust accounts for fully three-fifths of the rankings for *Fortune* magazine's list of 100 Best Companies to Work For—and that those companies on the list in 2007 averaged 18.1 percent shareholder return, compared to 10.5 percent for the S&P 500.[8]

Trust is a form of social capital, created in part by the company's sense of who it must be responsible to, as Dave Pollard points out in his book *Finding the Sweet Spot*. Those who are responsible only to their shareholders suffer low trust ratings in the marketplace, whereas those who see themselves as responsible to all stakeholders (and therefore would always include such costs as remediation of pollution or improving poor labor conditions in their cost-benefit analyses) enjoy the trust of all those stakeholders: employees, customers, neighbors, and so forth.

Pollard identified five bottom-line benefits to companies that have accrued enough social capital:

1. Customers feel good about supporting socially and/or environmentally responsible businesses, and are willing to pay higher prices.

2. Customers become allies in both product development and problem resolution.

3. Customers do your marketing for you.

4. You'll have an easier time raising capital from nontraditional funding sources, with fewer conditions.

5. You'll have lower risk of negative consequences from boycotts to lawsuits.[9]

Pete Blackshaw, Executive Vice President, Digital Strategic Services, Nielsen Online, and author of *Satisfied Customers Tell Three Friends, Angry Customers Tell 3,000*, identifies trust as the number one driver of brand credibility (out of six he identified for an article in *Marketing Sherpa*).[10]

To build that trust, businesses must:

➤ Deliver high value

➤ Ensure safety

➤ Dispense straightforward, unambiguous communication

➤ Respond predictably and appropriately to a crisis: "apologize for any wrong-doing and work to fix problems"

➤ Provide credible guarantees and warranties

Interestingly, all of the other items in his six drivers are really subsets of trust-building:

➤ Authenticity

➤ Transparency

➤ Listening

➤ Responsiveness

➤ Real data that substantiates the company's claims (e.g., through research or the customer's direct experience); Blackshaw calls this *affirmation,* but it would be more accurate to call it *substantiation.*

Among many other trust-builders, strong guarantees can jump-start consumer confidence. Want a great example of a powerful guarantee? As jobless rates climbed in the fall of 2008, Hyundai added to its already strong warranty against automotive failure a warranty on the ability of its customers to pay.

Anyone who buys or leases a new Hyundai and finances it through the company is eligible to simply return the car if faced with involuntary unemployment, medical disability, loss of driver's license for medical reasons, job transfer out of the country, personal bankruptcy if self-employed, or accidental death.[11]

This very creative risk-reversal strategy won praise from Patrick Byers on the Responsible Marketing blog:

> *Any automaker could have done this, but they haven't—yet. And Hyundai did it first.*
>
> *Not only will this drive word of mouth, it positions Hyundai as a company that cares—not just another automaker desperately trying to move metal.... With this program the car is returned without incident, the customer retains their dignity and Hyundai is the good guy.*[12]

Of course, within 10 weeks, other automakers offered similar programs.[13]

■ JOHNSON & JOHNSON: A LESSON IN ETHICAL CRISIS PR

In 1982, seven people died after consuming tampered-with, cyanide-laced Extra-Strength Tylenol—a popular seller for Johnson & Johnson. The company's response was nearly immediate and thoroughly centered on protecting consumers. Although the poisonings were localized and specific to one product, the company took no chances. It froze production, recalled all Tylenol products nationwide—31 million bottles, worth over $100 million—and offered a $100,000 reward.[14]

The company clearly put consumer safety ahead of its own profits. Though the loss was substantial, the resulting gain in consumer confidence allowed the company to recover quickly and gain wide respect.

Clearly, the company actually follows its own credo, which lists various constituents to which the company feels responsible, starting with health professionals and consumers, then employees, then local and world communities, and lastly, its stockholders.[15]

Contrast this firm commitment to ethics with some of the slippery tactics of other companies facing more recent safety scares such as Ford and Bridgestone/Firestone, which created PR and sales disasters for themselves by attempting to duck responsibility for SUV rollover accidents.[16]

For more on creating real loyalty, see Chapter 16.

■ ONE PART OF CORPORATE SOCIAL RESPONSIBILITY: STRATEGIC GIVING

More companies are switching from general corporate philanthropy to supporting social and environmental causes that directly align with their overall mission. For example, listen to Talia Aharoni, founder of Maala, an Israel-based social responsibility index:

> "I went to companies and showed them that they were giving money but not making any impact," said Aharoni. "They couldn't explain why they were doing what they were doing."
>
> Maala taught them to look at their donations as investments, not as contributions. In order to adopt this view, the contributions needed to demonstrate a fiscal and communal return, "an idea which companies found appealing."[17]

Aharoni's goal is to see social investment in Israel reach levels at least equal to its percentage in the United States.

In the United States, companies are also being forced to be more strategic in their corporate giving. Consultant Kellie A. McElhaney chides Ford Motor Company for its large contribution to Susan G. Komen for the Cure, a well-known cancer charity, not because the cause isn't worthwhile, but because she feels this particular cause is not in alignment with Ford's core mission. "There is no strategic link between the company's support of breast cancer research and the building of cars and trucks."[18] The company would be better served, she says, by donating to causes that address alternative fuels and global environmental or transportation issues.

She praises many companies whose charity efforts are much more aligned with their core mission. A particularly strong example is the dog food company Pedigree. In partnering with the American Humane Association to do a big public campaign around adopting abandoned dogs, the company brands itself as one that really loves animals, highlights the problem of dogs being killed when shelters can't place them, helps abandoned dogs find new homes, and positions itself as a choice for dog owners (and that's a whole lot of people) who care not only about their own pet but about dogs in general.[19] As of July 2009, the company's home page features a very visible banner with pictures of dogs and three links relating to dog rescue; it's actually easier to find the information on rescuing dogs than it is to find the product information. And a footer on every page of the site notes, "At PEDIGREE® Brand, everything we do is for the love of dogs, from the dog food we make to the dog adoption drive we support."

■ NOT JUST CORPORATE, BUT PERSONAL RESPONSIBILITY

Christopher Bauer, author of *Better Ethics Now*, points out that corporate responsibility must be based on a collection of individuals taking responsibility.

> *When we take full responsibility for our behavior—when we really own what we do and the impact of our choices—we immediately impose a range of extremely hardy pressures on ourselves to do the right thing. These pressures range from wanting to be proud of a job well done to wishing not to be humiliated or punished for doing the wrong thing. By contrast, the less responsible we feel for our actions or the less we care about their impact, the greater the distance we can create between ourselves and those extremely helpful pressures . . .*
>
> *Once you show employees that doing the right thing is a tool for their personal success and not just the success of your company—then it will be much easier to keep ethics problems from developing. Without that, the pressures to do otherwise will simply be too great for many people.[20]*

■ KEYS TO SUCCESS...*AND* HAPPINESS

Compare these scenarios:

➤ The doctor says your ulcer is a little better, but you're still over-doing it. You put in 65-hour weeks and you still can't get everything done. Your family life is suffering and your stress level is high. Much of your time is spent cold-calling people who don't even want to talk to you, let alone buy from you. And your best sales manager just got stolen away by your biggest competitor, taking with her a client list and inside knowledge about your company's business strategy.

➤ You're enjoying a quiet, relaxing weekend getaway with your family—a celebration of the big new client you landed. You got the contract because a previous happy customer, a competitor of your new client's, recommended you. That makes sense, because they've been so pleased at the way your services generated profits that they couldn't help spreading your name around. You also think back on the industry conference at which you spoke recently, and how, coming out of that event, your firm has joined with three others to form a strategic alliance that will build all of your businesses. Life is good, and you're glad to spend this time with your spouse and children. Only a few years ago, it seems that you never had any time to spend with them. You were spinning like a hamster on an exercise wheel—always working but never getting ahead. How glad you are that you've found a better way!

In the pages that follow, you'll learn how to begin setting a course for the smooth channel of success, instead of the rocky shoals of stress. And you will achieve this by helping others meet—or surpass—*their* goals.

■ THE MAGIC TRIANGLE: QUALITY, INTEGRITY, HONESTY

Ready for the big principle of this book? It's not a secret at all, just a simple truth. But it's crucial. Here it is:

Create value for others in everything that you do.

That's the magic formula. You help yourself best when you're helping others. And the way you do that is by basing your business on a solid foundation of three principles:

Quality, Integrity, Honesty.

Quality: Provide the best value you can.

Integrity: Run your business in alignment with your core values; don't try to be something you're not.

Honesty: Value the truth and be eager to share it with your prospects and customers, even if this means that it is not appropriate for a particular prospect to become your customer at this time.

Here's how Shel puts these core ideas to work in his own business:

Because I try to deliver extremely high quality while keeping my prices affordable, the value of my work to my clients is very high—and my customers become my marketing evangelists because they're excited and delighted by the impact my work has on their business. Integrity keeps me close to my core values. Those include making the world a better place, having work that I find meaningful, and enjoying a high quality of life. Out of honesty, I've turned down work projects because another person might be better equipped to do the job; out of integrity, I've refused work assignments that clashed with my values.

You may be surprised to find out that becoming super-rich is not one of my goals. In fact, it's integral to my value system to show ways of having a truly high-quality life, one filled with joy—expressed through travel, music, good food, and more—and to show that this can be done while living lightly and spending lightly. (In fact, my first web site, www.frugalfun.com, is dedicated to this idea.) I work because I enjoy what I do. I take great satisfaction in writing and speaking, and in knowing that I do these things quite well. I believe that the world becomes a better and more interesting place if I can create excitement for a book by an unknown author or explain to the world how to have fabulous vacations that don't cost much.

As for honesty, it not only feels like the right thing but it's also good for business. For instance, two of my books on how to save money on marketing covered much of the same ground. When someone ordered both books, I always explained that one of the books is all they need—and which one, and why. People are invariably shocked that I actually tell my customers that they should reduce the amount of my sale. I want a long-term customer relationship—and word-of-mouth buzz—more than the short-sighted short-term profit of selling customers a book they don't need.

■ WHO WINS WHEN YOU MARKET WITH QUALITY, INTEGRITY, AND HONESTY?

Your customers or clients will win because they realize you're not trying to cheat them. And they will so value the experience of being treated well that they will come back again and again—and tell others.

Your suppliers will win because they relate to your honesty and integrity, to your understanding that you're partners who can both go farther by helping each other.

Your competitors benefit, too, especially if they see that your ethical behavior opens the way for them to improve their own operating standards. As you make space in the market for quality, integrity, and honesty, you begin to see each other less as rivals and more as people who can work together to make things better. And we'll see a little later that with this cooperative model, you can help each other in many ways.

■ HOW THE MAGIC TRIANGLE POSITIONS YOU BETTER IN A TOUGH ECONOMY

When the economy contracts, as it did in 2008, businesses that use the Magic Triangle are better positioned to survive and thrive. You retain more customers—who help you acquire new business—and the lower price sensitivity of your loyalist customers means you enjoy higher profits. Thus, you have more surplus capital to invest in marketing, while your competitors pull back and retrench, focusing only on survival and not on growth or retention.

In fact, many experts pin a good part of the blame for the 2008 recession on unethical behavior. For example, a 2008 survey by Clemson University's Rutland Center for Ethics of 302 CEOs of companies with $10 million or more in annual revenues pointed out that many of these CEOs suffer from an advanced case of greed.[21] The Center's director, Professor Dan Wueste, claims that poor business ethics and practices directly led to the economic downturn, because when there's no trust, there's no confidence in the stock market:

> *The current crisis has everything to do with the failure to act in a way that would count as ethically acceptable. We start with the assumption that people will be acting rightly and not take unfair advantage of us. Then people do things to prove that we can't trust them (risky mortgages, frivolous spending). It's irrational to believe that trust will remain.*[22]

Green economist and ethicist Hazel Henderson, author of *Ethical Markets: Growing the Green Economy,* whose books have charted a better course since the 1970s, calls the ultraleveraged economy a "global casino," and noted that historically, overpumped economies have a tendency to "metastasize." This happened in 1929, for instance, and it happened in 2008. Her prescription includes new taxes on leveraged funds, reducing leverage ratios, eliminating subsidies for carbon-spewing fuels (including ethanol), reregulating the energy industry, and demanding greater transparency. Beyond that, she recommends a whole package of reforms:

> *Many more fundamental reforms are necessary: requiring central banks to use their more targeted tools beyond manipulating interest rates, e.g., increasing the capital reserves banks must hold and raising margin requirements on stock purchases. Reforming tax policies is urgent: taxing carbon emissions, pollution, waste, planned obsolescence and resource-depletion while reducing income and payroll taxes. Shifting the still-massive subsidies showered on the oil, coal, gas and nuclear industries to production tax credits can accelerate the growth of renewable energy. Solar, wind, geothermal, tidal, fuel cells, hydrogen, mass transit, smart DC electric grids as well as capturing the 40 percent of energy currently wasted in the US fossil fuel economy can shift human societies to the Solar Age.*[23]

But that's only the beginning. She sees this crisis as a fabulous opportunity to change the whole definition of a successful economy.

And as we change the financial games and fix accounting er-
rors in the global casino, we can also change the obsolete score-
cards. There is widespread public recognition in global surveys
of the errors of money-measured GDP growth, and correcting its
omissions of social and environmental costs has begun (www.
beyond-gdp.eu). Including all these factors and indicators of
health, education, poverty gaps, environment and quality of life
can help shrink the global casino and restore finance to its proper
function.

And as the economy spiraled down, poor choices by executives
with their hands out for a government rescue caused public relations
disasters. The lavish post-bailout parties thrown by AIG[24] and the
decisions by auto company CEOs to fly to Washington in separate
private jets[25] added to the perception that these business leaders are
completely clueless about economic responsibility, and that their lavish lifestyles and vast compensation packages are the first places to
look for cuts.[26]

Of course, there's a flip side. More and more companies are recognizing the need to take a strong public position in favor of ethics—
and, we hope, to act privately in ways that are congruent with that
commitment—and new organizations are springing up to support
that stand. For example, the Business Ethics Leadership Alliance
(BELA), organized by the Ethisphere Institute, requires a pledge to
honor four values: legal compliance, transparency, conflict iden-
tification, and accountability.[27] BELA's members—many of whom
have been heavily criticized on environmental and/or ethics issues—
include General Electric, Wal-Mart, and Pepsico, and the group is very
open in its mission to combat negative impressions left by unethical
companies.[28]

■ LESSONS AND ACTIONS

➤ Success in business is about providing value to others—the
Magic Triangle is your success formula.

➤ When values and value align, your chances of success are
greater.

➤ All things being equal, stakeholders prefer to do business with
companies they perceive as ethical.

Chapter 4

Marketing versus Adversarial Sales

■ MARKETING INSTEAD OF SALES

Some time back, Shel spoke on a panel of six people discussing sales and marketing for solo entrepreneurs. One of his copanelists was a sales jerk who monopolized about 70 percent of the panel's time and was thoroughly aggressive, rude, and arrogant. His advice to others was that they, too, should be aggressive. He went on and on about how you just have to pick up the phone and cold call, hour after hour, day after day. His theory seemed to be that if you were a thorn in the side of enough people, one or two of them would do business with you, just to get rid of you.

You probably won't be surprised that we disagree, strongly. With his approach, everyone loses. He's going to have to work 14 hours a day at alienating people in order to make a decent living. He's wasting a lot of effort that could be spent far more productively, and he's destroying the chance to build the long-lasting, positive relationships that turn prospects into customers voluntarily. What sales he gets will be in spite of his approach, not because of it—but eventually the numbers do add up to a livable income. We think he could sell a lot more and work a lot less if he followed our methods.

When Shel finally got his turn, he said, "Now, here's the difference between marketing and sales. I never make cold calls. I create marketing that has the prospect calling me. When I get the phone call or the e-mail, they're already convinced that I can help them. If I don't screw it up, I have the account." While this may be an oversimplification—sometimes he's on the short list of three or four vendors, rather than automatically chosen as the preferred vendor—it is actually the dominant marketing trend in his business.

Is this approach successful? Judging by how challenging it has been to carve out the time to write this book amid all our client projects, it has been quite successful. We spend a lot of time on marketing and virtually none on the actual sales process—until a prospect contacts one of us or makes a public appeal for specific types of help that we provide. Then we go right to discussing their needs. And here's the best part: We close a phenomenal percentage of those prospects.

Of course, this success did not happen overnight. But by focusing on helping others, by providing enormous amounts of useful and actionable information, we not only have full calendars but also stellar reputations.

Here is another key principle of ethical, profitable marketing—one that the sales jerk doesn't understand:

Conduct your business so as to build long-term loyalty.

When you get a customer, you want to keep that customer and build a sales relationship that can not only last for years but also create a stream of referral business. When you select and hire an employee, you want that person to stick around to repay the time and trouble you invest in the initial training, and harness the skills that the employee develops after a few years. When you select a supplier, you'd rather not have to go through the decision process and evaluate all the competitors again. And when you put time and energy into a joint venture, you'd like that cultivated relationship and hard work to result in long-term mutual success.

It is almost always much cheaper—and more profitable—to bring an existing customer back to purchase again than to prospect for and develop a new customer. Nortel cited a study showing that "a mere 5 percent increase in customer retention can translate to as much as a 75 percent increase in profitability."[1] Another source, the UK loyalty-marketing think tank TheWiseMarketer.com, claims that 5 percent more retention *"only"* doubles profits—but that "over only five years, a 70 percent customer retention rate loses 2 to 3 times as many customers as a 90 percent retention rate."[2] In a similar vein, ZD Net reported a Gartner Group finding that "it costs five times as much to find a new customer as it does to keep an old one. . . . [Gartner] estimates the cost of customer acquisition to be $280 a head, versus a mere $57 a head for customer retention."[3]

If these dollar figures were accurate, if you're selling something in the $100 range, you'd barely break even on purchases by your existing customers (subtracting not only the marketing cost but the actual production or wholesale cost of the item), and *lose* substantial amounts of money on every sale to a new customer. However, using more frugal strategies—which Shel discusses in *Grassroots Marketing: Getting Noticed in a Noisy World*[4] and on the Frugal Marketing web site, and Jay talks about in many of the *Guerrilla Marketing* books—you can slash the dollar costs substantially for both new-customer acquisition and retention. Other than paying performance-based commissions for referrals, Shel pays between $0 and $20 to acquire the rest of his clients. And since his primary customer-retention strategy is to deliver superior work at an affordable price and within a reasonable time, his cost to keep an existing client is essentially zero.

A broad-based study by Howard Seibel, for E-Metrics, showed new customer acquisition costs ranging from $8.66 for online travel discounter PriceLine all the way up to $700 for a mortgage origination. Most of the study's examples ranged between $14 and $300.[5] At the extremes, Harry Tennant and Associates found that Amazon.com had dropped customer-acquisition cost to $7,[6] while *Ward's Dealer Business* (an auto-industry trade magazine) cites a new-customer acquisition cost for car dealers of $1,000.[7]

The dollar costs may be overstated in the Gartner study, but the ratio of costs for acquiring new versus retaining existing customers still holds.

And how do you retain existing customers? By providing a delightful, high-quality experience during the buying process, by offering goods and services that offer genuine value to the customer, and by exceeding your own promises and your customer's expectations—*not* by making enemies of your customer during or after the sales process.

You also retain customers by listening to them. Ask regularly how you can serve them better (and change your company's behavior to reflect the answers), and give them other ways to be heard. Scott Stratten, of Un-marketing.com, suggests asking this simple question:

I would like to know from you what I should stop *doing, what I should* start *doing and what I should* continue *doing.*[8]

Now we begin to see the true shortsightedness of the sales jerk approach. When people buy in spite of your sales style and not because of it, there is virtually no chance for a long-term sales relationship. You've gone for the quick hit, and it will come back to bite you. By failing to deliver a positive experience to your customers, you've pretty much ensured that they will go elsewhere next time, and they will tell their friends and colleagues to do the same.

So, if this is true, why do so many businesses stuff their heads firmly into the sand and create marketing strategies, such as the following, that can only antagonize their prospects?

➤ Dishonest bait-and-switch tactics in the showroom

➤ Obnoxious unwanted—and untargeted—telemarketing

➤ Annoying saturation ad campaigns in electronic media

➤ In-your-face, unpleasantly loud tradeshow presentations

➤ An attitude from retail clerks that says, Don't bother me, I'm talking on the phone to my best friend

➤ Salespeople who can't listen or answer questions, and instead only recite their standard speech, regardless of whether it's appropriate or relevant

➤ Spam (junk e-mail) in which the marketer claims permission was granted to a marketing partner

Let's take spam as an example, because it's easy to find commentary about it. A successful Internet marketer, Paul Myers of www. talkbiz.com, complains bitterly about the invasion of his e-box by so-called permission marketers who never got valid permission to make the contact.[9]

Myers goes on at some length, attacking the tendency to add names to e-mail lists without explicit advance permission and the all-too-frequent claim that the information actually was requested—a doubtful claim when the e-mail goes to an inbound-only autobot address.

He concludes:

Building a truly responsive list of targeted buyers isn't hard. It requires nothing more than offering solutions to problems that people care about, and telling the truth.

People buy based on the relationship they feel with the list-owner. A relationship started in dishonesty and fostered by the belief that the subscriber has the intelligence of a week old pizza isn't conducive to sales.

Let's hear that last sentence again, Paul:

A relationship started in dishonesty...isn't conducive to sales.

These excesses are counterproductive in any marketing medium, not just e-mail. Years ago, some yo-yo actually placed an ad in Shel's local paper, with the headline: Sex.

Underneath it, "Now that I've got your attention . . ."

If this had been an ad for condoms, pregnancy counseling, treatment of sexually transmitted diseases, or one of a dozen other things, it might have been an appropriate strategy.

But it was an ad for a car dealership. In spite of the sexy models car makers use to sell their products, buying a car has nothing to do with sex. The attention that the ad got was entirely wasted. In fact, it was negative. How many people crossed that dealership off the list of possible places to buy a car, because anyone who would insult their intelligence with that ad was not a company they wanted to do business with?

And then there was the salesman who had an appointment to come to Shel's house and wasted over an hour on a presentation that should have taken 15 minutes, ignoring repeated explicit requests to move faster. Time is extremely precious. Shel desperately needed what he was selling, but the salesman's unwillingness to deviate from his prepared speech did not work. This would have been a fairly easy sale if he had been able to listen to what Shel wanted, answer the questions Shel asked instead of the ones asked by the hypothetical prospect in his presentation, and cut to the chase. Instead, Shel wrote a complaint letter to the company.

Telemarketing is usually done all wrong, too. It's gotten to the point where unless they already have a relationship with the company, many prospects won't even listen. If the product is actually of interest, they ask for materials in writing (and it's amazing how few of these salespeople actually follow up). And unless that interest is captured quickly, the prospect might just ask to be put on the Do Not Call list.

This is not a strategy for long-term success. One of the things they ought to teach in basic sales training is to approach the prospect the way the prospect wants to be approached. If the prospect asks for materials in writing and the salesperson can't be bothered to mail or fax some information, why should that prospect consent to a time-wasting sales call—to say nothing of an in-person appointment—just because that's the way the company would prefer to sell? Is it any wonder that society has such scorn for salespeople?

To get long-term positive sales relationships, treat your customer as an intelligent person, as a partner in your business. Marketing strategies that insult your customers' intelligence are a foolish waste of money because even if you get a one-shot sale, you haven't built a relationship. In fact, you've pretty well forced the person you duped to go elsewhere the next time, and that means you have to go out and expensively acquire another customer.

And if industry refuses to self-police, the threat of more government intervention looms. The FCC (Federal Communications Commission) Chief-of Technology, Edmond Thomas, warned attendees at an American Association of Advertising Agencies conference that obnoxious advertising clutter is out of hand. With up to 30 minutes of nonstop commercials, "You're almost forcing regulators to get involved."[10]

A year earlier, at the same conference, Yankelovich Partners presented disturbing findings:

➤ 54 percent steer clear of products that overwhelm them with ads.

➤ 60 percent had lowered their opinion of advertising in the past few years.

➤ 61 percent see advertising and marketing as "out of control."

➤ 65 percent feel constantly bombarded with advertising.

➤ 69 percent would consider products and services that skipped the ads.

➤ 45 percent felt advertising and marketing reduce quality of life.

➤ 33 percent would lower their standard of living if they could banish the ads.[11]

■ BUT WAIT—IT GETS WORSE

It wouldn't be so bad if win–lose marketers only shot *themselves* in the foot. Unfortunately, as soon as someone invents a new communication tool, somebody else figures out a way to abuse it.

E-mail is a classic example. E-mail at its best—in the form of discussion groups—may have been the single most powerful marketing tool invented in the twentieth century. (Social networking sites, a twenty-first-century invention, are starting to supplant it.[12]) E-mail allows instant communication, anywhere around the world, with many thousands of people on a discussion list talking about the exact subject where you offer solutions—as easily as you can send to your next-door neighbor.

It also allows something very close to real-time dialog with individual correspondents thousands of miles away. And of course, you can back up statements with spreadsheets, research sources, articles, and other data, either as file attachments or posted on a web page. For most users, in the United States at least, it costs nothing extra to take advantage of these tools. (Elsewhere, some people pay based on time online or bandwidth—and that's important information if you're in the habit of sending large files around.)

To a skilled marketer, e-mail was once the goose that lays the golden egg. But the abusers—spammers, con artists, scumware/spyware/virus programmers—are killing the golden goose. Consider this:

➤ Many users have filters that sort any unfamiliar e-mail addresses directly into the trash can.

➤ Some corporations use e-mail systems that automatically strip out attachments.

➤ Even if the recipient is hand-filtering, most e-boxes are so clogged with junk mail that it's easy to accidentally delete a legitimate message.

➤ Delivery reliability has dropped due to overloaded infrastructure.

➤ Some popular services, including AOL, Yahoo, and Hotmail, simply can't process the volume, and the recipient's e-mail system breaks down or is shut off for quota violation.

➤ Enormous numbers of e-mail addresses go stale every year.

For people who need to be accessible by e-mail—journalists, technical support people, and consultants who have an Internet-oriented clientele—this flood of bad mail becomes a huge burden.

And of course, we put up the same kinds of mental or technological filters against postal junk mail, telemarketers, junk faxes (illegal for years, but it doesn't seem to matter), and the barrage of ads that keep upping the ante—ads in toilet stalls, for goodness sake. Is there no sanctuary anywhere from bad marketing?

So now you know the truth: Part of why we're so zealous about the mutual benefit approach is that the win–lose people make it much harder for the rest of us. We're selfish that way. If we can convince a few people to change their ways, we'll have made the world a better place. And that's something we like to do.

■ LESSONS AND ACTIONS

➤ Intrusive traditional marketing can actually interfere with the buying process.

➤ Creating loyal, happy customers can slash your customer acquisition cost through repeat and referral business.

➤ Junk marketers can kill not just the sale but the entire medium.

Chapter 5

Sales the Right Way

Should you conclude from the last chapter that there's no place for salespeople anymore? Not at all. However, it is true that some businesses don't need a sales force if their marketing is properly effective, and it also means that successful salespeople will pursue a People First approach.

If you're going to do sales, start with sales consultant Jacques Werth's concept of High-Probability Selling. Figure out who really has a lot to gain by doing business with you and approach those people—*only* those people.[1] But don't approach them with the attitude that you have something to sell them; come to them from the point of view that *you're their ally*. They have a problem that you can help solve, or you have something that will free up their resources (for example, time, money, employee productivity). If the cost of not acting is seen as higher than the cost of taking action, you're very likely to make the sale.

Once you've begun working from that understanding, your customers will not even consider going elsewhere. Why should they bother choosing from other suppliers when you've already demonstrated your sincere and competent commitment to help them solve a pressing problem or use resources more effectively? Remember Shel's response to the sales jerk? The best marketing lets the *customer* decide that you are the right person for the job. Your own customers and prospects can even become evangelists for you, and—if you ask politely—will give you referrals or even introduce you to others.

Also, remember to match your selling style to your prospect's buying style. Introverted and extraverted, fact-driven and emotive, impulsive and methodical buyers all respond very differently. A sales process that works with one side of the pair will fail miserably on the other side, making the prospect feel violated instead of respected.

■ THREE WISE SALES STRATEGIES FROM THE UMASS FAMILY BUSINESS CENTER—AND ONE FROM SOMEONE ELSE

It was Shel's good fortune to be the long-time conference reporter for the UMass Family Business Center, which had a number of programs on sales and customer service over the years. These are programs aimed at businesses very different from a home-based service business: manufacturers, retail stores, hotels, and funeral parlors, among others. Just so you don't think that we're writing only from our own experience, or that these principles would apply only to information businesses like ours, here are some insights from others.

Mike O'Horo, of Sales Results, Inc., suggests an approach similar to Jacques Werth's: "Get permission from people who already want your product—and change the sales focus from an unwanted intrusion to a welcome—and rewarded—provision of service."

Create a profile of your best current buyers—then look for prospects that match that profile. When you find them, don't pitch. Identify the *demand trigger*: the problem your prospect urgently needs solved. Investigate collaboratively, ask questions, and listen. Switch to solution mode if the *prospect* decides to take action. When buyers conclude that you offer four or five times greater value than the perceived risk, they feel *compelled* to buy.

Don't focus on product features or even on generic benefits; stick to your client's specific and deep needs. Avoid the trap of pushing product. Don't be "the most expensive human catalog." O'Horo says the buyer cares only about how you can improve three factors: the effect the client desires, the relationship between value and investment, and self-interest/ego needs.

Independent of your offer, ask deep, probing questions:

➤ "What is the biggest problem you face?"

➤ "How important is this problem?"

➤ "What positive effects would you expect if you fixed it—and what benefit would that have for your business?"

➤ "How does the problem affect you personally?"

Once you've asked a question, "shut up and listen." From the buyer's answers, you will both recognize whether the issue actually needs attention. Then let the *client* conclude that the cost of inaction is too high.

Explore why the problem hasn't been solved. Ask, "What are the barriers to solving this problem?" Then determine how many others are affected. Ask, "Who, besides yourself, is the natural champion to lead the charge within your company?" Those people become natural allies in the selling process; they will be your sponsors or champions.

When you get positive responses to these types of questions, you've been given permission to sell together. As soon as you switch to telling, you've blown your credibility. If you're cross-selling outside your own expertise, bring in your resident expert: "Would you find it helpful to talk with someone who has solved this problem for many others?"

But you still need to differentiate your product from the competition—to show where you add the value. Show how you're different, *not* better. (Don't make the client feel stupid about an existing choice.) If you've set the sales process up along O'Horo's principles, the client often won't even consider anyone else's solution. You will have earned the right to advance to each successive next step.[2]

According to Susan Bellows, a sales trainer who uses David Sandler's Neuro-Linguistic Programming (NLP)–based sales methods, the chances of closing a sale are only 1 percent on a cold call. But the odds improve dramatically to 50 percent on a call with a referral and 80 percent or better on a personal introduction. So getting those referrals and introductions (right after the customer has bought from you is the best time, she says) will be a major shortcut to a successful sales career.[3] And of course your chances of getting referrals and introductions are far greater with methods that respect and value your clients and prospects.

For Alexander Hiam, coauthor of *The Portable MBA in Marketing* and many other books, the most important aspect of customer retention is providing a high-quality experience to the customer. That means not only an excellent product but also extreme emphasis on customer relationships—to the point where employees actually anticipate customers' needs, and propose accurate solutions to problems the customer may experience, but hasn't yet articulated.

For instance, if you sell photocopiers with a five-year lifespan, don't wait until the customers start to complain in the fifth year about high repair costs. After four years, send a mailing to your customers noting that their machines are aging—and you want them to know about your Borrow-a-Photocopier plan, in which they can sign up to use a brand-new loaner while their own machine is down for repairs.

Instead of an angry customer, frustrated that the equipment is down, you've created a loyalist who is aware that you'll go the extra mile, alerting your customers to an issue that hasn't even surfaced yet, and providing an easy solution. Better still, there's a good likelihood that they'll like the modern machine so much better, they'll purchase one.

But this attention to the customer's overall experience has to be genuine. Run the business the way you want to live. Relationships among employees and customers are interrelated. The way you treat your employees will be reflected in the ways they treat your customers. Employees who are valued, who are asked to contribute to the thinking behind a business, will be more likely to make that extra push so that the client feels the specialness of his or her own relationship with the firm.

Hiam cited a wildly successful company, Rosenbluth International—one of the leaders in the corporate travel market. This firm gets $3 million in new business every day and is growing at 15 percent a year. It does almost no traditional marketing, with an advertising-to-sales ratio of 0.00004. In an industry where a 75 percent retention rate is considered terrific, this company retains 96 percent of its 1,500 corporate clients. Rosenbluth will go so far as to open a new branch office just to serve a new account.

Says Hiam, "Build relationships, never lose a customer. You grow with your customers," so that a company that spends $1,000 with you in the early stages may spend $100,000 with you 10 years later.

When there is a customer service issue, make sure your employees' language is in harmony with the results you want to achieve. If the goal is to have a happy customer, it's not enough to simply address the customer's grievance. Use language that accepts responsibility and moves the customer's agenda forward. For instance, instead of responding in a sentence that begins, "We would...," take personal responsibility for the outcome by starting your answer, "I will...." By using the more immediate, direct language, you communicate to the aggrieved customer that you have accepted the challenge to make it right. *I* can't be brushed off on anyone else. And *will* expresses a commitment to take action. *We would* simply doesn't have this power.[4]

Craig Garber, another sales and marketing expert, noted in his newsletter that when you're selling high-ticket services in a competitive environment, you can be in a much stronger position to get work on your own terms if you avoid being trapped in the old-fashioned language of sales and proposals and bids.

So when the prospect requests a proposal, you respond instead with an audit:

> *Then, inside your audit or whatever you wind up calling it, you list all the remedies, all the solutions to the problems you've identified, and you let your prospect know that as part of your service or product or whatever it is you're selling, you're guaranteeing to fix these problems, and you extend some kind of an offer at a fixed price.*[5]

■ WHEN TO SAY NO TO A SALE

Let's turn for a moment from the idea of *selling* to the idea of *not selling*. When ethics are a major consideration in marketing, there will be times when you have to turn down work. One of the challenges, at least at first, is getting comfortable with this idea. This can be especially challenging if you're a small entrepreneur just getting started, and you're used to struggling hard for every last dollar.

When would you need to refuse an order? Here are several situations, and they all come back to our Magic Triangle:

➤ You don't have the appropriate solution; someone else is better equipped to solve the client's problem (honesty).

➤ There isn't enough time to do the job well (quality).

➤ You could do the job, but it's an area you're trying to get away from (honesty—to yourself).

➤ The client will obviously be so high-maintenance and/or so demanding that the job isn't worth the price you can charge (quality—of the client).

➤ The client asks you to engage in unethical behavior (integrity).

➤ The product is too shoddy and you don't feel good about working on it (integrity/quality).

➤ You find the job itself morally distasteful (integrity).

As an example of that last bullet, Shel was developing a relationship with a local PR firm that wanted to subcontract some copywriting assignments. The very first job he got was so clearly wrapped up in a cause that he has spent his life working against that it actually made him ill to look at the client's publicity fliers. Shel's only hesitation was knowing that the PR shop was overextended and needed materials on a short deadline; he didn't want to strand the woman who was subcontracting.

After spending an hour agonizing about it, he picked up the phone and explained that while he didn't want to leave her hanging, he couldn't in good conscience take the job—but he could still help her manage her overload by taking on a different client.

He was fully expecting that she'd be furious—but actually, she told him she respected his stance. She did take back the problem assignment and gave him one that he felt totally comfortable handling.

All marketers at some point are asked to take on poor-quality projects. When you're in that situation, just say no. If you think the product is shoddy, or a terrible value, or just doesn't capture your interest, you can't write decent copy or plan good strategy for it anyway—and the client will hate what you turn in. You need to feel good about the product in order to take on the job.

Shel implemented this policy many years ago.

I find that people respect me for this stance, and that I feel a lot better about the work I do. My conclusion? I should have started that policy years earlier. Now, when a client contacts me about doing some work, there's a clause in my return e-mail that allows me the right to back out of a project if I don't feel it's a good fit.

Interestingly enough, Arthur Andersen the person, the founder of the accounting firm that was driven out of business by its willingness to look the other way when major audit flags kept turning up at Enron, turned down a major account after refusing the company's request to engage in exactly the sort of unethical accounting that brought down his company almost 70 years later. He did this at a very early stage in his career, when he wasn't sure he could meet his next payroll. He told the company president that there was "not enough money in the city of Chicago" to change his mind.[6]

■ LESSONS AND ACTIONS

➤ People-centered sales methods are easy to implement.

➤ Sometimes, saying no to a sale makes more sense than saying yes.

Chapter 6

Expand the Model Exponentially—by Making It Personal

Sales clearly lends itself very well to a People First strategy—especially since so many companies are completely clueless about how to achieve their own goals by working collaboratively to meet each prospect's goals. But sales is only one among many marketing tools. Now let's look at how everyone can win when marketing through the media.

Media publicity is free, and is valued more highly than advertising because it conveys the endorsement of a respected third party: the journalist.

The trick to getting media coverage is to remember that the journalist does not care about you or your business. The journalist cares about the story that readers, listeners, or viewers will find so important that they choose it among all the competing stimuli and choices, and allow the journalist to tell the story for them, in words and images.

■ JOHN KREMER AND BIOLOGICAL MARKETING

Listen to an expert in working the media. John Kremer, author of *1001 Ways to Market Your Books* and one of the foremost authorities on book marketing in the United States, spoke at a conference where Shel was also presenting. Although he directed his remarks at authors, publishers, and book marketers, his wisdom applies to anyone marketing anything: a product, a service, an idea, an attitude.[1]

All marketing is essentially creating relationships: with press, distributors, printer, stores—the people who are helping your book get into the marketplace—and ultimately with your readers, who are going to create the word-of-mouth army that will sell your book. What marketing ultimately is, is making friends. All business success is determined by how good you are at creating and maintaining relationships—in any field.

Of course, coverage in the media helps you build those vendor relationships throughout the distribution chain, as well as create demand from the ultimate customer. Turning specifically to media relations, John says,

You act on your word, you stand by it, you give good service, you go to the aid of other people. That's all part of being a good friend. I pass people on, and people refer people to me—that's one of the best ways to build relationships with the media. You need to make it clear that there are things you can do to lead the media to other information—beyond their own agenda.

When you think of marketing as making friends, Kremer points out, it changes the way you market.

Make a database of 100 key media contacts who really need to know about your book. You'll get more sales by focusing in relationships with these 100 key people.

99 percent of all [efforts to contact] media is wasted. If you send 1000 press releases and 10 pick it up, the rest is wasted. Ideally, you put most of your emphasis into the 10 percent that does pay off. And do the follow up. There are some amazing mousetraps out there that nobody's beating a door to. Those inventors believed Emerson [who said, "Build a better mousetrap, and the world will beat a path to your door"], but it doesn't work that way. You have to create the path and pave it, and put in a landing strip for a plane or two.

He went on to broaden the discussion well past media coverage and out to the end user. He believes that if you turn your customer into a participant, that customer will develop an emotional attachment to your products. So, for example, let your customers have a say in choosing among different packaging alternatives or product names. In his case, he let visitors to his web site vote on which of two cover designs they preferred—and they overwhelmingly chose the one he liked less, so he followed their advice. There are also more subtle ways to get this feedback. For instance, "Get buy-in from votes on your web site. Offer a choice of one free report with several different titles" containing the same information. If there's a clear preference, that helps you name your product.

John has developed a new paradigm called *biological marketing*, and with his permission, we will share it with you:

> *Farmers have incredible ROI [return on investment]. They plant one seed of corn and get back 900. Nature does not follow physics. Instead of an equal and opposite reaction, there's an incredible multifold giving back. It follows biological laws, and when you give and share, it comes back to you in abundance. Physics says that the ultimate end of the universe is entropy. Biology says the opposite, that everything multiplies and becomes incredibly rich and diverse. That's the law of life. Physics is the law of non-life. And it's the laws of life that determine marketing.*
>
> *When you understand that, you know it's OK to give. The authors [or business owners] who are generous with their time get it back, they build legions of fans. That kind of relationship makes marketing fun and successful. You cannot replace it with mechanical rules, but once you learn it and take it to heart, that becomes the basis for success in anything you do. If you treat people right, it comes back over and over again. If you build a network of relationships, it's only three degrees of separation [versus the classic six to reach anyone in the world]. Another part of the law of nature is that you have to break out of your shell, just as birds and reptiles do. You can do it one person to one person.*

■ BOB BURG AND WINNING WITHOUT INTIMIDATION

We'll finish this chapter by telling you about a guy who has done more to improve our attitude than just about anybody.

His name is Bob Burg and he believes in *Winning without Intimidation*, which is the title of one of his many books.

Here's the basic premise. When you're in a situation where you aren't getting your needs met, find the best way to de-escalate potential conflict *and* get the results you want. He calls this principle *positive persuasion* or *winning without intimidation,* and he is a master at it. One of his books, *Endless Referrals*, applies this concept directly to sales. This book was published by McGraw-Hill and sold over 100,000 copies. His self-published *Winning without Intimidation* also

sold about that many, so clearly, Bob takes his own principles seriously. (Typical business books sell 10,000 copies or fewer; typical
self-published books are lucky to sell 2,000.)

When things could get heated, we take a deep breath, step back,
and ask ourselves, "How would Bob handle this?" And a lot of the
time, we're able to access that part of our brain that can figure out
what Bob would do, defuse the conflict, and achieve our goal. For
instance, if two people are publicly escalating inappropriately on an
e-mail discussion list, instead of writing a nasty public post to shame
the offenders into better behavior, we might ask the two offenders in a
polite private note, as a personal favor, to change their behavior. The
response from both is usually extremely positive.

As an ex-Chicagoan and an ex-New Yorker, raised in a loud, in-
your-face culture, we've also found Bob's approach helpful in talking
to people from a different, quieter cultural background—such as the
New England Yankee farm community where Shel now lives.

Burg's principles work not only in customer service situations but
elsewhere—such as employee relations. Workplace ethicist Christopher Bauer devoted his September 22, 2008, e-newsletter to reinforcing positive behavior from employees when you catch them doing
something good.

*Rewarding positive behavior beats the pants off negative conse-
quences for inappropriate behavior pretty much every time.*[2]

■ NETWORKING THAT WORKS

Ever go to a business networking function and watch some idiot pressing business cards into people's hands, grinning insincerely, giving
the elevator pitch, and moving on to the next victim? Eeeew!

Fortunately, there are much better ways to network. Bob Burg also
happens to be an expert on networking the right way, so let's start
with him. In his audio program, "Endless Referrals," he describes a
far superior approach:

➤ Observe the group and identify a few people you'd like to
meet, who seem very well connected.

➤ Focus on the quality and depth of the contacts, not on
quantity.

➤ Make contact, remember his or her name, and listen much
more than you talk.

➤ Find ways to do something nice for your new acquaintance right then and there—such as introduce someone else you've met because you feel they could help each other.

➤ Follow up rapidly with a handwritten thank you that doesn't hawk your products and services, and continue to follow up with nice little touches over time (for instance, sending news clippings that mention your new contact).

Eventually, that other person will begin to see you as a person who adds value in his or her life. Your contact will want to know more about what you do and want to know how to help you and refer prospects to you. Wow.

If that kind of approach feels scary, get a copy of Bob's program. He breaks down every step and role-plays it.[3]

A great tool with this kind of approach combines the power of online technology with the appeal of handwritten notes: SendOut-Cards is a service that can digitize your handwriting, create either a completely original and personal card or one from a template, and send the card or even a gift through physical mail. This service is relatively inexpensive and a lot more convenient than the old-fashioned method, and these cards have a lot of impact. You can learn more at www.BusinessByReferrals.net.

You can also take a more structured approach, such as joining a local chapter of Business Networking International (BNI), which gathers a team of noncompeting businesses together to serve as referral agents for each other. BNI is a commitment, with required attendance at weekly meetings at which members report on how many referrals they gave and received during the week, and their results. But for many people with a primarily local market, it's possible to build an entire business around referrals from the network, and there's a lot of safety built into the rigid structure. Most chapters will let you attend as a guest or substitute to check it out and see if it's right for you. Check out www.bni.com for more information.

■ LESSONS AND ACTIONS

➤ Biological marketing can create large results from small inputs.

➤ Winning without intimidation turns adversaries into allies, and networking the right way turns these allies into unending streams of referral business.

Part

II

The New Marketing Mindset

Chapter 7

The New Marketing Matrix

Time to blow apart some more conventional marketing wisdom. It's a common principle in the marketing world that you need more than one impression to move someone up the ladder from unaware to aware to prospect to customer to evangelist. Many marketers use the figure of seven impressions within 18 months. (Though, as the bombardment of ads increases, many would say that those seven impressions need to be much closer together, or that even seven isn't enough.)

So, in the traditional view, the more you rain down messages upon the head of any particular individual, the more you push that person toward being first a prospect, and then a client. This idea leads to saturation advertising—the sort of thing that Coca-Cola or McDonald's calls a marketing strategy.

But theirs is a strategy that only works if you have essentially un-limited resources. They can afford to throw away millions of dollars in advertising in order to ensure that everyone hears their marketing messages—because some percentage of people actually do respond to the constant bombardment. But as small business owners and man-agers, we cannot afford to buy that kind of saturation, nor should we want to. It's so much better to figure out who are our real prospects, and talk to them as colleagues in a mutually beneficial partnership.

There is a certain amount of truth in the theory of repetition, but it's only part of the picture.

Under the right conditions, even a single marketing message may be enough to move someone from totally unaware to writing the check. Here's our twist on the formula.

The effectiveness of your marketing depends on three variables:

1. The relevance of your message to an individual's wants and needs at that exact moment

2. The quality of the message—and that includes the perceived value of your offer, the sense of trust and reliability that you've

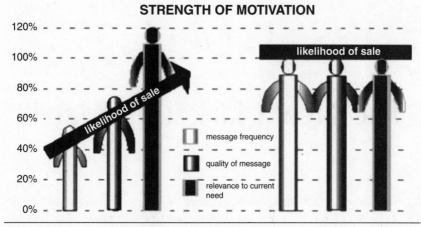

Figure 7.1   Strength of Motivation.

built, and the perceived quality of the product or service, as well as the quality of the user's experience of your marketing message (which, in turn, is created by the interplay of your message's copy, visuals, audio, and/or usability)

3. The number of times this individual is exposed positively to your messages

As shown in Figure 7.1, you are very likely to make the sale when all three of these variables are toward the top of the scale. But if any one variable is very high, a sale is quite possible even if the other variables are low. When they work in harmony or in sync, your chances are much greater. However, if one variable is strong enough, even if the others are weak, you can still close the sale (particularly if the strong one has relevance to current need).

In other words, if someone is looking for exactly what you offer, and you connect with that person through a beautifully crafted message that pushes all his or her hot buttons, that person might be ready to buy immediately, on the first contact. And if the desire is strong enough, that person will take action, right then and there. If the desire is not yet strong enough, it may take several more messages—different messages, not an exact repeat—to convince your prospect to become a customer.

The frequency axis is particularly tricky. In general, more *unique* messages move the prospect forward toward making the purchase—in part because, over time, increased frequency artificially increases desire, so that eventually, the perceived need to act on the desire moves up the ladder of the consumer's consciousness. However, repeating the exact same message in too close proximity will not be effective; it will start getting annoying very quickly. Think about watching a one-hour television show. If you see the same commercial at the beginning and end of the show, you're likely to be pretty tolerant of it. But if you see the same commercial at every single break, you might feel like throwing something at the TV after the third or fourth time it appears.

Yet if instead of the same commercial, the advertiser ran a series of six commercials, each of which stressed a different benefit, you'd probably still be listening by the end of the show, even if you felt the advertiser was overdoing it a bit.

Does that mean you should never repeat? No—just that you need to be careful. Here's a situation where more repetition would have increased the effectiveness. A local college FM radio station ran a Public Service Announcement (PSA) about why they had stopped streaming their programming over the Web, how new rules made it impossibly expensive, and it gave a URL for people to take action. As an occasional streaming audio listener, Shel was interested, but the spot was aired only rarely. The first few times he heard it while driving and couldn't write down the URL. Eventually, he did get the web address and did visit the site, but that was over a month after he first heard the announcement.

A greater frequency—say, once every couple of days—might have burned that URL into his brain and gotten him to click over a whole lot sooner. But the concept of the PSA—that streaming audio listeners have much to gain in creating pressure to change this new regulation—is definitely from the mutual-benefit book of strategies and tactics.

On the other hand, when someone is not a prospect, is not in the market for what you're selling, 20 messages will not move this person up the ladder. To use the same example, if Shel had heard the spot back in the days when he connected to the Web over phone lines at 2,400 bps, it wouldn't have mattered how often he heard it, he would never have been moved to action. Until he got broadband Internet, Shel was simply not a prospect for streaming audio.

■ PULL VERSUS PUSH

This might be a good time to look at the differences between *pull* and *push* marketing. Push marketing is the foundation for most traditional marketing. Focused heavily on advertising, push marketing happens when a company shoves its marketing at prospects. It's interruptive, sometimes even in-your-face. It shrieks, "You need to know about this, and you need to buy it! Now! Don't delay!" Push marketing wants to intrude, wants you to stop what you're doing and process this "important" information, all the way to the store.

Some would say that a marketer's job is to artificially create desire for a product, but we don't think that's following the Golden Rule. If a consumer is already in the market—for a breakfast cereal, a car, a computer, whatever—it's totally appropriate to create interest in your particular product. But to push a consumer with no previous interest toward a product that doesn't address that consumer's real needs and wants is dishonest—and not conducive to that all-important long-term relationship.

Pull marketing, on the other hand, allows the consumer to be in charge of the process. Someone decides to solve a problem, answer a need, or gratify a desire, and that consumer self-selects into a prospect. The prospect begins a research process to find the right solution, and the prospect chooses how to find messages that help refine the search. The research process could take just a few seconds or several years. It might involve such activities as:

➤ Entering a search phrase into Google or one of its competitors

➤ Looking up information in the Yellow Pages or in the classified pages of a trade magazine

➤ Asking friends for recommendations, or following recommendations from experts

➤ Consulting trusted sources such as *Consumer Reports*

➤ Reading product reviews on magazines or web sites

➤ Examining vendors' web sites, publications, and printed sales materials

➤ Initiating or following vendor-specific ("Does anyone have experience working with...") and general ("Who would you recommend to do...") discussions on Internet discussion groups and social networking web sites

➤ Participating in a focus group or beta test

In short, pull marketing is never intrusive. It's driven by your own customers. You can influence it but you can't control it.

And it works a whole lot better in our information-overloaded world. When people get hit with as many as 3,000 marketing messages every day, smart consumers have learned to filter out this barrage. They use technological tools, such as web browser pop-up blockers, TiVo, or the mute button, or they simply tape a TV show and fast-forward the commercials. They also use psychological filtering: mental cues that say, *this is an ad, ignore it.*

Unfortunately, the response of most marketers has been to up the volume, push harder, increase the frequency, and turn formerly ad-free spaces into commercial zones: to beat us into submission with even more and more aggressive push marketing.

So those who understand and use pull marketing have a huge advantage. We win in marketing by reaching the exact people who are ready to buy—with a message they can't resist, because it appeals directly to their current wants and needs. Pull marketing is really good at that.

Think about it. Say you're moderately interested in new technology and how computers continue to make our lives easier. Right now, it's a mild, purely academic interest. Marketing messages about the latest technologies catch some small part of your attention and you file them deep in the back of your mind. Then suddenly you try to boot your computer and nothing happens; it's dead. Now, when you see an ad or an article about the latest technology, you pay very close attention. Since you need to replace the computer, you think carefully about which of those new capabilities or customer service qualities are important to you—and very quickly, you research the available choices and place an order. If a marketer happens to send you a mailing about a special sale on exactly the computer you need, you'll order it. But if you'd gotten the same mailing a week earlier, you'd have tossed it in the recycle bin.

The change in circumstances—your computer breakdown—moved you instantly two rungs up the ladder from vaguely aware, right past prospect, and all the way up to *hot* customer, ready to move immediately.

The problem for marketers, of course, is knowing when that moment will happen—when changed circumstances convert someone from a nonprospect to a buyer—and how to be in the customer's mind at that magical moment, without having been a pest before the buyer made that transition. Here's where pull media, such as Yellow Pages, classified ads, and the World Wide Web, can have a huge impact. Pull media are customer-driven. They wait for a user to approach and pull the marketing information into their consciousness, unlike push media, which thrust messages into the audience's awareness without being invited in. When the customer is finally ready and turns to such a medium, where he or she is in control of the selection process, then a previous build-up of positive, nonintrusive messages over time can provide immediate advantage to the savvy marketer.

A real-life example: In the spring of 2002, Shel had a kidney stone, which caused extreme pain. He remembered that a former participant on a publisher's discussion list had written a book about kidney stone treatment—and that she had always been helpful and intelligent, not just about medical issues but about publishing topics as well.

Shel first tried entering her business name as a .com domain name; it didn't come up. So then he went to a search engine and searched for her business name plus the phrase "kidney stone." Instantly, he had her web site and ordered the book. Because she had, over a period of years, established herself as the authority Shel would trust if he knew someone with a kidney stone problem, he didn't want or need to sort through all the results for kidney stone treatment. Her prior participation had created confidence that she could help. Even though Shel used a pull medium, he'd already chosen the vendor; only if he'd been unable to locate her would he have explored other options.

Other writers also point out the holes in the standard formula of seven impressions. For example, Roy Williams's *Secret Formulas of the Wizard of Ads* refers to the APE, or Advertising Performance Equation. In his view, the effectiveness of your advertising is directly tied to other variables beyond frequency, including the prospect's personal experience with your firm. He says that if you multiply your "Share of Voice"—the percentage of advertising in your category that comes from you—by the ad's power to convince ("Impact Quotient"), you get "Share of Mind," and then, when you multiply the result by the prospect's "Personal Experience Factor"—direct experience of your company by the prospect—you can determine your market share. Multiply the Share of Market by the Market Potential (the number of customers actually out there), and you can determine your sales volume.

Expressed as a formula, it looks like this:

$$\text{Sales Volume} = \text{SoV} \times \text{IQ} \times \text{PEF} \times \text{MPo}$$

So customers who have positive previous experiences with a company are *far more likely* to respond to that company's ads than those with a history of bad experiences.[1]

Williams is onto something, but he misses one crucial point: advertising is only one part of marketing (often, the most expensive and least effective part). You can get to that share of mind and market without having to pay for it.

■ PRACTICAL PULLS

The secret to effective pull marketing is twofold. First, of course, you have to be found when your prospect is looking. Second and equally important, you have to position yourself so that your prospect decides on his or her own initiative to trust you with those hard-earned banknotes.

As you begin to explore this new and different world, you'll find dozens if not hundreds of ways to do that, most of which involve some way of providing useful content that positions you as the expert who can help. (Keep this in mind as you read Chapter 15 about effective marketing tactics; the combination is very potent). A few ideas:

➤ Articles and book excerpts that you can not only distribute to your own customer and prospect base but also seed out to infinite numbers of web sites, newsletters, and so forth

➤ Writing and publishing a book or e-book

➤ Speaking and coaching

➤ Introductory teleseminars, webinars, white papers, special reports, and so forth

➤ Trivia quizzes related to the problem you want to solve (two among many formats: "What you don't know CAN harm you," "Test your expertise against the pros")[2]

➤ Providing a do-it-yourself assessment tool that leads your prospect to the inexorable conclusion that he or she needs you

Amplifying that last example, consultant David Wood writes,

Assessments are a fantastic way to attract visitors. Assessments are quizzes and questionnaires that create an interactive experience for your prospects. "How Successful Are You?" "Are You Ready for a Relationship?" "Are You Stressed?" People love to fill them out and better yet, they like to pass them on to their friends . . . Once you have a visitor's email, you can contact them more to build the relationship you started with the give away. And you get a chance to show them what else you can offer them (i.e. coaching, an information product, a teleclass, etc.).[3]

One of Wood's clients

. . . has a great system for following up with potential clients who take the quizzes. He asks for their name and email address before

they hit the score button. He tells them where they are based on their score, and then follows up 6 times via an autoresponder specific to that quiz! The autoresponder messages are to upsell to his coaching.

■ LESSONS AND ACTIONS

➤ The effectiveness of marketing messages depends not only on frequency but also on the relevance and quality of that message.

➤ Customer-driven pull marketing is better positioned to succeed than company-driven push marketing.

➤ Once you've let your prospects pull themselves toward you, provide something substantial and useful enough to begin to cement their perception that you are the answer to their prayers.

Chapter 8

Abundance versus Scarcity

■ THE OLD SCARCITY PARADIGM

We've always heard that the pie is finite. If you win, someone else has to lose. There's not enough to go around. If you believe this, you're forced to spend lots of time and energy competing, striving to win, and defeating others.

But the whole premise of this book is that it's simply not true. There *is* enough to go around. Perhaps the distribution system needs some readjustment, but the pie keeps expanding. The eighteenth-century economist Malthus was wrong; the world produces enough for its growing population. And businesses can thrive and prosper without trying to drive their competitors out of business.

■ THE PROSPERITY CONSCIOUSNESS PARADIGM—AND ITS PROBLEMS

Some years ago, it seemed that all the buzz was about prosperity consciousness—about the idea that if you tapped into the right vein of the universe, you would be prosperous. Of course, with the stock market on a rapid-fire growth curve at the time, prosperity seemed to be very easy to achieve. Then the stock market tanked, and all of a sudden nobody was talking about prosperity consciousness—they were too busy surviving.

For marketing heretics like us, the idea never held much water in the first place. While neither of us is opposed to having material wealth, we recognize that money is not an end in itself, but a means. We use money to trade for purchases that make our life or the world better. The ability to trade for other things gives money value; without that ability, even a million-dollar bill would be just another piece of paper.

So, rather than Prosperity Consciousness, let's think in terms of Abundance Consciousness.

Rather than working toward material wealth in and of itself, Shel started focusing on the blessings in his life. And there were a great many:

- ➤ Good health
- ➤ A loving family
- ➤ A beautiful house in the country with wonderful friends and neighbors
- ➤ Enjoyable work that actually improves the world
- ➤ Community involvements that also make the world better
- ➤ The chance to travel
- ➤ An average of six weeks of vacation per year
- ➤ A house full of books, art, and music
- ➤ Schools that stimulate his children's creativity
- ➤ Nearby colleges and cultural centers that have amazing performances and lectures
- ➤ Closeness to nature, with terrific places to hike, bird-watch, bike ride, cross-country ski, and swim—either within walking distance or a very short distance away
- ➤ The pleasures of farm-fresh food and home-cooked gourmet meals, as well as the pleasures of sophisticated gourmet restaurant fare

He writes,

My life is one of great fortune and privilege, but not one that revolves around material wealth. I've learned to be a good shopper for what I want, and I've discovered that I can live a very comfortable, dare I say pampered, lifestyle. It seems to me that many people I know who have a higher income are actually less happy than I am. They always seem to be desperate to go out and make more and more money, while I make a comfortable living but leave lots of time in my life to walk in the woods, explore foreign cities, enjoy family time, attend concerts, and so forth.

Although I didn't yet have the phrase, Abundance Consciousness, to express this idea, my early thinking on this topic was what inspired me to write my fourth book, The Penny-Pinching Hedonist: How to Live Like Royalty with a Peasant's Pocketbook. *That book told every reader how to have more fun and spend less money doing it. I also was inspired to set up my first website, FrugalFun.com, back in 1996; it has grown to offer hundreds of articles that help people find abundance in their lives.*

The amazing thing is that when I opened my life up to that idea, the already abundant blessings in my life increased manyfold.

Jay, too, is an abundance thinker. As one of the best-known marketing authors in the world, he has no obvious need to cooperate with others. Some in his position would think they no longer need to be nice to others and wouldn't see any gain from helping them. But Jay discovered years ago that when he helps others, good things come back to him. He has a long history of giving support to younger, lesser-known marketing writers—and as a result of his willingness to collaborate, he has co-created far more books than he could write on his own, and his information empire is much more lucrative.

■ THE NEW VISION: NOT SCARCITY, NOT PROSPERITY, BUT ABUNDANCE

Here's another way to express that radical, heretical idea:

Your life can be abundant and full of blessings, with or without material wealth.

Abundance is fundamentally different from prosperity. Prosperity still works on the idea that you have to conquer others, that you have to strive for more money, and that the pie is finite; your gain is someone else's loss. Abundance says that the pie is infinite and that helping others is one way to help yourself—the more you help, the more the whole pie expands.

It also says that you have to act and believe in the whole process. If you think and act from a scarcity model, you will find scarcity. If the energy you put into the universe comes from the mindset that you can easily get what you need and more, that's what you're likely to find.

We've been talking about this idea long before it was popularized as the Law of Attraction, in the movie *The Secret*. Another piece of abundance and attraction thinking is that you can attract clients and customers who seek you out, instead of chasing them down and competing with others to get that business.

■ THE ABUNDANCE MODEL IN BUSINESS

Lots of things change once you start looking at business through the abundance filter. The biggest difference is that you don't need to feel threatened by your competitors. Because there is enough for all of you, you may even find that you want to cooperate. You can form alliances with others in your niche, and these alliances will be far more powerful than the group of you scrambling like mice to beat one another to the cheese—never realizing that the cheese is inside a mousetrap.

Businesses that you partner with will be more eager to put their relationship with you ahead of less ethical companies. They know that a joint venture involving you will have fewer risks and more benefits. They know that you are someone who can be trusted, and you won't be sucked into the abyss that swallowed Bernie Madoff, Enron, or Arthur Andersen.

Most importantly, you benefit yourself. Your business thrives, you feel good about what you do, and you build warm relationships based on the best human qualities. You walk the streets with a light heart and your head held high.

Listen for a moment to Internet marketing consultant B. L. Ochman of www.whatsnextblog.com:

> *I used to be afraid to put news about my competitors' e-books, newsletters and teleconferences in my newsletter. But I've completely changed my mind. I have begun to promote my competitors' works and to include them in the affiliate program for my e-books. I do teleseminars with them.*
>
> *Why? There is plenty of work to go around. People looking for Internet marketing are going to shop around anyway so why deny that fact? We can refer work to each other and we can enjoy the halo effect of being associated with smart, accomplished people. Try it, you'll benefit.*

Huh—what just happened here? As copywriters and marketing strategists, why on earth would we give you the name and contact info of one of our competitors?

Maybe, just maybe, it's because we really do believe in abundance thinking. We believe so much in it that on our web site www.guerrillamarketinggoesgreen.com/resources, you'll find a listing of Clued-In Copywriters, all of whom are our competitors.

And Ochman believes in abundance, too. When Shel wrote for permission to use her story in his earlier book *Principled Profit: Marketing That Puts People First*, she not only reviewed it in her newsletter but even connected him with a very well-known author who blurbed the book.

Yes, this philosophy really does pay back. Ochman, who had been living just blocks from the World Trade Center in New York City until 9/11, was having a fight with her ex-landlord; she'd had to move when her apartment became uninhabitable after the attacks, and the landlord was trying to retain many thousands of dollars that she would have paid in rent. She turned to her allies online, and within weeks, the pressure campaign she created accomplished the desired effect.

Our theory is that Ochman was able to get so much help from some of the world's heavy hitters in sales and marketing because she had long ago established herself as a person who doesn't just take, but gives—again, operating out of that abundance mentality. If she had been a cutthroat, if she had tried to steal business from her competitors or turn in useless work to her clients, would there have been a mass movement to come to her rescue? We strongly doubt it. First of all, she wouldn't have been known to the Internet communities where she turned for help. And second, people who had been burned would have sabotaged the campaign before it ever got started.

Let's look at another entrepreneur who has succeeded by embracing the abundance paradigm: Scottie Claiborne of Hullaballoo Entertainment. Recognizing that she was getting national and international traffic to her web site www.hullaballoorental.com for a local service (rentals of kids' inflatable play equipment), she turned her site into a directory so that no matter where you are, you can find the nearest vendor. Then she sought out other companies and asked them to list on her site. In other words, she drives traffic to businesses that could be thought of as her competitors. She believes that her listing of other sites is directly responsible for her Number 1 rank at Google, which in turn generates lots and lots of traffic directly.

The site was successful very quickly, and she branched out into selling the equipment to other companies—all of whom know her company because she's been funneling inquiries to them.[1]

■ LESSONS AND ACTIONS

➤ Abundance is different from—and more powerful than—scarcity, or even prosperity.

➤ Giving people, who act from abundance, create a reservoir of goodwill that they can draw on in times of need.

Chapter 9

Build Powerful Alliances—with Competitors, Too

The word *"guerrilla"* traditionally implies an armed struggle. In war, the usual way to neutralize an enemy is to render that enemy impotent through dramatic losses of personnel and resources. You drive out the oppressor by making the cost of an invasion or occupation too high.

But Guerrilla Marketing has never been about shooting your opponent. Marketing guerrillas outflank the competition by moving swiftly, nimbly, and unexpectedly. We find and exploit new markets before the big, slow-moving household names even know there is a new market. And sometimes we're out again before they even come in.

Another way to disarm your competition is to turn those companies into part of your marketing team. By working together, you leverage the strengths your former opponent already has. You tap into the markets your so-called adversary already created.

Yes, we're talking about cooperating with your toughest competitors. This is a strategy that:

➤ Gives you access to an existing and proven market

➤ Lets you take a privileged position in the customer's mind, because you have the powerful endorsement of a company he or she already trusts

➤ Allows you both to be stronger by enabling initiatives that would be too big or too expensive for either of you to do alone

➤ Eliminates the wasted energy you previously spent fighting each other, putting each other down, or battling negative perceptions you created about each other

In many cases, the cooperation is going to be some kind of "joint venture" (JV)—a fancy phrase that simply means working together with another business. JVs might range from a simple comarketing deal such as stuffing fliers for each other in outbound orders or giving a purchase link in an e-zine, all the way up to a full-scale corporate merger. In between, there are many rungs on the ladder: project-specific partnerships, bundling products from different companies to add value, handing out a freebie from another business as an incentive award, and on and on it goes.

Since for many people, the idea of working with a competitor feels peculiar, we'll start with some examples that show how very easy it actually is to work with people in the same field. Then we'll look at some more Guerrilla JVs for businesses that don't compete directly.

■ TURN YOUR COMPETITORS INTO ALLIES

➤ Get to Know Other People in Your Niche

When you notice a new arrival in the marketplace—or if you enter a market new to you—pick up the phone and get acquainted. Become active in trade associations in your industry and in your geographic area (for example, Chamber of Commerce or neighborhood business association). Participate in Internet discussion groups with others in your own or closely related fields. Talk shop, discuss approaches to problems, let each other know about events or opportunities of interest. Know each company's unique selling proposition (USP), which is the key reason why it makes sense to do business with that company. That way, you'll know when and where to refer accounts that aren't quite right for you.

Key Guerrilla Principle: Find out how you can provide assistance to the other person—before you bring up your own wants and needs.

➤ Market Together, Cooperatively

Here's a wonderful newspaper co-op ad from 11 local florists, who teamed up just before Mother's Day (see Figure 9.1).

By joining forces, the consortium could afford a big, noticeable ad. An ad one-eleventh the size would have been easy to ignore, but this

You wouldn't buy your groceries from a **florist!**

So, why buy your plants from a **grocer!**

For the healthiest plants and flowers, it makes sense to buy from a grower or florist... not a grocer! We can tell you how to expertly care for everything you purchase. Our commitment to our customers doesn't end when we make a sale. It just begins. And we're proud that our reputation for quality and service grows stronger every year. Come check-out our selection!

Always in Bloom
220 No. Pleasant St.
Amherst
253-5545

Child's Flower Shop
80 Maple Street
Florence
584-6689

Main Street Florist
89 Main Street
Easthampton
527-9536

Mt. View Greenhouse
26 Strong Street
Easthampton

Dwyer Florist
202 Main Street
Northampton
584-3784

Wildflowers of Williamsburg
Colonial Shoppes, Rt. 9
Williamsburg
268-9330

Spuds & Buds
Rts. 5 & 10
South Deerfield
665-8371

Florence Village Flower Shoppe
29 Keyes Street
Florence
584-9595

Nuttelman's Florist
Corner of Woodlawn
Ave. & Prospect St.
Northampton
584-2272

Truehart's Garden Center & Florist
25 College Highway
Southampton
527-5047

Luci's Country Greenery
100 Elm Street
South Deerfield Center
665-2997

Remember Mom with flowers! Mother's Day — Sunday, May 10th

Figure 9.1 When joining together, 11 competitors can afford a big, dramatic ad.

one filled a quarter-page (in a large-format broadsheet newspaper) and demanded to be noticed.

Another example: In publishing, many small presses will include a flier for a complementary book from another publisher as they ship out orders. For the very low cost of printing and mailing the fliers, participating publishers get to reach an entirely new audience. Sometimes, publishers will even sell a bundle consisting of their own and other firms' books, gathered together at a value price.

It's not just small companies doing this, either. Some of the largest and most fiercely competitive corporations in the world engage in joint ventures regularly. The first car Shel ever bought new was a 1988 Chevrolet Nova, which was essentially identical to the Toyota Corolla. Built by Chevrolet to Toyota's specifications, it was a marvelous car, and about $2,000 less than the same car with the Toyota logo. More than 20 years after production ended, there are still plenty of them on the road. Similarly, the popular Ford Escort wagon was really a Mazda, and on and on.

Think about the package delivery business. FedEx and the U.S. Postal Service have a very interesting arrangement. The USPS subcontracts intercity air transportation of Express Mail and Priority Mail to FedEx, which gets a substantial new revenue stream and makes use of otherwise wasted air freight capacity. And meanwhile, FedEx has installed thousands of drop boxes at post offices around the country, thus helping its consumers avoid pick-up charges and making shipping with the company incredibly convenient.[1]

For service businesses, sometimes your biggest competitor is not another company, but your prospects' ideas of doing it themselves. Certainly, this is true in the writing and consulting that we both do for a living. Most people believe they can write well; few understand the difference between putting sentences together on paper to convey information—something most people *can* actually do themselves—and writing materials with a sharply defined focus and a powerful call to action, or a news hook. Only a very small percentage of businesses ever hire outside professional copywriters. Large firms hire this skill internally, and many small firms use their own (untrained) marketing departments.

The companies that write their own marketing materials will usually never know the "opportunity cost" of going it alone, that is, how many more sales they could have gotten by using a professional. But we've learned not to try to convince them; it's much easier to leverage the interest from a prospect who already knows it's time to hire out the copywriting. And our marketing strategy focuses on both making contact with that already-convinced audience and facilitating our existing clients' desire to demonstrate to—and convince—the "unbe-lievers."

Professional writers compete not only with homegrown do-it-yourselfers but also with software tools. As an example, résumé shops around the world saw their markets contract when Microsoft started bundling a résumé template in Microsoft Word. During the boom times when companies would hire any warm body, people could get by with that approach. But in a leaner economy, a low-quality, formu-laic résumé probably won't properly highlight the client's strengths or minimize weaknesses, the format may not be appropriate, or per-haps the writers haven't focused their résumé on the target market. It's up to the professional résumé writers to point out these deficiencies and demonstrate how their value is more than worth their price.

This is an ideal situation for résumé writers to comarket and make that value infinitely clear, just as the florists did in their coopera-tive ad.

➤ Refer Business to Each Other

Typically, you will each have areas of specialization that you do better than others. So if you get an inquiry from someone best served by your competitor, you help the customer by playing matchmaker. And your competitors will do the same for you. With both competitors and complementary businesses, you may choose to pay or charge a referral commission, or simply pass appropriate clients to each other.[2]

Very early in his business, which he started in 1981, Shel discov-ered the power of this kind of marketing:

> *My business started primarily as a typing service, but very quickly, I branched out into writing résumés and marketing ma-terials. I joined a local association of secretarial services, and because people knew my specialties, I got a lot of résumé work through referrals.*
>
> *At the same time, after my first two tape-transcription assign-ments, I decided I really disliked that part of the business and began referring those jobs out to other services.*

This kind of cooperation always has three winners: the client, of course, who gets the best providers for the services he or she needs—but also both the referring and the receiving businesses. You don't let the things you dislike get in the way of doing what you enjoy and excel at, yet you're able to keep your clients happy when they need those services.

Wendy Shill Kurtz, MBA, APR, CPRC, president of the PR firm Elizabeth Charles & Associates, LLC, www.elizabethcharles.com, has a similar outlook:

> *I disagree with the premise that there are only two types: winners and losers. All too often, we as professionals tend to overlook the basic concept we learned in childhood, "Do unto others as you would have them do unto you." I have found that some of my best referrals have come from vendors and those competitors with whom I maintain a sense of "we're in this together," rather than "we're out to beat each other to the top."*[3]

➤ Subcontract, Joint Venture, or Even Merge

If one of you has too much work and the other has too little, doesn't it make sense to work with a professional that you trust and even it all out?

Create temporary joint ventures, where each of you is a partner. After all, if fierce competitors like Apple and IBM could join together (with Motorola as a third partner) to develop the Power PC chip architecture, surely you and your competitors can put aside your differences. These could be equal or weighted partnerships.

In some cases, if you work well together, and enjoy advantages of scale, increased buying power, and so forth—and your corporate cultures harmonize well with each other—a permanent merger or acquisition may even make sense.

➤ Help Out When You Can, and Reap the Benefits

In the earliest days of Shel's business, one of his competitors called and asked if he needed any office supplies. He wanted to place an order with a large mail-order wholesaler and didn't need enough to make the minimum. That phone call has saved Shel thousands of dollars, because he hadn't been aware of this very inexpensive supplier. Shel not only added his order to his competitor's but for the past 27 years, he's ordered from that company—at a deep discount.

And when that competitor later moved out of the area, he was one of several who sent all their clients to Shel when they closed their shops.

He got the initial call—*and* the later referrals—because they were on friendly terms and had often sent each other clients.

Lesson: be there if your competitors fold. If you've maintained strong positive relations, if you've cooperated on several projects, if your competitor leaves the business, *you* will get the referrals.

The above examples are only a small slice of what's possible. Dave Pollard lists six different large categories of JV possibilities, and his list isn't even comprehensive (leaving out, for instance, best-practices training):

1. Collaboration on large projects that either need extra horsepower or complementary skills

2. Cooperative purchasing

3. Research and development, including new products

4. Marketing

5. Cross-industry licensing

6. Leveraging skills[4]

■ YOU'VE DONE THE HARDEST PART—NOW, NETWORK WITH COMPLEMENTARY BUSINESSES

Psychologically, it may be pretty hard, at first, to accept the idea that your competitors can be extremely powerful allies in growing your business. That's why we put it first in this section. We wanted you to see that these techniques work even with the people you might have thought you were least likely to develop partnerships with. The ideas in the next sections will seem easy to implement after you've already started thinking about how you and your competitors can help each other.

➤ Online Joint Ventures

Partnering with established businesses can completely reinvent your business model. Consider the way Amazon.com birthed the modern affiliate program by syndicating the ability to have a bookstore—without needing inventory—to thousands of web site partners, around 1995 or 1996. All of a sudden, those sites and newsletters had a way to offer their members relevant, highly targeted titles from the convenience of home, with no need to carry inventory, no need to worry about selection, and even a small income stream.

It was a brilliant move, and it took Amazon from a relatively small startup to the best-branded bookseller online—because it seemed back then that if you visited ten sites, five or six would have an Amazon store.

Amazon's strategy is a case study in what marketing legend Alex Mandossian calls "the paradox of syndication"[5] —that restricting your presence to your own web site is counterproductive. The more channels that offer a company's message (or products), the faster it grows. This is true both online and off. Consider how the power of syndication built such brands as Dear Abby, the Peanuts comic strip, and every chain store franchise you can think of.

Mandossian developed this theory after years as an active promoter of Internet-based JVs. These are extremely common in the Internet-marketing superstar world, where you find the same gurus speaking at each other's conferences and endorsing each other's products. We believe that one of the reasons this small group has generated so much wealth is this strong cooperation. Rather than make all the sales on the basis of your own client and prospect list, by cooperating with other businesses to reach their lists and cutting them in on the profits, you reach a far larger audience and make many more sales.

But there are special considerations in setting up Internet JVs. Master copywriter and commercial writing coach Bob Bly outlines some of the concerns he has when he's approached. Recognizing that if you over-e-mail, your readers start unsubscribing, Bly figures he has 100 slots a year to promote other people's products, and each one should be worth at least $4,000 to him if he wants this aspect of his business to bring in $400,000. This means a 20 percent commission on a $20 book isn't going to cut it. He suggests you answer three questions when approaching "gurus" about partnering with you:

1. Who are you and why do you know the guru? Are you a subscriber? Have you bought product? Attended a workshop?

2. How would your product directly benefit the guru's subscribers?

3. What payout terms are you suggesting? (The guru looks for 50 percent on a product price of $20 or more, though a lower percentage is acceptable if the price is above $1,000.)

Send this information and offer or provide a free review copy of the product. The good gurus will want to kick the tires and make sure they can see the value in the product, so they can honestly enthuse about it to their audience.[6]

➤ **Geographic Alliances**

If your business uses a retail model—you have a storefront or office where your customers and clients come to you—geographically based partnerships make a lot of sense. It is in everyone's interest to draw people into the area where your businesses are located. And that area can be as small as a single office building, a strip mall, a city block—or as big as an entire state or country. This is why Chambers of Commerce and neighborhood business associations get organized and why economic development offices and tourism departments promote their region as a place to locate or visit. But that's only the beginning.

Some other ways to cross-promote:

➤ Organize and promote a special event that draws traffic. It could be as simple as a group promotion with 20 percent off any one item, or as complex as a street fair with live concerts, children's activities, dignitaries, and so forth.

➤ Market the neighborhood or region as a destination. In Minneapolis, the many restaurant owners along Nicollet Avenue banded together and dubbed it "Eat Street"; they even posted permanent banners proclaiming this to all who pass by—and even people who live in distant suburbs recognize the destination.

➤ Seek partnerships with complementary businesses in the neighborhood. *Cooperative Life Leader* magazine reports that a food co-op in Durham, New Hampshire, invited the weekly farmers' market to set up shop outside the store.[7] The existing storefront provided a natural base for the farm stands, and customers seeking fresh produce were drawn into the store to buy other natural foods.

Join with your neighbors to advertise the neighborhood. There are many ways to do this: list several businesses in one ad; give more space to one business at a time, rotating through all the members; or create and distribute a group flier, web site, ad-supported map, catalog, or discount coupon book.

Organize together under an association banner for neighborhood-improvement projects—anything from a group litter-pickup to creating public pressure to close down health and safety hazards—and tell the media what you're doing.

If there's a major attraction nearby, work with the local tourism bureau to develop a brochure about other nearby attractions (including yours) that the large attraction can distribute. The participants can reciprocate, of course.

► Other Joint Ventures

Geographical proximity is only one possible bridge to collaboration. Consider a tiny startup that joined forces with the largest and most powerful player in the entire computer industry, in order to supply operating systems for the giant's new line of microcomputers, back in 1981. If you knew it was Microsoft and its partnership with IBM, you get the gold star.

If you're in a service business, there are many opportunities to partner with complementary services. For instance, wedding planners, caterers, banquet halls, photographers, florists, and musicians can cooperate to provide a one-stop wedding service. And if your business is not local, your partnerships can spread around the world.

The partnership can be active or passive—and sometimes can lead to whole new opportunities. A marketing-savvy graphic artist brought Shel and a local web designer into a three-way pitch meeting to produce some collateral and a web site for their local Board of Realtors.

The organization had asked the web designer to register a very obscure domain name that only had meaning for them. When they heard the domain name, Shel and the graphic artist exchanged looks and told the organization why the domain name they had picked would be a marketing disaster. They told the executive director to imagine giving out that name on the radio, and to look at a name that would reinforce the group's identity and message. This was a free consultation; they didn't even know if they had the job yet. But the whole room brainstormed a bunch of better domain names as a result.

Years later, Shel got a call from the president of the largest real estate firm in the service area. He had been impressed at that meeting and came to Shel to rewrite the firm's entire collection of a dozen or so brochures—a very juicy assignment. By advising the client that its present course was strewn with obstacles, Shel had unknowingly put himself in the position to receive a much, much larger assignment: one for which he was not competing against any other copywriters.

Most of our JV relationships are far less formal. We often recommend vendors who provide complementary services: graphic design, search engine optimization, web site coding, press release distribution, and so forth. Rather than tit for tat, it's "what goes around comes around." And other professionals who offer similar services send us referrals, using one of three models:

1. Informal referrals, in which no money changes hands
2. Formal referrals, where the receiving business owner pays a commission (Shel, for example, pays 10 percent on the first order)
3. Subcontractor relationships, where just one business works directly with the client, and farms out other services as needed (in some cases marking up the subcontractor's service)

■ SOCIAL PROOF—TURN YOUR CUSTOMERS AND SUPPLIERS INTO EVANGELISTS

If mutual-success cooperative approaches work well horizontally with competitors, won't they also work vertically? The people who choose to do business with you and the people with whom you choose to do business are your natural allies. We are ardent believers in the marketing power of "social proof": convincing people to take a certain action because a critical mass of the populace, or of people they respect and trust, have told them to do so. Testimonials, endorsements, referrals, and other social proof techniques allow your customers, others in your networks, and perhaps even celebrities, to do your marketing for you. (Note: Disclose any kind of money exchange in securing the endorsement, including affiliate relationships. We've marked affiliate URLs in this book with the symbol λ.)

➤ Use Testimonials

Use testimonials in your advertising, or submit testimonials to other businesses. If you're delighted with a product or service, offer a testimonial for that company's ads. Jim McCann's wildly successful 800-FLOWERS was plugged in national TV and print ads by AT&T— because McCann praised the telecommunications giant's toll-free service. It would have cost him millions of dollars to get the exposure if he'd paid for it himself.

On a much smaller scale, years ago, Shel offered a local telephone book publisher this plug:

I track my sources of clients, and Yellow Pages advertising brings in about 70 percent of them. Right now, I'm in the Pioneer Valley book and three Nynex books. Amazingly enough, Pioneer Valley is outpulling all three Nynex books combined. Keep up the good work!

—SHEL HOROWITZ, Author, *Marketing Without Megabucks: How to Sell Anything on a Shoestring*; Director, Accurate Writing & More, Northampton, MA

Not only did the company run this testimonial in local papers—and yes, Shel heard from several people who saw it—but it also showed its gratitude by throwing in a few hundred dollars in upgrades to his own ads in its book. Meanwhile, he got his name, his firm name, and the name of his then-current book plastered all over the phone book's three-county circulation area.

Not a bad deal for something that took about 3 minutes to write and maybe 30 minutes to negotiate.

If you do print or broadcast advertising anyway, and if your clients say nice things about you, ask permission to use their quotes in your ads. If the ads are on radio or TV, ask if they'll let you tape them reading the quotes. (For ideas on how to get really great testimonials, see Shel's earlier book *Grassroots Marketing: Getting Noticed in a Noisy World.*)

Even if you don't advertise, you can grow through referrals. It could be as simple as handing each client a business card and saying, "If you have friends or colleagues who need this service, please spread the word." And sometimes the client will turn to you and say, "I actually know several people. May I have a few more cards?"

And this works online, too. If you participate in any online groups (and you most definitely should), leverage the enthusiasm of your clients who participate. Make it a practice to ask people who've used your services and been enchanted by them to mention their delight to the list. So over a period of years, participants in this community will hear dozens of people exclaim about your skills and expertise.

Shel, for example, has developed a reputation for writing terrific promotional materials, even on tight deadlines:

Some of these publishers may go months or years between new titles. But when they have a new book coming out, they need to find someone to write their publicity. I post frequently and helpfully to this group, and many of my posts subtly demonstrate (often by using examples from client work I've done) the advantages of having press releases professionally written—something that's particularly true in the book industry, where it's very hard to get press coverage through "ordinary" press releases. And at the end of my post is my signature, an electronic business card that mentions my writing services, along with contact information and the slogan, "I make the world insist on learning why you're special." (To keep it fresh, I do change the signature every once in a while, or use one of the many alternate versions I've developed.)

Of course, Shel actively cultivates and nurtures this reputation. Here's a post he sent to one of those lists.

Just opened an envelope from <a list member and client> to discover a review of his book. Other than two paragraphs added at the beginning, it's almost identical to the press release I wrote.

This is not all that unusual. In fact, the one time I saw a New York Times story covering a book I'd written about, I was amused to see that this bylined article by a well-known columnist (no, I won't mention names!) took several entire paragraphs straight out of my release.

That's OK! That means that I did my job right and the journalist thought it was good enough. I am long past the need to see my own byline attached to my words.

So what's the lesson here?

Lesson 1: When sending out book press releases, always send your best work. Not only does it increase the chances of coverage, but it may be used essentially as is.

Lesson 2: Never send anything you'd be ashamed of if it landed in print.

The unspoken Lesson 3: Shel's press releases are so good that a reporter for the *New York Times*—probably the toughest paper in the nation to get media coverage in—lifted large portions and plopped it into an article. Shel can write you a press release that could get noticed and used by major media. But he didn't have to beat his readers over the head with that information. It was there as part of a long-term relationship of trust and expectation of quality that he has built over many years.

A publisher in the final stages of bringing out a new book sees this message and signature, remembers all the previous posts from others about Shel's excellent skills, quick service, and affordable prices—and calls or e-mails asking if Shel can do some writing.

His participation on these lists brings in thousands of dollars a year with a marketing cost of zero. Sometimes it will start with a very small job, perhaps a single press release—but his happy clients often come back for many other projects. Some of the people on these lists have done many thousands of dollars' worth of business with him.

One of his clients was initially somewhat skeptical about whether Shel's approach was actually better than what he'd been doing on his own. So he ran a test. He sent out a press release Shel had written to one group of journalists and one of his own press releases to another group. He reported back to the entire list that Shel's release had pulled six times as many responses as his own effort, and he has since come back for many projects.

Many vendors who participate in these lists—designers, editors, even an intellectual property lawyer—find that listmates account for a substantial percentage of their client load. Nor is it something found only on that particular list. At least as far back as 1995, when Shel was just beginning to explore this powerful technique, Jay included it in his book *Guerrilla Marketing Online* (co-authored with Charles Rubin).

Even better, you may actually get referrals from members of the list who have *not* used your services themselves. That may include industry gurus who list you in the resources sections of their books and web sites and newsletters.

This is a form of viral marketing, to use the phrase popularized by the brilliant marketing visionary Seth Godin in his book *Unleashing the Idea Virus*. Viral marketing uses resources far beyond the marketer's own organization to spread the message very rapidly, much as a virus spreads through close physical contact. The classic case is Hotmail, which grew amazingly rapidly by advertising its free e-mail services at the bottom of every outbound message sent by its users.

Hotmail was the fastest growing subscription-based service in world history, achieving an astonishing 12 million subscribers in its first year and a half. About 150,000 new users signed up every day, and they gave the company significant demographic information about themselves. By 1998, it was the largest e-mail provider in the world, dwarfing even America Online.[8] Microsoft bought it in 1997.

Juno, its nearest competitor in the free e-mail arena, acquired only about a third as many users in its first several years. Hotmail spent only $500,000 on marketing to acquire its first 12 million members; Juno, in contrast, spent $20 million.[9]

The difference? Hotmail pioneered the tagline ad and got the first-mover advantage.

Enlisting your customers to do your marketing can work in any demographic, in any industry. MarketingSherpa.com reported on an online magazine's success with teens—an audience traditionally difficult to sell to. The magazine *Kiwibox* simply asked its readers to not only make referrals but actually open up their e-mail address books to the company (with some privacy safeguards). Perhaps because the teens themselves create the magazine's content, the campaign was shockingly successful: a 29.34 percent increase in memberships.[10]

Much-published marketing author Marcia Yudkin, citing a booklet by sales consultant Paul Johnson called "Let Your Customer Sell You," talks about the art of asking for small favors. When someone gives you a testimonial, he or she has made an emotional commitment to you and your product. And the person who has done you a small favor may then be more willing to do you a larger favor.[11]

If the favor is a testimonial, your clients not only publicly state their commitment but also cement the reasons why they felt so good about you in their own minds. You may well get more referrals or more work assignments.

Johnson believes that one of the best times to get a testimonial is when you haven't heard from the client in a while. By writing the testimonial, the client is reminded of the value you created. But we disagree; we think it's better to get the testimonial when the fabulous job you did is still fresh in the client's mind.

And that relationship can be easily rekindled, even after an absence. For instance, you could send a quick note—perhaps accompanied by a small gift or a discount coupon for a future order—that says, "I just wanted to thank you again for your beautiful testimonial, reprinted below. For six months, it has helped me turn prospects into clients. I'm honored and gratified by your continued faith in my work."

David Frey, one of America's unsung marketing geniuses and author of *Marketing Best Practices* (see www.guerrillamarketinggoes green.com/resources), notes that you can use your clients and customers as case studies and write articles or white papers about them. If you publish articles in magazines, you're not paying for advertising; with many publications, you even get paid. Again, they get exposure, you get exposure, and you show how you've solved a problem for them. (Get their written permission ahead of time, of course.)

Frey also suggests giving out an award to a big customer or supplier. By so doing, you can build brand awareness, customer retention, and the opportunity for quite a bit of publicity and marketing oomph.

➤ Explore Co-Op Advertising Programs

Explore co-op advertising programs, where a supplier partially subsidizes the cost of a retailer's ads and in-store displays. Many manufacturers will provide logos, sales aids, and actual dollars to help you tell the world that you carry their products. You can sometimes also get this kind of help from credit card companies, retail co-ops, professional associations, and so on.

➤ Develop Incentive Programs

Institute cooperative loyalty, referral, and incentive programs that not only keep your customers coming back but also have your partner businesses actively recruiting new customers for you. These programs offer wonderful opportunities to partner with other merchants. Find complementary businesses whose offerings will resonate with your customers. You offer a reward from the other firm, which in turn rewards its own customers with something from you. This is something some of the country's largest corporations do. For instance, a cereal box may have a coupon good for a bottle of juice from a different company, or a fill-up at a gas station gets you a deep discount on a car wash. By using goods and services from other businesses as rewards in your loyalty and incentive programs (and vice versa), you have the benefit of reaching their customers as well as your own.

You can operate similar programs, not only to reward your own customers for frequency and amount of purchase but also to actively solicit referrals. If a customer sends you a customer, it's nice to say thank you. This could be just a quick note (handwritten and mailed, if you want maximum impact). But if someone sends a whole bunch of clients, a small gift is probably appropriate.

And unlike the frequency reward, where it makes the most sense to bring in other businesses, here's a perfect time to use your own offerings as a reward, so that your own client comes back to you again. We might give one of our books as a thank-you to a marketing client who has sent a large amount of business, for instance.

Larger companies have been known to be very creative with this, too. Intercontinental Hotels, one of the largest hospitality chains in the world, got an unheard-of 1,766 percent response on a promotion that enlisted their top rewards program users to bring in more business. In other words, the company *got responses from almost 18 times more people than had originally received the offer.*

The company offered triple reward points for a three-night stay, and provided codes to share the offer with three friends. Every single person who received the initial mailing shared the offer, and the promotion went viral.[12]

Talk about a triple-win. Intercontinental added substantial immediate revenues with all those three-night stays, paying only in slightly decreased revenues much later, when the new guests qualified for a free stay or other reward. The elite customers felt special, honored for their patronage. And the new guests started their guest careers with a big head start toward free lodging.

If one of your sales staff has been a super-achiever, a reward is certainly appropriate. (Set it up as a policy, with performance levels quantified, so you won't get accused of favoritism.) To create incentives within your own organization, partnering with other businesses once again expands the market for everyone. If you're friendly with a restaurant owner, see if he or she will donate a free dinner for two as a sales achievement award, in exchange for publicity in your company newsletter and on your web site. (As a side note, you can use this strategy in your outbound marketing, too. Donate a door prize to your local Chamber networking event, for example.)

➤ Bundling

Bundle complementary products and/or services together. Make life easier on your customers by arranging to provide all the pieces of the right solution, even when that means pulling them together from different vendors. Enhance your offer by combining complementary products that add value, for less money than buying them all separately. And of course, all the participating suppliers share the marketing cost, and all benefit by reaching each other's customers.

Here's a real-life example. To compete with integrated software that includes a word processor, spreadsheet, database, and graphics package, four different software companies bundled these four functions together. The word-processing company coordinated marketing.

Using the same principles, a carpenter, plumber, electrician, and painter could offer a one-stop home repair clearinghouse. A rental car company, airline, and hotel chain could join forces to offer a great one-stop deal for business travelers. A used-car dealer could team up with a car wash and an oil change service. The possibilities are limitless.

➤ Networking

Network with organizations that service your customers and become a preferred or endorsed supplier. When you provide products or services through an association, several wonderful things happen:

➤ You reach the organization's membership at no cost, through its newsletters, web site, and other promotional materials. Sometimes, this could be tens of thousands of members.

➤ You receive the organization's implied endorsement, and thus, the members are predisposed to choose you (and even recommend you to their own networks).

➤ The members will benefit from a better price, and the organization can receive a donation or a sales commission. Because you had no marketing cost, this is an easy benefit to offer.

➤ Enlist Your Customer's Help for Charity

Enlist your customers' help for programs that benefit both of you: environmental or charity initiatives, fundraising for independent stores, and so forth.

For the last several years, a local bank in Shel's community has divided $50,000 among a number of local charities. The bank's customers get to vote on how the money will be divided, by nominating their favorite organizations. The bank apportions the grants according to the number of votes, above a very low minimum number. But only customers can vote. Of course, if you don't already happen to have an account there, the bank will be glad to set one up. Needless to say, this bank gains a lot of new accounts as people sign up to support their choices.

And don't be afraid to embrace more controversial causes, if your demographics support it. Sure, everyone loves to help charities that are working on curing various diseases or solving poverty problems. But there's definitely a place for being willing to take a position, even if it's not universally popular. If there's strong alignment between your market and your chosen cause, doing so will build your reputation as a firm of integrity and courage, while allowing you to benefit from the exposure you get. The Body Shop, an international personal-care products firm founded by the late Dame Anita Roddick, embraced numerous controversial causes and used its stores to build awareness. Ice cream maker Ben & Jerry's probably did more than any other company to popularize the idea of business as a tool to fund social change.

While Ben & Jerry's was known for its social activism when the company was controlled by founders Ben Cohen and Jerry Greenfield, the company continues at least some significant social commitment under the current ownership by multinational food giant Unilever. Consider this note that the advocacy organization Common Cause sent to all its members with the subject line, "Yes Pecan!":

We've got BIG news. And it's pretty sweet.
    For the month of January, Ben & Jerry's is renaming its butter pecan ice cream flavor to "Yes Pecan!" and donating a portion

of the proceeds from scoop shop sales of the new flavor to the Common Cause Education Fund!

We're honored to be working with Ben & Jerry's to celebrate the spirit of activism and the newfound optimism that government can work for the common good.

Here's how you can help:

➤ *Find your local Ben & Jerry's scoop shop and get a cone of "Yes Pecan!" Proceeds will benefit our efforts to help citizens make their voices heard in the political process.*

➤ *Join us on Facebook! Ben & Jerry's is also donating $1 for each person who signs up on our Facebook "cause" during the month of January or who donates to the Common Cause Education Fund, up to $10,000!*

➤ *Tell your friends about these easy (and delicious!) ways to help Common Cause. Forward this message to your friends, and if you're on Facebook, invite them to join our cause.*

I'm off to get some ice cream. Best wishes for a happy and healthy new year.
Sincerely,
Bob Edgar
and the rest of the team at Common Cause[13]

Consider some of what this message accomplished. It:

➤ Reached hundreds of thousands of Common Cause e-mail subscribers with a time-sensitive call to action

➤ Built incentive to patronize Ben & Jerry's during its winter slow season

➤ Reinforced the branding for Ben & Jerry's, Common Cause, Facebook, and President Barack Obama, whose campaign slogan was "Yes we can!"

➤ Publicized Common Cause's Facebook cause page

➤ Raised matching funds for an organization in financial need

In short, a four-way win whose only downside (the $10,000 maximum outlay) was more than made up by the promotional value. Very strategic—and totally replicable.

Smaller companies can create less dollar-intensive promotions that similarly benefit themselves and others. For instance, Green America's *Real Green* newsletter has a column that spotlights member discounts from a variety of eco-friendly firms. One recent issue features three natural apparel/accessory companies and a green flooring company. How many thousands of people learned about these not-terribly-well-known companies from reading this newsletter or browsing the GreenAmericaToday.org web site? The organization claims to have redirected over $100 million toward its strategic partners in 2008 alone, while channeling $1 billion in donations to good works.[14]

Of course, the charity-alignment strategy works for right-wing causes, too. Companies such as Coors in the 1970s and Blackwater (or Xe, as it became known in early 2009) today are known for their support of the radical-right agenda. But don't champion causes your market hates. Whole Foods CEO John Mackey's August 11, 2009 *Wall Street Journal* op-ed opposing health reform instantly led to a nationwide backlash. As of October 1, 35,725 people had joined Facebook groups urging a boycott.[15]

Earlier, we talked about other campaigns where businesses assist schools, human service agencies, and other worthy causes. People are always predisposed to become your customer if doing so helps the community in some tangible way. And if your offer is good enough that it could stand without the charity tie-in, you should be able to market it very successfully by stressing the community benefit. (Of course, if your prospects don't see your offer as a benefit to themselves as well, you'll have a much harder time making the campaign work. But if you can get your prospects to buy in to both the community benefit and their own self-interest, you should have a very easy time with the campaign.)

This attitude can even help for-profit businesses without a charity tie-in, under the right circumstances. Many, many local, independently owned businesses have turned to their customers for help in staying afloat against predatory competitors or other adverse circumstances (such as a fire). One common strategy is to turn to your customers to raise capital, by providing scrip (money that can be used only in your business) worth more than the cost of buying it. For instance, you can sell $20 scrip that can be redeemed as $25 store credit. Of course, this only works for businesses that have had a community spirit and are known not only to treat their customers as allies but also to create a truly special environment. In other words, these are business owners who have been practicing the principles of this book from the moment they first opened.

► Framing and Social Proof

Social proof can be a two-edged sword. It's very easy for a crowd to convince itself that bad behavior is socially acceptable. In a must-read article, Brian Clark points out the danger: a negatively phrased message might actually *encourage* the behavior it tries to prevent, by planting the idea that because so many people do it, it must be okay. He cites a fossil park that put up signs to prevent vandalism and theft, but because the signage focused on the problem, the number of incidents went up. A sign phrased positively about protecting the common heritage reduced the incidence.[16]

Framing is an extremely powerful technique in business, non-profits, nongovernmental organizations, and politics. It's a matter of creating the imagery in words, sights, smells, sounds, tastes, and touches to move your audience's thought and emotions where you want them to be. And framing is especially valuable when it hooks into core values. Thus, the anti-abortion movement went mainstream when it stopped describing itself as *"anti-abortion"* and began calling itself *"pro-life."* It's really hard to "be perceived as against life," and *"pro-choice"* doesn't have the same oomph. When the pro-choice position finds a metaphor as powerful and laden with values as the anti-choice, that pendulum will swing.

Similarly, the Obama presidential campaign with its uplifting messages of "yes we can" and "change" was a powerful message to the American public. The campaign's elegant use of social media to empower volunteers, supporters, and contributors in two-way communication; its soaring oratory; its transparency; and its focus on core values such as bringing people out of poverty and achieving peace spoke to people who had been battered by physical, economic, and social storms; watched their leaders get caught in a web of secrets and lies; and seen their country's standing in the world, its budget surplus, and its considerable post-9/11 political capital depleted.

■ IT'S NOT ABOUT TRANSACTIONS, IT'S ABOUT RELATIONSHIPS

So far, we've talked about ethics and values, charity partnerships, green initiatives, and customer retention/loyalty-to-evangelism programs. What do all these strategies have in common?

Each of these approaches shifts the customer interaction from a one-time transaction to an ongoing relationship.

And customers crave that relationship. Roy Williams cites an MIT study that watched buyer behavior on a best-deals web site. Although the study authors fully expected that nearly 100 percent would choose the lowest price, Williams wasn't surprised that "51 percent scrolled down from the lowest prices at the top of the list to buy from a better-known retailer down below, voluntarily paying several dollars more."[17] According to Williams, many businesses draw about equally from both transactional (price-sensitive, looking to squeeze out all they can from you, support-intensive but not necessarily appreciative) and relational (appreciative, long-term, repeat, loyal) customers.

Relationship-oriented customers account for far more profitability, create far less hassle, and are much more likely to refer others. Those are the customers you want to reach out to, and nurture. Some businesses go so far as to deliberately disincent the bottom 10 or 20 percent of their market: to drive these transaction-based, high-maintenance, low-profit customers elsewhere. However, since you don't know which of your transactional customers will become relational, we prefer strategies that convert transactional customers to relational ones.

■ LESSONS AND ACTIONS

➤ Neutralize your enemies not by disabling them but by befriending them or even joining forces on projects.

➤ Gain access to their existing complementary markets, and work together to build new markets—increase the pie for everyone.

➤ Compete effectively together against do-it-yourselfism or deep-discount nonspecialists.

➤ Build additional alliances with competitors as well as customers, suppliers, nonprofits, and businesses in a completely different market.

➤ Incorporate social proof such as powerful testimonials.

➤ Frame your discussions to emphasize positive rather than negative steps and harness core values.

➤ Understand and harness the difference between transaction- and relationship-oriented customers. Move people from encounter to prospect to customer to fan.

How the Abundance Paradigm Eliminates the Need to Dominate a Market and Allows You to Better Serve Your Customers

Once you get rid of *I win = you lose*, many new horizons open up. Cooperation can take the form of trade associations, referrals, virtual partnerships, subcontracting arrangements, and more. These are all different ways of achieving the same result: With enough work to go around, you can help each other.

Professional associations offer a number of benefits: sharing resources through joint purchasing power, learning from those who've gone before (from both their successes and their failures or mistakes), building the overall market, or simply having someone you can comfortably talk shop with or ask for advice on a problem client.

If you have too much work, farm some out to your competitors in a subcontractor arrangement. You pay them, the client pays you somewhat more, and you're assured that if you have more work than you can handle, not only do you keep the client but you get the work done by someone you can trust to do it right.

Or create a *virtual partnership*. Here, you actually join forces with a competitor to do a project together, kind of like a joint venture except that you dissolve the partnership once the job is complete.

Say you're offered a project with a short deadline, too large for you to do completely within your own company. If you can work with other shops to do pieces of it and then assemble the entire project together as a finished whole, everyone benefits. But if you can't cooperate, you'll either be forced to turn down the project or work under such pressure that you do a bad job and kill any future business with that account. Whether it takes the form of many people doing different parts of one task (for instance, translating a large book to get ready for an international conference) or complementary tasks (such as the plumbing, electrical, and cement work on a construction site), working together enables you to complete the job faster. In this way, you spread work around and make impossible deadlines not only possible but much less stressful (and more lucrative, since you can charge a premium for rush work).

■ THE DEATH OF MARKET SHARE

You hear it constantly: "We need to gain market share."

Our question is Why?

If your business has enough, why would it possibly be a problem if others have enough as well? In fact, a rising tide is more likely to lift other boats. More for them may very well mean more for you as well.

Consider a famous case: PC operating systems. In the beginning, believe it or not, Apple pretty much owned the market. The Apple II line had dominance in both hardware and software, in large part because the first PC spreadsheet—VisiCalc—was available first on that platform. The rest of the PC market was divided among companies like Tandy, Commodore, and Kaypro. When IBM entered the hardware market in 1981, the equation changed. First, IBM already had tremendous brand equity, which Apple did not have back then. Second, IBM actively courted business software developers in a way that Apple and the others did not. All of a sudden, the personal computer world was flooded with much more powerful word processors, databases, accounting programs, and so on. Thus, the business community migrated to IBM's platform. When Apple came back into the fray in 1984 with the original Mac, it quickly made inroads in graphic design, publishing, and educational markets. But because there weren't any good databases, those businesses already on the IBM platform tended to stay there, and businesses that were getting their first computer naturally chose IBM.

The computer war might still have gone either way. But then IBM did something very clever: the company opened its architecture. All of a sudden, many companies were making IBM-compatible computers, selling them cheaply, and driving a vast expansion of the overall market. IBM's market share went down but its sales went up, because a smaller piece of a much larger number turned out to be larger than the largest piece of a smaller number. The small fry with shallow pockets went to clones. But those who valued IBM's reputation for quality and support, or who didn't want to be bothered when it turned out that some of the clones weren't actually all that compatible, were willing to pay the premium price IBM commanded.

The Mac market stayed strong in education, publishing, advertising, music, and video, where factors such as the much faster learning curve, better graphics capabilities, or the ability to see work on the screen as it would appear in print were more important. But more and more offices were buying computers, and they were mostly buying IBM.

It became essentially impossible to run a business without a computer. Then the computers became inadequate for newer software and had to be replaced. Next, Windows (from the user's point of view, essentially a copy of the much friendlier Mac operating system) reached maturity right around the time the Internet became popular, and users demanded full color, fast processors, and large hard drives. And people bought again. And again.

Thus, by creating an entire new class of competitors, IBM helped itself. And Microsoft, supplying DOS and Windows operating system[1] software to IBM and all the clones and productivity software to users on both the Mac and Intel platforms, was sitting pretty.

At one point, Microsoft had nearly 90 percent of the operating system market, leaving most of the remainder to Apple. More recently, inroads by Linux and other open-architecture systems have brought Microsoft's percentage down, but it's still the dominant player, by far. (Interestingly, even without selling operating systems, Microsoft has historically sold—and still sells—more software for the Mac than any other software maker.)[2]

Yet Apple Computer has been highly profitable even during the downturn. In the last three months of 2008, Apple took in a record $10.17 billion (up over a billion dollars from the previous year). Of that amount, $1.61 billion was profit.[3] Apple's growth has been quite rapid. In 2001, the quarterly numbers were just $1.5 billion in revenue, of which $40 million was profit.[4] Seven years later, the quarterly profit was greater than the overall revenue had been.

Could you make a comfortable living on those numbers? With an installed base of tens of millions of users, the Apple OS could be a big, promising market for software developers. In fact, Apple—even when its installed base was only a few million—often served as a testing ground for some of the most popular business software out there. PageMaker, Quark XPress, Adobe Illustrator, Photoshop, and even Microsoft Excel were first piloted on the Mac platform and then rolled out to the admittedly much larger DOS/Windows world. In fact, AOL, which was originally developed for the Commodore 64, was ported to the Mac as a product called AppleLink long before it was available for Windows computers.

Unfortunately for Apple, the lack of good visual programming development tools, the lack of support from the company, and various other factors mean it's not enough to simply look at the market numbers. Development costs and headaches are far higher on the Mac side, and of course, the number of prospects is smaller. What Apple is running up against is the 80/20 rule. If a company can achieve 80 percent of its potential customers with 20 percent of the work, why should it spend 80 percent of its resources for the remaining 20 percent gain? That, and not market share, is the reason why few developers bring out innovative Mac-only products anymore.[5]

Apple's solution is worth learning from. Failing to dominate in personal computers, the company looked to bring superior products to vast untapped or poorly tapped markets that appreciated them. The runaway success of both the iPod and iPhone show that this high-risk strategy can work, if executed properly. But the utter failure of its first PDA, the mid-90s Newton, demonstrates that superior technology is not enough. The innovation has to provide enough practical utility to leapfrog existing competitors. This was a lesson that Apple took to heart in both iPod and iPhone. An iPod is much easier to carry and offers more music choice than a Sony Walkman; an iPhone has a lot more functionality and user-friendliness than a BlackBerry or ordinary cell phone. And both products became category killers.

In a service business, market share is even less relevant than it is in manufacturing. In a product-based environment involving manufacturing or high-volume retail, economies of scale allow a market leader to command more favorable terms than smaller competitors. But these simply don't apply in most service businesses. Every service business offers a USP. For a copywriting shop like Shel's, it might be the ability to deliver fast, effective copy with a quick turnaround. For a baker, it might be the luscious chocolate filling that only this one shop offers. For a lawn-care business, it's simply the time and trouble the homeowner saves by farming the work out to someone who will show up every two weeks and never need a reminder. And if even 200 lawn-care businesses each service 25 households a week in a community with 50,000 lawns, that still only serves one-tenth of the potential base. Even though the market may appear saturated, there's plenty of room to grow. Too, those 200 lawn-care businesses can expand to other product lines. Chances are homeowners would be delighted to hire the lawn-care person they already know and trust to prune trees, remove leaves, set up a composting system, perhaps even plow snow in the winter.

This idea works in the real world, even with much larger entities. Which was the only U.S. airline to show a profit in the aftermath of the World Trade Center attack? Southwest Airlines. In their history of the company written some years earlier, Kevin and Jackie Freiberg quote Southwest's founding CEO Herb Kelleher:

> *Market share has nothing to do with profitability. Market share says we just want to be big; we don't care if we make money doing it. . . . To get an additional 5 percent of the market, some companies increased their costs by 25 percent. That's really incongruous if profitability is your purpose.*[6]

Does this mean market share is *never* a consideration? Or that you can't attempt to grow your market share without being predatory? No, in both cases. When you enter a new market, you need to calculate whether it will be worthwhile for you, and that means figuring out how much you'll sell. If you're entering a market that already exists, you need to calculate what percentage of the market will shift to you, how you'll attract them, how you'll draw in new customers who hadn't yet seen a need for what you offer. In short, you'll need to have some idea of how large a piece of the market will become your customers. However, ultimately, the number you really need to look at is how much money you will make, and not how that number relates to your competitors' performance.

Shel's friend Eric Anderson, president of the consulting and computer services firm FutureThru Group, Inc., www.futurethru.com, will disagree with us here. He believes market share is actually quite important, but we're not so far apart in our thinking. He points out that market share has little to do with your competitors and everything to do with your customers. Just to let you make up your own mind, here are some of his thoughts.

> *Within constraints, market share matters intensely. It may matter less in some areas, but in general, it is often a significant indicator of the financial leverage a product might have. . . .*
>
> *Market share is not about competition. Market share is about your customers, and it helps you in three ways.*

First, market share trends tell a company how well it is continuing to serve its customers. Declining market share indicates there is a problem. It could be that service, quality, price or some combination has slipped. Declining market share is a warning to the company that it is doing something wrong someplace.

While increasing market share may indicate that a company is fulfilling customer needs, it is possible to "buy" short-term market share gains that hide underlying problems.

The second property that market share brings is the ability to innovate and to spread development costs across a greater base. For example, Company A has 60 percent of the market and Company B has 40 percent.

Both companies discover that 10 percent of the market want Enhancement X.

Because Company A has greater market share, it can spread the cost of the enhancement across a greater customer base than Company B. Company A then has a lower cost of producing the enhancement per unit sold than Company B. Company A can pass the savings along to customers and/or retain it as profit.

Finally, if external financing is a consideration, banks, other lenders, or outside investors are going to be concerned about market share. Investors want to make money on their investment, and market share provides an indication of the security of their investment. If you have a small market share or declining market share, the chances of raising outside funding, if it is needed, become increasingly difficult.[7]

Anderson's comments lead directly to the next chapter: are there cases when market share really does matter?

■ LESSONS AND ACTIONS

➤ Market share is often the wrong thing to measure.

➤ Opening up the PC architecture to competitors and giving up market share saved IBM—keeping Mac architecture closed almost killed Apple.

➤ Existing market penetration can position you to open up new markets among existing customers.

Chapter

11

Exceptions: Are There Cases When Market Share Really Does Matter?

Although, in many cases, the concept of market share actually gets in the way of success, there are situations where there really are winners and losers. We'll look at some examples in this chapter. But even in such cases, you can win the race through ethical, Green behavior that leaves your opponent standing and your conscience intact. It's all too easy to fall back into the old ways, but once you go for throat-cutting, you poison your own well. Be the best, get the prize—and look at yourself proudly in the mirror afterward.

Here are four situations where you may have to modify the mutual success approach. But even if you do, it does still work.

■ MAJOR MEDIA

Media coverage would seem to be a zero-sum game. Although anyone can get into local newspapers or on small market radio shows, the most coveted slots are quite a bit tougher. A newspaper or broadcast station has a finite amount of space; if you get in, someone else doesn't.

Still, over time, that finite space is actually quite expansive. If a TV show uses two guests per show, five shows per week, that's over 500 guests a year. Each newspaper feature writer might profile four people in a week; that's more than 200 a year—and the paper might employ a dozen feature writers, so you have 2,400 chances each year in that paper.

93

You'd expect someone of Jay's stature to get quoted frequently in the media, and he does. But Shel, who is far less of a celebrity, also usually scores 30 to 50 media interviews a year and has been mentioned or featured in plenty of major media. And you can get major media too, with a cooperative approach that recognizes that you must offer the media what they need: a source who is interesting, informative, and sometimes entertaining, and who talks about issues important to that medium's customers.

Formulate your media contact materials to make it obvious that the media outlet's readers, listeners, or viewers will learn something interesting and/or be entertained. In some cases, it may even make sense to suggest other businesses that would also be good sources for a roundup story, or to assemble a panel for a TV or radio show or speaking event. You may even find that not only do you do your competitors a favor and get them free publicity but you're also able to differentiate your USP even more clearly. You demonstrate the ways you are different from them.

What if a competitor gets the coverage? The old, ineffectual response would be to call up the editor and complain. And all that does is ensure that that journalist will *never* use you as a story source, unless it's bad news or a scandal.

Here's one among many more effective strategies: write a letter to the editor, thanking the publication for the good story about your subject area and volunteering some new angle. You get the exposure, you're noticed as someone with something to contribute, and you may well get the call the next time that topic is covered.

In fact, that's one among many techniques to be perceived as a *thought leader*. Rachel Meranus, writing in a 2006 article for *Entrepreneur,* offers other strategies to build the perception that you're a thought leader, worthy of media coverage.[1] Once you identify a few key publications that you'd like to feature you, tilt the odds in your favor:

➤ Study the publication's editorial calendar, and pitch articles that align with the featured topics (either as a writer or a source) well in advance of the issue's closing date.

➤ Tie your pitch to larger social trends, and give the big-picture broad-based view of your company's role.

➤ Follow news closely, and contact the press instantly when a relevant story shows up.

➤ Conduct surveys (and release the results to the media) that "suggest a course of action, particularly one that supports your company and its business strategy."

Shel's book *Grassroots Marketing: Getting Noticed in a Noisy World* goes into extensive detail on how to gain media publicity and how to turn that publicity to your advantage as you market your products and services.

■ EXTREMELY LIMITED OR SATURATED MARKETS

Here is another scenario that challenges the idea that everyone can win: What if there aren't very many customers, and a sale to you means that someone else doesn't get one? If there are only 10 customers in the world for what you do, you probably want all 10.

Have we finally come to a situation where marketing from the abundance paradigm doesn't work?

Even here, there are many ways to achieve your agenda and be loyal to your principles.

You could be like Microsoft or General Motors and buy out your competitors. That's certainly a win–win if you've made a fair offer.

A more affordable strategy is to make it clear that working with you has advantages to the client: better service, a more thorough understanding of the client's needs, and/or a more favorable financing structure, for instance. Without putting your competitors down, you provide the information necessary for your prospects to choose you. The benefit extends to your customers, and you're not trashing your competitors, even if you're not actively working with them.

You can even do this with price shoppers, even if you're not competing on price. When someone asks about price, you should provide the information, and then follow immediately with, for example, "The other question you should be asking is, 'What are your qualifications?'" You may find that a lot of people book an appointment then and there after hearing your response to a question they hadn't even asked.

But still, situations will come up where a competitor is obviously better qualified than you to handle a particular client's circumstances. And that's where it's important to remember that you serve those clients best by referring them to another business. It doesn't take many referrals before those competitive business owners realize that while you will certainly attempt to close the sale when someone is considering you, you always have the client's interests at heart and that inspires you to refer the work to other shops when that's the best way to meet the client's needs.

Another strategy is to expand the market. If you're competing against do-it-yourselfers, approach your business competitors and discuss a cooperative marketing campaign to show people why they should have it done professionally. The ads and publicity materials, of course, would list all the contact info for the participating shops and would expand the pie for everyone. Recall the florist example in Chapter 9.

The hospitality industry has clearly been successful with this approach, as the following examples demonstrate. Bed-and-breakfast reservation services are common. You travel to a city and either call the local reservation service or visit its web site. When you contact the service, the reservationist knows which innkeepers have rooms available in what price ranges, can tell you which is the best fit for your needs, and will take your reservation over the phone or online. On the restaurant side, many cities have organized massive cooperative promotions, such as a Taste Festival where dozens of restaurants offer small, inexpensive samples of their most popular dishes, and thousands of consumers go from booth to booth, trying new foods. After the festival is over, these people seek out the restaurants they liked and enjoy the full dining experience.

There are a number of other ways to cooperate with competitors for mutual benefit. Formal or informal associations can develop new markets for all members. As an example, let's say that a group of writing instructors band together. Maybe the basic market for fiction and poetry workshops is fairly saturated, but the group hires an outreach person to open doors in corporate training, senior centers, prisons, and schools, to partner with college and university creative-writing programs, and to create a public relations campaign encouraging writing among sectors of the public that haven't tried it before. Thus the organization can create an elevator under all of its members' feet. Rather than carving up a small market into tiny slivers, the group expands the market collectively, and all its members benefit.

Or consider those chiropractors who practice a particular approach to spinal care called Network Spinal Analysis. Network practitioners are a small subset of chiropractors in general, and those who coexist in the same geographic area often do quite a bit of cooperative marketing, refer patients to each other, and choose to work on each other.

A third benefit-focused strategy is to diversify. Three times in the history of Shel's business—first with term-paper typing, then with his wife's writing workshops, and finally with résumé writing—he found that a service line was very strong for a few years, but because of technology, saturation, or other factors, that market largely disappeared. In all three cases, by the time the market dried up, his company had already been offering new products and services and was not only able to recover but actually able to increase both his hourly rate and profitability in those new areas.

Would he go back to typing term papers, even if the market were still there? Definitely not. Every time there has been pressure on a market that had previously generated the largest share of his income, he was already in a new, better, more enjoyable, more lucrative market—and had the opportunity to develop new skill sets that are much more in demand, and for which his clients cheerfully pay a good deal more money. These days, Shel's biggest clients are usually writers who want to become published authors. And typically, these are people who work intensely with him for several months at a time, to create books they can be proud of. It takes a whole lot of press release clients to equal the income from one book shepherding client.

Finally, the fourth strategy is to go after a niche. This is an excellent strategy when you're facing changing technology, or you're feeling pressed by a deep-pockets competitor.

Think back 100 years. There were still many companies making horse carriages and buggy whips, but cars were beginning to displace horse carriages as the preferred mode of transportation. Still, even now, there is a place for a buggy whip or carriage manufacturer—serving the tourist carriages that roam through New York's Central Park or New Orleans's French Quarter. It's a much smaller market, one that a mass manufacturer can't profitably serve. But for one or two companies that go after that market, it can be a nice profitable niche.

We have a friend who is a hand-bookbinder. Although the vast majority of books are bound by high-speed machines, our friend never lacks for work. He restores old books for libraries and private collectors, and creates works of art out of new books. Once again, the industry couldn't support thousands of hand-bookbinders, but it does support dozens.

■ PREDATORS

We can hear you thinking: Marketing That Puts People First is all well and good if you have competitors that think the same way. But what if your competitor is a cutthroat trying to drive you out of business? You can nicey-nice yourself right into bankruptcy.[2]

If a Wal-Mart or Home Depot, with its vast purchasing power and potentially predatory practices, moves into your territory, striving for total market share, how do you deal with that?

Interestingly enough, independent hardware stores and lumberyards continue to exist, despite pressure from homeowner superstores. Some of their survival has been due to developing cooperative approaches. To name one example, they've formed purchasing co-ops that can purchase goods at competitive prices. If a single hardware store were to buy inventory on its own, it might actually be cheaper for the store's purchasing manager to go to Lowe's or Home Depot and buy at retail. But by joining co-ops like Service Star or Tru-Value, they not only gain enough purchasing muscle to buy cheaply, but also get the marketing benefits of a national or regional brand.

When competing with a Wal-Mart—or for that matter, a BJ's or Costco—the local stores that thrive are those that don't get into a price-cutting game. Lacking the ability to purchase warehouse quantities, they look to compete on value, not price. They find the places where they can offer better service to their customers than the giants can, stress the importance of community-based retailing, and show the win–win advantages of a strong local-business sector.

Of course, if you've created a brand-new market, your calculations need to be figured differently. How many people will you convince of the desirability of your new approach, and how long will you have before other companies move into the territory you've created?

We've already discussed some ways to survive and thrive when a large, well-financed competitor enters the market. But sometimes, with someone who is actively trying to own the entire market, you need a tougher approach. If a competitor comes in determined to drive you out, and brings a huge amount of firepower to bear, you certainly need a response. And in all likelihood, you won't have the budget to fight fire with fire. When you face massive ad campaigns in the Yellow Pages, local newspapers, and electronic media, you're not going to be able to spend your way out, because the other business may have deeper pockets or a willingness to lose money until it can drive competitors out and they can own the market.

So what's a small-business owner to do? How can you survive an onslaught by a well-funded competitor who doesn't understand that there's enough to go around?

Here are two excellent approaches:

1. Identify and *use* the communication strategies—and product offerings—where you're better than they are.

You have your customer list; now is a great time to do some postal or electronic direct mail. *You* have carefully built up local contacts in the press. Explain to these contacts how you'll meet this new challenge—and what it would mean to the community if you can't. *You* have the benefit of your existing store traffic while the new competitor is under construction. Think about how you can create allies out of those visitors. *You* have access to nimble, innovative marketing methods that nonlocal chain superstores simply cannot use, because they have to spend months learning about them and then seeking approval from headquarters. *You* can compete as an equal, perhaps a superior, in cyberspace—because *you* can spend the time to optimize your pages for your own local area, for your own special product mix and USP, and for the value that you add to the equation when a customer chooses to do business with you.

Seth Godin talked about this recently:

> *What's being rewarded now is insight, authenticity, and innovation, and speed, and alacrity, and flexibility, none of which we associate with General Motors, none of which we associate with giant companies and organizations . . . what we're seeing now in times of rapid change and in serious recession is organizations that can bring smart, connected, motivated people straight to the client. Those organizations that can tell the truth, that organization that can change quickly, that organization that can synthesize lots of ideas all at once, those organizations are busier than ever . . . the opportunity you have when you're small is . . . to say, "If you need this, we are the single best choice." . . . If you're a small business, change is your friend. If you're the Chrysler Corporation, it's the enemy.*[3]

2. Try a little marketing jujitsu. In jujitsu, you use your opponent's greater strength and redirect it so that your opponent, and not you, feels the brunt of the blow. In jujitsu, you can flip someone much larger than you over your shoulder and onto the mat. So, in a situation where your competitor insists that there is a winner and a loser, you want to be the winner.

Here's where the political capital you've built up over time can really help. If you have been in business several years, filling a unique niche in a special way that's meaningful to your community . . . if you've been regularly supporting local artists by exhibiting their art on the walls or giving them space to perform . . . if you're known as someone the community can turn to when it needs someone to sponsor a Little League team, chair a civic improvement committee, or raise money for the local hospital, now is the time to harness some of that good karma you've been spreading around all these years.

Write your customers and explain that you've tried to approach the new store from the standpoint that there's enough to go around, but they're not playing fair. They want to drive you out, and you need community support to stay in business. Ask not only for people to patronize you but ask for other kinds of help: testimonials, buying scrip to generate extra cash, even outright donations. Flood the market with testimonials that not only show what you've done for them as customers, but what you've meant to the entire community. Approach reporters on your beat to do a story on you. Expose the competitor's predatory policies and show how they're selling below your wholesale cost (if that's true). Bring in your existing, nonpredatory competitors for a joint effort. And most of all, show how you are different—and better. Show where the dollars go—how dollars spent in your store continue to circulate locally, whereas dollars spent in a big chain store are sucked away to a distant corporate headquarters.

All this information is out there. There's even an activist, Al Norman, who has made a career out of blocking Wal-Mart and other megachains from entering a community. He spends the entire first part of his book documenting the impact these superchains have on the existing retail environment. Then he shows, step by step, how he organized to keep Wal-Mart out of Greenfield, Massachusetts. He has gone on to consult with many towns and block superstores elsewhere. His book, and two other books about surviving near a superstore, are listed on www.guerrillamarketinggoesgreen.com/resources.[4]

If someone comes in and starts undercutting your price, it won't take much to find their weakness. One service business owner faced down a deep discounter by offering to fix the competitor's bad jobs. A little creativity can go a long way against a predatory competitor.

Consider the strategies of Dave Ratner, owner of three pet food stores. His flagship store shares a parking lot with a Wal-Mart, and Ratner is making a new career speaking about innovative success strategies that surpass the category killers. For instance, he displayed a cheap Wal-Mart fish tank along with a sign about why he'd never sell that model because he wouldn't want to be responsible for dead fish. See more at www.DaveRatner.com.

By forcing a win–lose model on you, the competitor takes a loss. But you and your customers win, and your community wins because this approach strengthens local businesses that keep dollars circulating in the community.

In all the years Shel has been in business, he has come across only one competitor who was hostile. Shel called him up within a few weeks of his first ads on a friendly get-acquainted call, but it was clear he had no interest in being friendly. His business lasted just about a year; Shel's firm has celebrated its twenty-eighth anniversary.

■ CROOKS

There are two kinds of people who engage in fraudulent behavior. One kind is naïve. As writers, we run up against this frequently. We discover an article that one of us wrote, reprinted without credit, negotiation for reuse, or payment. When we investigate, we find that the violator is simply ignorant. He or she does not realize that this is our property (not to mention a big chunk of our livelihood), and that we have the right to get paid for it. By treating them nicely, we convert nearly all of these people into paying customers, and everybody wins.

But then there are the real crooks: the ones who write piracy software that steals affiliate commissions or banner impressions, try to steal millions of dollars through fraudulent chain letters, simply refuse to pay their bills or deliver the goods and services their customers paid for, break into a store with guns pointed and demand the money, or steal identities and credit card numbers to run up big bills before they get another card number and start all over again.

If someone is deliberately trying to cheat you, there's no point in being nice. Bringing your competitors along on the success train does not extend to thieves. But the rest of you, the honest ones, who are already working together in all these other ways, can get rid of the problem faster by banding together. You can lobby, you can organize suppliers, you can inform the public, and you can press for action through the police and courts much more easily than you could if working alone.

■ LESSONS AND ACTIONS

➤ Initiate people-centered strategies for working in saturated or limited markets.

➤ Be an ally to the media.

➤ Put predatory competitors and crooks in their place.

➤ Survive and thrive in rapidly changing markets.

Chapter 12

Some *Real* Loyalty Programs from Big Companies

Do you think a loyalty program is just a business card that gets punched for every purchase, and after 10 punches the customer gets 1 free? Sorry, but that's not really a loyalty program, just an incentive to come back. If the loyalty is only for the free gift, it's not solid.

Compare the punch card with some big-company approaches that really do build loyalty.

■ SATURN

It wasn't so many years ago that buying a car was a horrible chore. You came into the dealership fully expecting a hostile, manipulative environment. But even before the Internet made it possible for consumers to be far better informed, Saturn revolutionized the way cars are sold—and sold a huge number of cars in the process.

Saturn is a part of General Motors, the largest U.S. car maker, and one firmly rooted in the old, adversarial ways. But Saturn did a number of things differently. It created a feeling of pride and ownership among its employees that enabled the car line to quickly develop a reputation for quality. Its design standards emphasized safety but did not compromise value, economy, performance, or comfort. And the Saturn dealer network—many of whom also operated traditional showrooms selling other brands—treated the customer as a valued part of not just the sales process but the entire idea of driving a Saturn. The customer-really-counts philosophy even extended to its ads, which have often featured ordinary people who drive Saturns.

When you walk into a Saturn dealer, you're given a friendly greeting and you're told who can answer your questions. There's no pressure. Your contact will helpfully assess your needs and suggest a vehicle that will work for you. And if you decide to go forward, the price is already set—at a level that provides very good value to the consumer and very good profit to the manufacturer and dealer.

It's all spelled out in the Saturn Consultative Sales Process, which says, among other things, "All customers shall receive a thorough interview in order for Sales Consultants to determine their wants and needs" and "All customers shall receive open and honest treatment about all elements of the transaction price."[1]

In J.D. Power & Associates' annual automotive sales satisfaction study, Saturn ranked Number 1 seven out of eight years. It was the only nonluxury brand to earn top ranking in both Power's Customer Service and Sales Satisfaction indexes; the only other brand that achieved both the same year was Lexus, in 1994.[2]

Unfortunately, the brand hasn't kept pace with the trend it pioneered. Since Saturn introduced its new dealership style in the early 1990s, many other dealerships have followed suit. By 2008, Saturn had fallen to 11th place in sales satisfaction—behind not only several luxury brands, but also Buick and Mercury.[3] As part of its massive restructuring in late 2008 and early 2009, GM announced plans to close or sell off the brand, and following the collapse of a buyout deal in September, said it would shut the division.[4]

Still, even if GM closes the division, Saturn's pioneering ability to reframe the customer experience will last. Quality of the experience in the dealership is still crucial. J.D. Power and Associates notes that "'Hassle-free' negotiation continues to be a leading reason why buyers choose to purchase from one dealer compared with another dealership."[5] But Saturn's slippage, combined with only so-so reliability ratings,[6] may have a lot to do with why the brand is in serious trouble.

■ NORDSTROM

How did Nordstrom become one of the largest department stores in the United States, opening numerous new locations while some of the oldest and greatest department stores went out of business? It certainly wasn't on low prices.

Nordstrom built a reputation for excellent service—for going so far out of their way to assist customers that word spread far and wide.

Living in an area where Nordstrom hadn't reached yet, Shel first learned about Nordstrom from Guy Kawasaki's book *The Macintosh Way* in the 1980s. Kawasaki cited several examples of excellence, and

Nordstrom was among them. The store has been known to accept returns of heavily used merchandise that probably wasn't even bought there. Instead of focusing on short-term profits, the company went after long-term consumer loyalty and word-of-mouth brand building. If you return an item of clothing that no sensible store would take back, and you get full credit, aren't you going to shop there over and over again—and tell your friends?

■ STOP & SHOP'S TWO PROMOTIONS

Your collaborators in marketing don't have to be in the same market at all, or even be a business. Nonprofits or businesses from an entirely different sphere can make excellent partners.

A lot of years ago, Stop & Shop, a large New England supermarket chain, teamed up with Apple Computer for a very innovative promotion. Many others have copied it since (and for all we know, Stop & Shop may not have been the first), because it created huge customer loyalty for both companies and also helped the communities where it was offered.

Here's how it worked. Customers saved their register receipts and turned them in to their children's schools. The schools counted the dollars spent toward points, and those points were redeemable for computer equipment from Apple. Of course, Stop & Shop drew customers from other stores, and Apple trained new users in its own operating system from a young and tender age. Since the Apple operating system had less than 10 percent of the market, this campaign established a vital new base of Apple-oriented computer buyers, who would be buying systems of their own in a few years.

Stop & Shop had another great win–win powerhouse a few years later: a no-fee frequent-flier credit card that earned a mile for every dollar spent, and two dollars for every dollar spent at Stop & Shop. Unfortunately, after about four years, the sponsoring bank was bought out by a large conglomerate that eventually killed the program. But many of those former airline customers stayed with the grocery chain out of habit.

■ OTHER AFFINITY PROMOTIONS

Many other businesses have teamed up with schools, offering books, supplies, training, and other benefits at certain dollar levels. And many businesses and nonprofit organizations have also benefited from affinity programs of one sort or another. Working Assets was perhaps the first to team up a long-distance telephone plan with a social benefit to political organizations that its members support. In this case each organization in a pool selected by the members received a substantial contribution. Now there are a number of others, including at least one company whose phone plan is actively sold by the members of the beneficiary organizations, and each person who signs up benefits the group under which he or she was signed up. For instance, the National Writers Union (NWU) offers a phone plan and gets a percentage on all its members who participate. Members are encouraged to refer their nonmember friends, too.

And, of course, there are affinity credit cards. Sometimes it seems every college alumni association must have one. These cards work because they provide ways for members to help the organization, just through the purchases they already make.

■ LESSONS AND ACTIONS

➤ Saturn and Nordstrom: Companies that have win–win partnerships with consumers.

➤ Apple and Stop & Shop: Companies that have win–win partnerships with other businesses *and* consumers.

Chapter 13

Marketing Green

As we've already discussed, customers want to do business with companies who share their values—and these days, those values include strong awareness of climate change and other environmental issues.

We live in a powerful time: Finally, the environment has penetrated our collective consciousness deeply enough to move a whole lot of people toward Green lifestyle changes. At the same time, technology (especially the Internet) has made it possible to run a global business with little or no staff or resources, and without a big infrastructure.

This opens up all sorts of opportunities for the Green Marketing Guerrilla who honestly fits into this market.

■ HOW YOU BENEFIT BY MARKETING GREEN

When you look at all the advantages of running a Green company, it's hard to understand why every company in the world hasn't shifted.

➤ Green goods and services are much easier to market.

➤ They often command a premium price, and thus are more profitable.

➤ Green goods and services are better for the environment: They use fewer resources, less energy, and more organic and natural materials—and thus create less pollution, have a smaller carbon footprint (which means they don't add to the global warming problem), and are easier to dispose of.

➤ Against conventional wisdom, they can actually be cheaper to produce, if properly designed (see the profiles of Amory Lovins and John Todd in Chapter 19).

Worldwide, consumer consciousness on these issues is growing by orders of magnitude. As recently as 2004, discussions of climate change and sustainability were rarely heard in mainstream discussions; now those discussions are everywhere. One example: *Plenty* magazine named "10 ideas that will change our world"—and 6 of those 10 (turning waste into new inputs, Green affordable housing, Green media, Green jobs, carbon labeling, and pay-as-you-go energy retrofits) are directly and explicitly rooted in Green thinking. The other four all have a Green component.[1]

Areas of living that we used to take for granted are now being reexamined under a Green microscope. Suddenly, Green is an issue in every single industry.

Another example: The very successful e-zine *Healthy, Wealthy, and Wise* recently ran an article on choosing a Green pediatrician. The doctor-author writes, "As you did when choosing an ob/gyn, you want to find a pediatrician who is top-notch medically. How much better if he or she is also on the journey to an environmentally sustainable perspective on pediatrics!"[2]

The more effectively a company can demonstrate commitment to environmental values, the easier it will be to convince those consumers to channel their business to that company. Here are some examples.

➤ The hotel industry's change in towel washing policies had essentially no consumer resistance because this cost-cutting move was successfully marketed as a Green initiative.

➤ A shift among publishers to slash print inventories and eliminate the practice of allowing bookstores to return unsold books was made for both environmental and economic reasons.[3]

Conveniently enough, many Green initiatives not only make the company more attractive to consumers but they actually cut existing costs. And those are the ones that can survive corporate restructuring. If they actually both save money and make money, they won't be on the chopping block when the company faces hard times or a new management team. As Joel Makower puts it in his book *Strategies for the Green Economy*:

Companies that don't leverage their environmental achievements and commitment in a way that produces business value often find that green is the first thing to go when times get tough—when there's a change in leadership, when shareholders raise questions, or when your company otherwise finds that being seen as an environmental leader is no longer convenient. On the other hand, if you can say, "Our sustainability initiatives have reduced costs and boosted revenue by creating new markets, adding new products, and deepening loyalty with customers," this creates a long-term justification for a sustainability strategy and for environmental issues broadly.[4]

Reframing this discussion in line with the abundance mindset we discussed earlier, Melissa Chungfat advises companies to "move away from the language of sacrifice. Find ways to talk about how your product or service is easier, healthier, more convenient or lower maintenance. Be positive and solutions-focused." She also suggests pointing out actual achievements, rather than sometimes-vague commitments.[5]

Still, let's contrast better and worse ways to call attention to this, using three companies in the printing industry.

One printing company ran an ad in a local business publication noting that 60 percent of its electricity came from renewable hydropower and asking prospects to choose this company if commitment to sustainability was "as important to you as it is to us." The main text of the ad uses light and dark type (all capitals) to form the shape of an electrical plug. Outside of the main text is the logo and a brief explanation of the Forest Stewardship Council and the printer's name and contact information. The headline simply named the printing company followed by an ellipsis (...) and the word *Unplugged*.

This ad combines a happy accident—that the company's local utility happens to provide clean hydroelectric power—with a true environmental commitment, the Forest Stewardship Council (FSC) certification, a very big deal in the paper and printing industries.

As we see it, it's a step in the right direction but also a lot of wasted opportunity.

First of all, the headline doesn't tell the story. It's focused on the company, has no benefit other than to arouse just a slight bit of curiosity about why a printing company might do acoustic music. Then the mix of light and dark type, all of it dense and all in capitals, and with words broken across lines in mid-syllable without even hyphens is just too hard to read. And it takes at least two glances before the image forms itself into an electrical plug.

If the only environmental claim had been the bit about hydroelectric, the ad might have been discredited entirely as an attempt to capitalize on something the company doesn't even control. FSC certification, however, is real, and it can provide a great marketing advantage to savvy printers. But this genuine advantage is buried two-thirds of the way through the copy. So, unfortunately, the most effective part of the ad is the little freestanding FSC logo in the bottom left corner.

Wouldn't it be stronger if we wrote the ad, something like this, and matched it to a design that was much clearer in its environmental benefit (like a tree)?

Headline: If You Care about the Environment...Choose a Printer Who Shares Your Commitment

Body: We've only got one planet. Printing the old way is pretty hard on the environment. That's why (Company) is taking every Green step we can:

➤ In May 2008, we were certified by the Forest Stewardship Council (www.fsc.org) so you have complete assurance that all our paper is made from sustainably harvested lumber, free of dangerous pesticides or genetically modified trees, and respects the economic and spiritual well-being of indigenous people where the wood is grown.

➤ 60 percent of our energy comes from nonpolluting, renewable hydropower.

➤ Of course, you can get your printing done on recycled paper; we'll even help you choose the right stock.

➤ Outstanding integrity, customer service, and print quality, for over 100 years[6]

The ad in Figure 13.1 appeared in a book-industry trade magazine, which was perfect targeting.

This Webcom ad ran in a special online issue of *Book Business* previewing Book Expo America (BEA),[7] the U.S. publishing industry's largest trade event. The clear call to action is to book an appointment at BEA. In short, the targeting is basically perfect. And amid all the ads from printers in that publication, this was one of the very few to have any point of differentiation related to the environment. The FSC logo is there, and FSC certification is also mentioned in the color-screened text. The ad is attractively designed, although the daisy collage is kind of hard to figure out. In our opinion, another graphic element might have been better. And it's very much on-message: Book publishers

Figure 13.1   Book Expo Ad.

who care about the environment will want to know more. Of the two URLs, one is the home page and the other links to a request form for eco-friendly paper samples.

This ad obviously cost quite a bit more than the Unplugged ad, but it's easy to see how the dollars spent will be considerably more effective in bringing in new business.

Of course, we're big believers in maximizing the leverage of a display ad by driving traffic to an appropriate web page, and there were a couple of opportunities Webcom missed. The company already has a very informative web page covering Green printing issues (emphasis on education, not sales) at www.webcomlink.com/enviro, but this isn't mentioned in the ad. It would have been perfect to say something like, "If you'd like to know more about Green printing options, we've set up a special web page with information, resources, links, and more, at www.webcomlink.com/enviro," and then on the page itself, which doesn't have any call to action as of this writing, a link back to the paper-sample request form listed in the ad. Also, in any medium that doesn't make the links clickable, it's good to use very short URLs that are hard to mess up when retyped.

Still, it's light-years ahead of what most companies are doing.

And here's a third example, very low cost, and very eco-friendly, from the Fidlar-Doubleday electronic newsletter:

TURN GREEN INTO GOLD

Following the first Earth Day in 1970, communities raced to introduce recycling programs and plant trees. Over time, interest in environmental issues waned, but now it has resurfaced in an almost over-the-top way. Companies promote everything from carrots to cars as organic, all-natural, recycled, biodegradable, ozone-friendly and carbon-neutral, with new terms introduced by marketing geniuses daily. This has created skepticism from consumers, leaving companies that are truly interested in eco-safe initiatives wondering how to rise above the vague and dubious assertions of their competitors.

There is no universal approach to going green, but there are a number of steps a business of any size can take to quickly reduce its environmental footprint and legitimize its environmental marketing efforts.

Green your operations. Whether your office is a factory or a penthouse, you can green your operations by using energy-efficient lighting, using local materials and supplies to reduce transportation emissions, and using recycled or reusable products. Set your office printers and copiers to print two-sided by default, create computer files instead of paper files and implement green and sustainable systems and policies.

Green your marketing. Make sure your message is rooted in a sincere effort to be socially responsible. Clearly define the eco-friendly qualities of your product or service, and publish supporting data in your marketing collateral and on your Web site. We can show you the least wasteful way to design and produce a project by introducing post-consumer recycled content, non-chlorine bleached papers, low-polluting inks and two-sided printing options. Include a reminder for the customer to recycle your printed materials.

Green your stakeholders. It is important to engage your employees, shareholders, suppliers, customers and community in your environmental efforts. These groups influence market and buying decisions, so the opportunity for gaining competitive advantage is greatest when you align your corporate strategy with stakeholder values. Consider producing an annual sustainability report as a tangible reminder of your long-term commitment to environmental stewardship.

At the end of the day, it is your actions, not your marketing claims that determine whether your company is green. By adopting a proactive approach to sustainability, you will effectively balance your financial objectives with social and environmental considerations, leading to higher sales, increased market share, happier employees and a better future for all.[8]

This is a classic example of marketing by supplying information. In the short space of 379 words, it provides a ton of useful and easily initiated tips, including some that don't have any bearing on the company's own offerings.

And now, look at this:

We can show you the least wasteful way to design and produce a project by introducing post-consumer recycled content, non-chlorine bleached papers, low-polluting inks, and two-sided printing options. Include a reminder for the customer to recycle your printed materials.

What a clear, specific reason to do business with this company. Phrased as an invitation to accept help, it's exactly the kind of hype-free, ultratargeted marketing we advocate (going to an audience of existing customers and prospects) delivered in a way that's totally consistent with the Green message. No four-color ink was spilled to create or deliver the message; no trees were cut down to print it. Yes, there could be a more explicit call to action, but the message is there, embedded in a solid and useful information piece.

■ PACKAGING AND VALUES

Like Fidlar-Doubleday, lots of other companies use low-cost/no-cost methods to spread the word about their ethical and environmental commitments. And for those who sell physical product, the packaging itself is a fabulous marketing tool for conveying values as well as product benefits. Instead of paying for advertising, you're letting shoppers see your values message as they shop, and allow them to make the decision that your product is worth buying.

The food industry is particularly good at this.

➤ Gary Hirshberg started Stonyfield Farm Yogurt (now the market leader in organic yogurt) without an advertising budget. Instead, he used his container lids to push for action on global warming, public transportation, and so on—and boosted revenues by an astonishing 26 percent.[9]

➤ Nature's Path, an organic cereal company in Canada, printed educational information about organic farming and nutrition on the *insides* of its boxes.

➤ Major food conglomerates such as General Mills, Unilever, and Starbucks have been incorporating more and more information about the social, health, and economic benefits of their products, and/or buying up successful eco-friendly companies (including Stonyfield, Ben & Jerry's, the personal care company Tom's of Maine, and many others).

Of course, you can find many examples in other industries, too. Some of the most successful not only educate the consumer but actually turn that consumer into a Green champion and educator. For example, Procter & Gamble's Tide Coldwater brand focuses its entire marketing on the community benefits of saving energy as well as the monetary benefits to the consumer who won't have to pay to heat all that water. Tide partners with the Alliance to Save Energy to publish energy-saving tips (not just about laundry) on the product's page,[10] which on March 21, 2009, featured a TV ad that talked about powering a city with the energy saved by cold-water washing. Jacquelyn Ottman, author of *Green Marketing: Opportunity for Innovation*, reports that Tide Coldwater's initial campaign in 2005 let consumers actually calculate how much energy they were saving, individually and in conjunction with everyone else who took the Coldwater Challenge.[11] The campaign also included a number of viral elements.[12]

Green messaging is showing up in every corner of society. In a recent news video, Autodesk, a computer-aided design software company, touted its software as a greener tool to design greener buildings.[13]

Other initiatives are much less public, but still quite dramatic. For example, cruise ship operator Carnival's many brands incorporate numerous environmental programs that far exceed government requirements: separating waste streams, refilling ink cartridges with soy ink, breaking down biological waste in an aerobic digester, switching some lighting to LED. However, few passengers are aware of any of this.[14]

And Microsoft, listening to employee feedback, made a conscious choice to reduce cafeteria waste, including switching from landfill-clogging polystyrene hot cups to compostable cups—and plates and cutlery, too.[15]

Even as massive and diverse a company as Cox Enterprises, with 83,000 employees across multiple industries (newspaper, radio, TV, automotive, and Internet advertising) saw enormous changes after instituting a corporationwide environmental awareness program.

> *In the first eight years, the company kept 37.7 tons of obsolete electronics out of landfills . . . saved more than 2 million gallons of water per year by switching to waterless urinals . . . switched 98 percent of its fleet to low-emission vehicles (among many other initiatives).*[16]

■ LOCAL AS GREEN

As the world becomes ever more conscious about environmental impact, opportunities abound for smart entrepreneurs. One huge opportunity is the Local Economy movement. As consumers become aware of the environmental and economic impact of transporting products across the country or around the world, many consciously seek out locally based alternatives. Benefits include not only reducing carbon output but also keeping money and jobs in the consumer's own area while reinforcing local and regional identity. Shoppers may even choose a local conventionally grown or processed product over an organic or all-natural one from far away, to minimize their carbon footprint. Combine Green engineering or organic agriculture with a local economic base, and you're golden.

In the next few years, we predict that entrepreneurs who create locally based alternatives to faraway products will grow rapidly. The E. F. Schumacher Society, a leader in sustainability thinking for decades, recently highlighted the tremendous possibilities of this trend:

> The late Jane Jacobs brilliantly argues that the best strategy for economic development is to generate import-replacement industries. She would have us examine what is now imported into a region and develop the conditions to instead produce those products from local resources with local labor....
>
> An independent regional economy calls for new regional economic institutions for land, labor ... [that] cannot be government-driven ... free associations of consumers and producers, working cooperatively, sharing the risk in creating an economy that reflects shared culture and shared values. Small in scale, transparent in structure, designed to profit the community rather than profit from the community, they can address our common concern for safe and fair working conditions; for production practices that keep our air and soil and waters clean, renewing our natural resources rather than depleting them; for innovation in the making and distribution of the basic necessities of food, clothing, shelter, and energy rather than luxury items; and for more equitable distribution of wealth.
>
> Building of new economic institutions is hard work ... fine beginnings are being made in the development of local currencies, community supported farms, regionally based equity and loan funds, worker-owned businesses, community land trusts, and business alliances for local living economies.
>
> These initiatives are motivated by the affection that the citizens of a region have for their neighbors and neighborhoods; for the fields, forests, mountains, and rivers of their landscapes; for the local history and culture that bind these all together; and for their common future.[17]

The Schumacher Society has sponsored the research and development of an alternative local currency; BerkShares, usable in Berkshire

County, Massachusetts, which passed $2 million in late 2008.[18] Many other local-economies groups around the world have local currencies, including Ithaca Hours, in Ithaca, New York, founded in 1991 and now accepted by over 900 businesses. Businesses that want to cultivate a local-first mentality gain a built-in marketing channel (plus community credibility) by accepting their local currency and participating in the meetings, business fairs, and other events.

In the Pioneer Valley of Massachusetts, Communities Involved in Sustainable Agriculture (CISA) has been building consciousness about buying local for more than a decade. This trade organization for farmers started a Local Hero campaign that involves farmers, retailers, and consumers. The region has experienced a huge shift in favor of buying local that extends well beyond food products. And if the group ever decides to go national, it already owns a great web address that could accommodate regional subdomains. You can find this organization not at CISA.com or .org, but at www.buylocalfood.com. And yes, there are measurable results: Sales of organic farm products in Massachusetts more than doubled from $7.8 million in 2002 to $17.5 million in 2007, agritourism in the state soared from $665,000 to $5.3 million—an *800 percent increase*—in the same period, and both the number of farms and the total acreage farmed in the state increased during those years.[19]

Interestingly, small local farms can be far more profitable than big corporate ones, especially as energy prices spiral up. Writing in the *New York Times*, restaurant chef Dan Barber notes:

> *Small farms are the most productive on earth. A four-acre farm in the United States nets, on average, $1,400 per acre; a 1,364-acre farm nets $39 an acre. Big farms have long compensated for the disequilibrium with sheer quantity. But their economies of scale come from mass distribution, and with diesel fuel costing more than $4 per gallon in many locations, it's no longer efficient to transport food 1,500 miles from where it's grown.*[20]

At least one national association already exists: Business Alliance for Local Living Economies (BALLE), www.locallivingeconomies.org. Founded by Judy Wicks of the White Dog Café, a successful socially conscious restaurant in Philadelphia, BALLE provides education to consumers and support to businesses around the importance of buying local. And some local Chambers of Commerce are also moving into this territory, which clearly helps their members. Businesses that can position themselves as the locally owned, locally produced alternative can harvest deeply from their local markets.

■ GLOBAL AS GREEN

The flip side of the buy-local movement is that in our increasingly globalized economy, enormous opportunities are opening for nimble companies who can make sharp turns in the global arena. Mark Schapiro, Editorial Director of the Center for Investigative Reporting and author of *Exposed: The Toxic Chemistry of Everyday Products and What's at Stake for American Power*, noted in a radio interview on February 24, 2009, that because environmental and safety standards for cosmetics/personal care products are much tougher in the European Union than in the United States, U.S. companies that meet the stricter requirements have access to the entire EU market.

And U.S. consumers will discover the tougher labeling and ingredient standards and demand them for themselves. "There are levels of disclosure required on European products that are not required on American products. We live in a global economy. So that information is going to start making its way back here to the United States. And I think it's going to start creating some interesting tensions when people start seeing information disclosed there that's not disclosed here."[21]

Extrapolating from that, it seems obvious to us that the first U.S. cosmetics company to start heavily marketing its own compliance with the European standards and what that means for consumer safety and environmental protection, could score a huge first-mover marketing coup even in the U.S. market, and cast doubt on the offerings of many of its competitors.

Other aspects of the global economy can also be harnessed to your benefit as you demonstrate your company's ethics and principles. If you supply the vast majority of consumers who don't want to give up nonlocal foods, educate them on the importance of dealing fairly with suppliers in developing countries, and offer fair-trade certified products they can feel good about, you're well positioned for success. Similarly, if you are selling organic clothing, craft items that benefit a women's educational co-op, natural and renewable building materials, traditional toys that are guaranteed to be safe, or even recordings of indigenous music from around the world, and you can show that you're giving back to the communities that supply you *and* those that purchase from you, consumers will be predisposed to support you.

■ USING THE RIGHT LANGUAGE

All these examples show the importance of using the right language to get your Green message across. Futerra Sustainability

Communications, a UK marketing agency specializing in Green approaches, studied the effectiveness of various terms in sustainability marketing.

The study found that language emphasizing empathy, personification, action, and intellect (e.g., *smart, conscious,* or *savvy*) was highly persuasive, as were phrases that focused on connectedness and the big picture (*one planet living*). Terms that ranked poorly included *eco-safe* and *conflict.*[22]

Language that positions the company with a friendly, human voice also works well. Consider Tom's of Maine, a natural personal care products company (now owned by Colgate-Palmolive). Tom's packaging always includes a friendly, down-home note from founders Tom and Kate Chappell. And the web site's product page proclaims, "since 1981, we've proudly listed every ingredient, its purpose, and its source on our packages, so you know what you're buying."[23] There's also a prominent link to the ingredients Tom's refuses to use, again with reasons why.

Green marketing expert Jacquelyn Ottman emphasizes the wisdom of this approach and its applicability to other companies. This level of transparency, she says,

> *Is unprecedented in the history of consumer goods! Can you do this with your product's ingredients? How many of them may contain warning labels? (Crest and Colgate each do.) For Tom's, listing the ingredients, such as natural spearmint oil, helps get consumers over any price barriers at the point of sale. They are choosing a brand with natural ingredients and recognize that it must come with a price.*[24]

As an aside—the right language is important in any marketing campaign, not just the Green ones. To cite one of thousands of examples, social media strategist Chris Brogan attributes the iPod's success to Apple not getting bogged down in megabytes, sampling rates, and so forth, but to position it as a player that holds 1,000 songs—cutting straight to the core benefit and bypassing all the technobabble.[25]

■ DON'T GET STUCK IN THE GREENWASHING SWAMP

Failure to be careful about language can lead to serious backlash. If you talk to marketers who are gun-shy about Green marketing, it's likely because they've been accused of *greenwashing*: putting a Green spin on something that's not all that Green when you look closely. Companies or even whole industries that try that gambit can experience serious backlash, and then it becomes much harder to convince consumers that the company has begun to work seriously on Greening itself.

Look what happened to Nestlé after it ran an ad promoting one of its bottled water brands as an eco-friendly alternative in the *Toronto Globe and Mail*. Five major environmental groups lodged an official complaint charging violation of the Canadian Code of Advertising Standards as well as environmental claims guidelines set by Canada's Competition Bureau and the Canadian Standards Association.

The legal complaint cites three claims in the ad:

1. Most water bottles avoid landfill sites and are recycled.
2. Bottled water is the most environmentally responsible consumer product in the world.
3. Nestlé Pure Life is a Healthy, Eco-Friendly Choice.

In the statement, the coalition said,

"Based on our review of the representations made by Nestlé Waters in this advertisement, it is clear that they are not supported by fact—we believe this is an outrageous example of greenwashing," says Beatrice Olivastri, Chief Executive Officer, and Friends of the Earth. *"The truth is that many water bottles are not being recycled, a phenomena that Nestlé Waters itself—in direct contradiction to its own advertisement—admits in its 2008 Corporate Citizenship Report." Olivastri points out that Nestlé Waters states in the report that many of its own bottles end up in the solid waste-stream and that many of them are not recycled even though they are recyclable.*[26]

Of course, Nestlé could have easily avoided the specific Canadian complaint (and resultant bad publicity) by being more careful in its copywriting. It wouldn't have helped with the growing perception that bottled water is inappropriate in most situations precisely because of its severe environmental consequences[27]—but rewriting the claims as follows could have rendered this particular complaint moot:

➤ *Many* water bottles avoid landfill sites and are recycled.

➤ Bottled water *could be considered an* environmentally responsible consumer product, *especially* in *parts of* the world *where tap water is not safe to drink.*

➤ *Pure, clean water such as* Nestlé Pure Life is a Healthy Choice.[28]

By contrast, no amount of copy tweaking could save the nuclear power industry from being accused of greenwashing. The *New York Times* reported on January 1, 2009, on initiatives by two different European power companies, offering so-called Green nuclear power to their customers.[29] And this response was posted the same day:[30]

> *Anyone who buys into the lie that nuclear is green needs to take a serious look at the environmental impact of . . .*
>
> > *Mining and milling and transporting and processing uranium*
> >
> > *Radiation leakage during normal operation*
> >
> > *Catastrophic environmental consequences of a major accident or serious terrorism incident (and in the US, no meaningful financial liability on the part of the utilities)*
> >
> > *Need to isolate extremely large quantities of toxic wastes for a quarter of a million years! (How many objects survive from even 1/10th as long ago?)*

Still, even very mild claims can lead to greenwashing accusations. Lexus was forced by British authorities to yank an ad containing the seemingly innocuous claim that one of its cars was "perfect for today's climate." Regulators felt the ad "was likely to reinforce the impression that the car caused little or no harm to the environment and was unlikely to clarify for readers that the headline claim was intended to refer to the economy as well as the environment."[31]

To us, this is more than a bit over the top. That phrase could be interpreted in a dozen different ways that have nothing to do with climate change. It's like the lawyers who force a peanut processor to warn on the label that the package of peanuts contains peanuts. And with this kind of backlash, it's understandable that companies are reluctant to make Green claims.

So how do you avoid being tarred as a Greenwasher? It's very simple. Create genuinely eco-friendly innovations in your processes, sales and support structure, marketing, supply chain, and every other area of business—and don't say anything that isn't totally true and verifiable.

TerraChoice, a consulting firm specializing in environmental marketing, lists "six sins of greenwashing" on its web site:[32]

1. Hidden trade-offs that highlight leadership on one environmental issue while burying areas with less progress

2. Lack of proof for claims (as in the Nestlé example, above)

3. Vagueness of catch-all terms like eco-friendly, all-natural, and so forth
4. Irrelevance (such as a claim that could apply to every product in the category—e.g., being free of a banned substance)
5. False claims
6. Green claims for a harmful product that shouldn't be offered in the first place (e.g., tobacco, toxic lawn chemicals)

■ THRIVING AS THE BAR IS RAISED

Right now, it's still possible to draw on any Green initiative as a positive point of differentiation, a way of moving consumers toward your brand. But that first-mover advantage won't last. Over the next few years, as company after company makes a commitment toward sustainability, marketing messages will have to do a better job of heralding why this particular company is special. Just as in 1995, it was enough to say, "We have a web site," but by 2000, you needed "Visit our web site to find these resources," and in 2010, it's "Visit our web site so you can have real-time input into developing our next products . . . to have conversations with a community of product users . . . to get faster and better support." Green messaging will have to get more specific and highlight advantages better.

Smart marketers will start improving their Green messaging now, so they'll be prepared and positioned when the shift happens. Here are some (among many) messages that will likely have sticking power:

➤ Eco-aware and eco-friendly since our founding in 1898

➤ We went Green in 1980, and we're still Green today

➤ You save money and time because our Green initiatives allow us to pass on the savings

➤ 30 years using recycled materials

➤ Every purchase you make helps fund sustainable development of indigenous farmers in (country)

➤ We're training tomorrow's construction workers in solar installation, so they can have jobs and you can save money

➤ Rethinking transportation (housing, agriculture, health care) for a sustainable tomorrow

➤ Small steps to big improvements

➤ Partner with us to save the world

■ LESSONS AND ACTIONS

➤ When using Green marketing, make sure the customer can find your true environmental message—and make that message believable.

➤ Be genuine and avoid greenwashing.

➤ Grab the early-mover advantage now, before you become just another voice in the crowd.

Part

III

Hands-On with Cooperative, People-Centered Marketing

Chapter 14

Getting Noticed in the Noise and Clutter: A Brief Introduction to Effective Marketing Techniques

In this part of the book, you'll learn how to take the principles we've been talking about and apply them in real-world marketing. Although we don't have the space for a full discussion of practical marketing here, we can give at least a brief summary. If you want more, please check out *Grassroots Marketing: Getting Noticed in a Noisy World*, Shel's comprehensive book on how to market effectively for maximum impact at minimum cost—as well as Jay's numerous books, especially *Guerrilla Marketing for Free*. We also both offer huge amounts of practical marketing advice at www.gmarketing.com and www.frugalmarketing.com, a direct example of the demonstrate-your-expertise model we discussed in Chapter 7.

Not surprisingly, many of these techniques are totally suited to Green, people-centered marketing.

The reason is that ethical, Green, win–win marketing methods work better. These strategies are cheaper, more effective, and easier to implement than the typical win–lose strategies. For instance, if your operating costs are lower, your prices can also be lower—or your service standards higher. And you may find ways to shine a spotlight on your suppliers and customers, and bring them along with your success.

If your next proposed marketing or customer service initiative meets the criteria in the checklist below, the chances are good that it's in harmony with the abundance mentality, and that your prospects will see your message as beneficial:

➤ Incorporate top-quality customer service into every aspect of your business. Train your staff in how to greet customers in person and over the phone, how to resolve complaints and follow up to make sure they're resolved—and how to go the extra mile so the customer really feels special. Empower your workers as much as possible to satisfy customers. If you've reached out to an ethnic or subculture community, have people on hand who come out of that community, speak the language, understand the cultural context, and can make customers feel welcome. Remember how much easier and less expensive it is to get more business from an existing customer than to recruit a new customer—*if* that customer had a positive experience. But it has to be genuine. When researching an earlier book, Shel saw a sign at a well-known national chain that talked about how its employees were all empowered to help—but when he called to get the wording of the sign so he could put it in this book, he was told, "I'm not allowed to give that out; please call our corporate headquarters." Worse, his wife had a mild customer service request that should have been easy for such an "empowered employee" store to accommodate. Yet the manager told her that company policy prevented him from doing what she asked, and the store lost their business as a result. In other words, the company didn't take its own message very seriously, so how could anyone else?

➤ Target your marketing to your exact audience—and, as much as possible, *only* your exact audience. Don't waste your money annoying people who are not your prospects.

➤ Treat your prospects as intelligent, thinking, feeling people. Don't ignore their emotions, but create marketing materials and campaigns that engage your prospect both intellectually and emotionally. Those that only involve emotions and ignore rational thinking too often come across as patronizing, or just plain poorly thought out—while those that ignore emotions come across as limp and boring.

➤ Be sensitive to the cultural nuances of your target audience. This means knowing the demographics and psychographics, using the right media to reach your particular set of prospects, and creating marketing that resonates with the people you most want as customers. If you have a storefront in East Los Angeles, run Spanish-language radio ads on Spanish-language radio stations—and make sure every shift includes several employees who speak Spanish fluently. If you want to reach the deaf community, mention in print media that your event will be interpreted into American Sign Language (ASL). If you sell luxury goods, a soft-spoken, elegant ad campaign on the local classical music station may be appropriate. If you run a feed store out in the country, sponsor a tractor pull or cow-milking contest and put notices in the local shopper or underwrite the swappers slot on an AM talk station. If you run a trendy downtown eatery, open your doors to a free 5 P.M. gourmet appetizer tasting, and publicize it by distributing fliers the previous day as commuters leave their offices. If you sell heavy metal CDs, organize a concert of local artists and get a rock station to co-promote it. If you sell high-end computer processors, a multifaceted Internet campaign makes sense. If you're a deep discounter, distribute money-saving coupons on cheap newsprint.

➤ Be scrupulously honest in every headline, claim, or offer (more about that follows), but still use copy that makes your audience sit up and take notice.

➤ Always take advantage of every honest chance to build your reputation. Turn your customers, your employees, and your competitors into evangelists for your business.

■ HONESTY IN COPYWRITING

Everybody knows you win new customers by making outrageous claims, right?

Wrong—unless, of course, they're true.

If you want words to sell a product, that product should be strong enough to do so without tricking the buyer. True, if you trick someone, you might make a one-time sale, but you've lost a customer for life. Whereas if you show the merits, back up your claims, and focus on the way this product solves a problem, eases a hurt or fear, or satisfies a need, you build a lifetime relationship.

Oh, and one more thing. When you look in the mirror, you'll see someone who is doing good for the world. Lies and trickery won't accomplish that. It feels so good when you can honestly say, "My soul is not for sale."

Without tricking people, you want your marketing to capture interest, move the reader to action, and still feel good about yourself in the morning.

Yes, it can be done. We do it for clients and for our own businesses every day.

There's a fine line between making something sound as good as possible and deceptive, overblown hype. Don't cross it. Many wise people have advised that it is best to underpromise and overdeliver.

It works pretty well in face-to-face sales, or even on the phone. If you surpass the customer's expectations, you have a very loyal customer who becomes an evangelist for your brand.

So, for instance, when a client submits a job and asks for an estimate of the cost and turnaround time, and you've already established yourself in the prospect's mind as the preferred provider, you may want to quote toward the upper end of the possible range. Since usually it takes less time and comes in cheaper than your estimate, your clients will be simply delighted. (Of course, this strategy is considerably less effective if you're competing on price and delivery with a host of other vendors. The strategies we're talking about are designed to elevate you out of that commoditization and into the much less price-sensitive market where the customer is totally convinced that he or she wants to do business with you.)

Those who overpromise and underdeliver, however, have just sacrificed a long-term client relationship for the quick sale. And that is in fundamental conflict with the People First approach. Your customer loses because a shoddy product, or one that is inappropriate for the stated need, doesn't solve the problem and therefore was a waste of money or because the customer's experience didn't even meet minimum acceptable standards. And you lose because all that careful buildup, all the time and expense of wooing a customer, has been wasted, and you have to do it all over again.

That kind of negative branding is really tough to overcome. So there are practical as well as moral reasons to do right by your customers.

At the same time, if you're relying on written words to make a sale, underpromising may not be enough to get the order, especially if you're using a medium that doesn't offer visual, sound, or sensual clues (for instance, text-only e-mail). Your writing alone must be persuasive. It must convince the vaguely interested thinker to become a prospect, and then turn your prospect into a living, breathing customer. So in copywriting, underpromising is not the best approach. You want to promise exactly what you can deliver, because to offer less means you might lose the sale, whereas to offer more leads only to disappointment and its resultant problems. You want to move your prospect to action, and then create an experience where the customer feels rewarded for having taken that action.

This can take some practice, and you may benefit from bringing in a professional copywriter who is clued in about writing copy that is gripping and action-oriented, but not hyped or overselling (a number of copywriters, including Shel, are listed in www.guerrillamarketing goesgreen.com/resources).

■ COPYWRITING BASICS

In the following sections we discuss a few basic principles of effective copywriting.

➤ Understand Your Audience and Your Medium

If you write the same way for a press release as for a direct-mail sales letter—or use the same ad on a highbrow, low-key classical music station as on an in-your-face, loud, and brassy rock or hip-hop station, your marketing will be a failure. You must know your audience and reach them with an on-target approach.

And this is true even within genres. The same sales letter or press release won't be equally effective to every target audience. You have to craft it to reflect the people encountering your marketing message.

Here's a concrete example. In a three-town state representative race, one candidate took the time and trouble to individualize his campaign mailer for residents of each town, talking about the issues that were important in that specific town. Another candidate sent a very general vote-for-me letter and the sample ballot for the largest of the three towns, which happened to be his hometown. His marketing simply ignored the other towns.

Who do you think won the election? Yup, the one who customized his mailers for his audience. Of the losing candidate's votes, 87 percent were from his own town (where he came in first, but led the overall winner by only 16 votes). By making no effort to reach voters in the other towns with a targeted message, he was destined to lose.

➤ Focus Your Copy on Why It's to Your Prospect's Advantage to Do Business with *You*

So many marketers focus their copy on *I, me, we.* Guess what? The prospect doesn't care about that. The prospect wants to know how you can do one or more of the following:

➤ Solve a pressing and urgent problem

➤ Relieve pain or fear

➤ Improve his or her financial condition, health, romantic life, or skills and knowledge

➤ Provide entertainment or other stimulation

Here are two brief (slightly modified) sections from the much longer copywriting chapter in *Grassroots Marketing* that summarize this very important point:

Great Copywriting

Many experts cite the AIDA formula: Attention, Interest, Desire, Action [and one expert, Jeffrey Eisenberg of Future Now, adds an S at the end, for Satisfaction].[1] I've expanded this to ten points. Great copywriting

1. *Catches the reader's attention with something relevant;*
2. *Addresses the reader's fears, anxieties, and/or aspirations;*
3. *Stresses specific benefits to the user, not the features that lead to those benefits;*
4. *Offers to solve the reader's problem, in the most specific terms possible;*
5. *Provides the reader with a chance to acquire something of clear value—but only for a limited time;*
6. *Pulls the reader toward an immediate action step;*
7. *Shows the consequences of a failure to act;*
8. *Includes solid, substantial validation of your claim by someone else (a customer, an expert);*
9. *Backs up claims with comparisons to competitors and a strong guarantee; and*
10. *This should be obvious—provides the necessary order form, address, and/or telephone number to allow the reader to move forward.*

You probably won't get all 10 in every marketing document, but strive to include as many as you can. (The book goes on to explain each of these 10 points in detail, with examples.)

Ogilvy's Principles

The late David Ogilvy, founder of Ogilvy & Mather, one of the world's largest and most successful ad agencies, was a believer in research. Based on extensive testing, he developed guidelines for effective ads. He scattered them throughout his book Ogilvy on Advertising:

➤ *If five times more people read headlines than body copy, your headline must sell—or you've wasted 80 percent of your ad dollars. Promise a benefit in your headline to attract four times as many readers.*

➤ *For the same reason, mention the brand name in your headline.*

➤ *Headlines below an illustration have 10 percent higher readership than headlines above the picture—but never put the headline under the body copy.*

➤ *Caption every illustration and use sales copy in the caption. Captions have much higher readership than body copy.*

➤ *In designing art, focus on one person, not a group—or focus on the product.*

➤ *Keep the language simple and the copy interesting (and that lets you use long copy, which Ogilvy favors).*

➤ *Use a great lead.*

➤ *Six times as many people read editorial copy as read ads. So consider making your ad look like a story. Ads that look like editorial content can get past the reader's automatic filter against advertising. Thus, full-page text-heavy ads with drop capitals [the first letter set in very large type, hanging down a few lines], serif type [the tiny feet at the edges of certain letters], black ink on a white background, set in three- or four-column type, without the company logo, can work very well.*

➤ *Short lines increase readership.*

➤ *Devices such as bullets, asterisks, and arrows help readers into your copy.*

➤ *Draw attention to key points with bold, italic, call-outs, bulleted or numbered lists, etc.*

➤ *If using long copy, break the page up graphically: use a two-line subhead between your headline and the body copy, start the body with a drop cap (13 percent increase in readership!), use no more than 11 words in the first paragraph, and use subheads every couple of inches. And use good leading [vertical spacing between lines—pronounced ledding]—it increases readership 12 percent.*

➤ Stay Believable—and Stay Connected to Your Customer

Because we are so barraged by marketing messages, all of us have our guard up. We have very good B.S. detectors, and if we catch a whiff of something that smells too good to be true—or, for that matter, smells just plain rotten—that prospect is gone.

This danger signal can be subtle. Drs. Judith Sherven and Jim Sniechowski talk about the difference between *technique acting*, where the actor goes through the motions of showing emotion but doesn't internalize it, and the much more effective *method acting*, where the character actually feels the emotions. By extension, they note, marketing that focuses on *techniqued* approaches is rejected as hype. As soft-sell marketers, they understand the value of technique, but combine it with genuine emotional interest. "Your intention is to create and maintain an authentic, heartfelt emotional connection with your customers . . . while preparing your customers to buy what you offer." As one example, phrase your action message as an invitation, not a command.[2]

Building on that, Sherven and Sniechowski state that the best type of selling is service to your customer, that it's actually spiritual—even sacred—because your genuine emotional connection to the customer creates mutual respect and safety. Hype would be a violation of that carefully nurtured relationship.[3]

➤ Provide Hype-Free Incentives

Just because your marketing is honest doesn't mean it can't sell. You want to create a value proposition—the perceived difference between what the package costs and the value the buyer receives. This proposition needs to be so strong that it moves the prospect from "I'll think it over" (translation: lost sale) to "I need this NOW!" In other words, you need to make an irresistible offer.

First, create such strong value in the prospect's mind that it seems downright foolish to turn down the benefits. Here are two, among many, ways to do this:

1. Cram your marketing pieces with *fascinations*: teasers in the copy that hint at secrets and benefits of the product but don't tell how to implement (this is great for information products such as books and special reports). Here are a few (out of 52, plus four testimonials and a rock-solid guarantee) from a salesletter Shel wrote for a client selling the audio recordings from a marketing conference.

➤ Where to find products you can sell at a 20,000 percent markup

➤ Should you copyright your products? The answer may surprise you!

➤ The secrets of putting together value-added premiums that cost almost nothing, yet allow you to charge twice as much money—while almost eliminating refund requests

➤ How Gary Halbert sets up his envelopes for success—right down to what kinds of stamps do better than others

➤ What *never* to do at the end of a sales letter page

➤ What Karen Myers says to her buyers to make them feel *great* as they part with hundreds of hard-earned dollars

2. Include add-ons—perhaps good for a limited time—that are so desirable, they increase the prospect's interest in the offer: information products, consulting and training, free trial membership in a continuity program, access to superstars.... (We recommend bonuses rather than discounts, or discounts that don't cheapen the perceived value of the product, such as free shipping.)

Lisa Sasevich, author of *The Invisible Close*, notes that she helped one of her clients reach a 60 percent close rate on a high-end personal services offer by offering a tiered incentive: sign up within a week and receive a great bonus package; *sign up that same day* to receive an additional bonus worth hundreds of dollars.[4]

■ LESSONS AND ACTIONS

➤ Use the six-point check list for designing customer-focused promotions.

➤ Remember: Honesty, not hype.

➤ Reread the 10 points for great copywriting.

➤ Ogilvy's 12 principles of advertising are essential.

Chapter 15

Practical Tools for Effective Marketing

Guerrilla Marketing enables you to take advantage of some of the very best low-cost, high-impact marketing tools. Here's a very brief look at win–win approaches in traditional grassroots marketing.

■ MEDIA PUBLICITY

Coverage by the media conveys an implied endorsement by an objective, trustworthy source—something you can't buy with any amount of advertising dollars. Therefore, take full advantage of opportunities to promote yourself through media publicity; even a complete unknown ought to be able to do at least 20 media interviews per year. That includes radio, print media, Internet-only media such as e-zines, and even a little television. Both Jay and Shel are frequently quoted in major media, including the *New York Times, Christian Science Monitor, Boston Globe, Los Angeles Times, Entrepreneur, Inc., Fortune Small Business,* Microsoft's bCentral small-business web site, *Woman's Day,* and a host of smaller media.

The best media publicity is a home run. It builds credibility, increases your branding and visibility, draws the attention of other media, and stimulates lots of direct sales. Any marketing that can hit all four of those bases is clearly a winner. But even if all you get is first base—credibility—it's worth doing. If all you get is a one-sentence quote in the *New York Times,* your press kit can now legitimately say that the *New York Times* found you a worthy story source.

But what do the media get out of it? Although getting major media coverage is fiercely competitive, the media need stories. Broadcasters (in the United States, at least) are required by law to provide a certain percentage of public service programming. Print media must fill a *news hole* in order to wrap content around the ads.

We've already talked about how you can bring your competitors (or colleagues in different parts of the country, or clients, suppliers, etc.) into news and feature stories by suggesting their names for a roundup story, where the media outlet interviews several people in a field. If you each present a different perspective, you should all get some coverage. But that's only one among many ways to get the benefits of press coverage.

If you're a good writer, consider writing and placing your own articles, or even a regular column. Many, many extremely successful marketers batch up a bunch of articles and self-syndicate to dozens of publications and web sites. In many cases, the only compensation is a detailed resource box explaining who they are, what they can do for people, and how to get in touch. Other marketers prefer to make the articles themselves into an income stream and are much more selective in the markets they penetrate, but get paid as much as two dollars a word to place their articles. Of course, they usually get a much smaller bio, and interested prospects have to track them down. Therefore, you may want to mix both approaches, as we do. We have some articles available for free reprint, with certain conditions. But if we create new content for a publication, we expect to get paid for it.

Still, sometimes the exposure really does pay off. Shel did not get paid for an essay that Mark Joyner included in his book *The Great Formula*—but he gets several client inquiries a year from that book, including one in November 2008 (years after the book was published) from one of the largest charitable organizations in Britain. How else could Shel attract that kind of a stellar client from half a world away? And without that essay, would Mark have given Shel the name and contact information of his editor at John Wiley & Sons, and would Wiley have published the book you're holding in your hand?

An even better trick than approaching the media cold—even if you have a great story, they are so deluged, they may miss it—is to provide useful information to journalists who are already working on relevant stories. Most of Shel's top-tier media appearances came through a service that actually transmits information about what journalists are seeking sources for which stories. This is the secret of how a lot of publicists get ink and air time for their clients. PR firms currently pay $3,600 a year to get this information; however, we have a colleague who is the service's only authorized reseller. He supplies journalists' query feeds to individual clients for only $99 per month.[1]

You can sign up at http://snipurl.com/nv6p λ. Another similar service is http://helpareporter.com, which is free.

■ COVERAGE IN DO-IT-YOURSELF MEDIA

In today's wired world, it's so easy to set up a blog or e-zine or print newsletter that anyone can become a media outlet in minutes. And it's much easier to get coverage in these tiny, obscure outlets than in the big mainstream newspapers and magazines. So if you've got a hot new product, consider a virtual tour of blogs and e-zines, from the comfort of your own home or office.

But does anyone actually read them? Oh, yes. Here are two examples.

One of those independent media outlets, a tiny little print newsletter with a circulation of just 3,000, sold over 70 books for Shel, at full list price plus a shipping markup.

On a larger scale, *Marketing Sherpa* reports on an amazing blog-tour success story. Darren Barefoot and Julie Szabo, coauthors of *Getting to First Base*, targeted 50 blogs, then ranked them into top 10, middle 20, and bottom 20 (using number of e-mail and RSS web-based newsfeed subscribers; rank on Technorati, Google, Alexa, and Compete; number of comments on the blog—much of this information is very easy to get). The top tier received handwritten, perfumed letters in postal mail, with personal notes demonstrating familiarity with the blogger's work and providing a link to a unique landing page, where the blogger saw a video that mentioned that blogger by name. The book was actually about social media, so it was well-targeted—and the authors included a charity component, too.

The campaign actually got coverage on 178 blogs (well over three times the number they targeted). Six of the top ten responded, including superbloggers Seth Godin and Lee Odden.

This underscores one of the key advantages of blogs (and social media generally). Bloggers read and comment on each other's blogs, and if they like something they read, they'll spread it around. And not only did it go viral, it sold books, with some blog sites converting as high as 6 percent, and YouTube videos pulling 7 percent (most direct-mail marketers are delighted to get just 2 percent).

About 35 percent of our buyers came directly from blogs that we pitched. The rest is comprised mostly of Google, which, indirectly, is largely thanks to the blog coverage, other blogs and sites, and direct visitors.[2]

■ **TWENTY-FIRST-CENTURY TOOLKIT**

Your media tools have to evolve along with your definition of media. The old-fashioned press release, too often a dry recitation of the journalist's classic 5 Ws (Who, What, Where, When, Why/How), was only mildly effective even in the 1970s. It may have gotten ink, but that doesn't mean it got read.

These days, it won't even get ink. But fear not: there's still plenty of space for creative press releases that tell the story *behind* the story in attention-getting ways. A few pointers:

➤ Incorporate social media and/or multimedia features in your release to make it easy to share. Consider how this press release at www.pitchengine.com/free-release.php?id=5538, announcing a well-known Internet guru's hire by a press release distribution company, includes the following:

One-click links to share a mini-version on Twitter

A slightly larger version on Friendfeed and Facebook, or the whole thing on a whole raft of social bookmarking and content-sharing sites

A shortened URL aliased to the page

Numerous hotlinks to read more in particular areas

A reader comment section, just like most blog pages

Several versions of a summary, including a bulleted list

A color photo

It wouldn't have been difficult to add a brief video or audio and transcript of Brian Solis (the guru) as well.

➤ Figure out the *real* news angle. When Shel was hired to write a press release for a book on electronic privacy, he didn't bother with an expected and boring headline like "Electronic Privacy Expert Releases New Book." By asking himself questions like "who cares?" and "what's in it for the reader?" he came up with "It's 10 O'Clock. Do You Know Where Your Credit History Is?" In the social media example above, the real story was Solis's view that social media press releases have come of age—which could easily connect to his new job.[3]

➤ Target the right audience. Don't send your news about corporate raiders to gardening publications.

➤ Remember that the media no longer stands between you and your public. A search engine, link, or blog post could bring readers right to your press release, without involving any journalists at all.

➤ When possible, be personal—and that doesn't just mean using mailmerge to call someone by name, but researching the publication and the writer, as Barefoot and Szabo did to get their 178 media hits.

All these techniques make it easier for journalists to do their job and run your material and easier for the public to share with their own networks.

■ SPEAKING

Like the media, meeting planners have a lot of time to fill and are always looking for speakers who can capture the audience's interest and impart useful information. (They are *not*, however, looking for a blatant sales pitch from the podium.) Again, there's a large mix of free, low-paying, and highly paid opportunities, and you can expect to spend a few years working your way up the pay ladder.

But even if you speak for free, you'll have the chance to sell informational products, to distribute handouts that include information not only about your topic but also about how you can help your prospects, and how to get in touch. And if you provide solid, useful information—especially if you can do so while entertaining your audience—you'll find that, yes, prospects in the audience seek you out to consult, to buy your products, or to hire you for another speech. And, of course, the meeting planners will remember the good job you did for them and spread your name around to others who can use you. After all, if you deliver more than an audience is expecting, that reflects favorably on the meeting planners, and on the audience's willingness to come back and pay another registration fee the next time that planner offers an event.

You'll find a number of practical tips on speaking in the back issues of Shel's Monthly Frugal Marketing Tips, available at www .frugalmarketing.com/marketingtips.shtml.

■ INTERNET DISCUSSION GROUPS AND SOCIAL NETWORKING SITES

The Internet is such a powerful marketing tool that in *Grassroots Marketing*, Shel wrote over 35,000 words—nine very full chapters—about it.[4] We talked earlier about reaching *only* your actual prospects. What makes the Internet so potent for marketers is the incredible segmentation of interest groups, and one of our very favorite items in the Internet marketing toolkit is participation in discussion groups.

If you're not familiar with them, these are communities of interest that come together in cyberspace, through e-mail, the Web, social media sites like Facebook, threaded bulletin boards and forums, or Usenet newsgroups. These different technologies accomplish the same thing: they draw a group of like-minded people together to talk about something they all have in common. And they are a lot of what makes the Internet special, because instead of speaking to a local interest group with 20 or so people at a meeting, you're in front of hundreds or even thousands of like-minded people around the world—often including some of the top names in the field, as well as people just starting out with a new interest.

No matter what topics interest you, there's bound to be a discussion group about it. These are the epitome of the People First mindset, and watching them for over a dozen years has helped formulate a lot of the core thinking in this book. Just at random, searching Yahoogroups.com—one of the major places to locate e-mail discussion groups—for "wine" returned 5,564 different lists. "Fibromyalgia" returned 1,336 results, and "garden" yielded 32,876 lists.[5]

The culture is focused around giving information; sharing success stories; and asking questions to improve your products, your business, and the quality of your business thinking. People subscribe to lists that interest them, choosing by topic from literally hundreds of thousands of possibilities. From around the world, members chip in to share their expertise.

Many marketers have found that helpful participation brings them work. For Shel, discussion list participation has been his largest single source of both new marketing clients and paid speaking gigs. And he has some thoughts about why:

> I do take the time, week after week, to answer questions and provide a lot of information. That turned out to be an amazing credibility builder in the group, and clearly motivated some of my earlier clients to try me out. Once I had satisfied a few folks, my reputation—and sales—built very quickly.
>
> Interestingly, when I first began to participate, my original agenda in posting was not to get clients, but to be consistently helpful to others—so that when I asked a question, even a really dumb or off-topic question, other people would answer it out of loyalty, because of the useful advice I'd given over time. It is definitely easier to get your questions answered if you're willing to give of yourself.

Over the years, I've provided hundreds of hours of free consulting to these lists—but I've gotten back far more than I've given out. The discussion groups I've participated in have provided me with everything from market research to new product ideas to computer technical help.

Together, the list members create a resource that is more valuable than any newspaper or magazine, because it's based on the real-life experience and academic knowledge of hundreds of people out there in the trenches. Helpful advice comes from superstars in the field, who still find it useful to participate, and also from unknown people quietly succeeding in their own niche—people whose advice you would never have stumbled upon if you were looking for it on your own, because it's not in the traditional literature. List culture also creates genuine community. People start to really care about each other's successes and trials, not only in the business context, but as one human being to another. And if there's an opportunity to get together face to face, you feel as if you're meeting old friends. Even a shy person will feel as if he or she already knows a lot of people, and the interactions can shortcut a lot of the getting-to-know-you stuff—because you really do know each other already.

There is an added benefit. Since feeding articles to web sites and publications is a great way to market yourself for free, or maybe even get paid, some of your best posts can be recycled into articles or even books, and spread around to reach new audiences.

Discussion lists exist in several different technologies; choose one that's comfortable for you. Until 2007, Shel used e-mail discussion lists almost exclusively, because most of them are available as a digest of all the posts for a day, which he can then print out and read easily off-screen. (His eyes get tired from working at the computer all day.) Other people prefer newsgroups or Web-based forums.

For the past couple of years, Shel has also participated in social networking communities such as Facebook, LinkedIn, Plaxo, and Groupsite. All of these sites and their many competitors offer numerous interest groups. Typically, you can set the systems up so you receive e-mail notices of new group activity (or you can just visit the web site often enough to stay current). ·

Remember, too, that one major—and little-talked-about—aspect of social networking sites is that hundreds of millions of people now have a Web presence, even if they don't have a business. MySpace and Facebook profiles, especially, provide a way to research people on the Web who might have been harder to find before. But now, using tools like Facebook's Friend Finder, you can connect with niche audiences on the consumer side: fans of a particular obscure music group, for example. If you've got a product geared toward that market, you're going to be a very happy marketer (never spam, however).

These newer platforms also offer many options to spread your visibility. For example, it's easy to automatically feed your blog into your Facebook and Twitter profiles, and then anyone who has connected with you might see the notice that you've got a new blog entry. You can also feed your Twitter tweets into the Facebook status update, and that in turn flashes across the screens of your Facebook friends—at least those who've enabled that feature.

Twitter is a particularly amazing phenomenon. Whereas Facebook and the others allow greater flexibility in what you can post, Twitter is rigid. There are only three things you can post on Twitter, and all of them have to be kept to 140 characters at a time. You can post:

> An open message

> A message directed to a specific person, but that anyone can look at—these start with the @ sign, followed with no space by the recipient's screen name

> A private message to a specific individual who is following you

Using a hashtag (#) immediately in front of a codeword, you can also make your tweets searchable. So, for instance, searching for #bbash brings up all the Tweets relating to a conference where Shel spoke.

With Twitter, it's all on the Web, but you get e-mail notices whenever someone new follows you, or whenever you receive a private message. Even though you only hear news from people you're following, one click loads the profile of anyone mentioned in a message—whom you can then follow, in one click.

What can you do in that tiny little canvas of 140 characters? Quite a lot. In a great article on his favorite Twitter moments,[6] David Spark showed how real people have used the service to save substantially on purchases, respond instantly to customer complaints, slash customer service response time, track loved ones through natural disasters, receive real-time information about cities they're visiting, even get unstranded by the side of the highway.

Smart businesses in both B2C (business-to-consumer) and B2B (business-to-business) markets harness Twitter to manage reputation, build communities, respond to customers, hawk new features or products, and offer discounts or other promotions:

➤ Dell, the huge computer company, attributed $1 million in revenue from March 2007 to December 2008 just from posting discounts on Twitter. For a company the size of Dell that may seem to be small potatoes, but keep in mind those sales cost nothing to acquire except 30 seconds of someone's time to post the Tweet. And for a solopreneur, $1 million is far from chump change.[7]

➤ Chelsea Green, a publisher with a large line of sustainability books, flags blog posts and video appearances by its authors along with general sustainability links and commentary, does giveaways—and has over 3,000 followers.

➤ Frank Eliason, Comcast's Director of Digital Care, has pretty much single-handedly turned around Comcast's once-sorry reputation for customer service, through his ComcastCares Twitter account. Tweets like "@frankgorton I see the trouble call and line check scheduled but I think it is modem/router. I have been seeing trouble w/WCG200" help customers troubleshoot and direct a repair team in when necessary (and save money by not sending them when the problem can be fixed remotely). For the company that infamously kept a repairman on hold so long he fell asleep on the customer's couch,[8] this is major rebranding.

➤ Cisco, a major B2B player in computer networking, has one Twitter account just for highlighting the company's sustainability practices. CiscoEcolibrium mixes Tweets like "Curious About Cisco Going Green?!?!: Check out this video: http://tinyurl.com/au6uss #green" and "blog post: Top Ten Ways to be Greener through Better Networking http://tinyurl.com/blajqy #green" with general commentary about Green initiatives elsewhere and general Twitter chitchat. Of 20 posts from January 21 to March 18, 2009, six apparently directly promote Cisco initiatives, and several more discuss networking generally. But others discuss carpooling, the Obama environmental agenda, and so forth, so the balance will keep people interested.[9]

➤ An Australian tweeter, iconic88, offers 25 Twitter-based customer service tactics, including providing "WOW options" to dissatisfied customers, collecting testimonials and case studies, integrating with Skype or other voice-based system, and more.[10]

➤ Peter Shankman of helpareporter.com (HARO) Tweets last-minute requests from reporters needing story sources at his outbound-only helpareporter account (he has another account, skydiver, to interact with the Twitter community); he closed his PR agency and makes a seven-figure income by selling ads on the free service.[11]

Here are some other benefits

➤ Find—and share—great resources: useful articles and blog posts, audios, upcoming teleseminars. A certain percentage of these can link to content you've created without alienating people. (If you're perceived as doing nothing but pumping salesy messages out, a lot of people will unfollow you.)

➤ Get direct access to movers and shakers who are extremely open and accessible on Twitter. (As one example, follow Guy Kawasaki and send him an @ message responding appropriately to one of his Tweets—you're very likely to get a personal response.)

➤ Grow your own community and get connected with people you ought to know about. (Twitter spreads virally; you will notice an @ Tweet that looks interesting, click to the recipient's profile, and begin following that person. Often, you'll get followed back—and of course, others will also start following you, if they like what you post to those they're following.)

➤ Follow up media leads of reporters looking for sources, by following @helpareporter and @Profnet.

➤ And, yes, develop a number of new friendships, both online and in person. (Twitter participants often gather face-to-face in "Twee-tups.")

➤ Create and run Twitter-based charity events or discussions.[12]

Warning: You can also fritter away vast amounts of time following links and so forth, so be disciplined. There's a whole industry of no-cost third-party tools to improve the Twitter experience, such as TweetDeck (which, among other things allows you to create a separate feed of the people you most want to follow, and also allows you to respond or retweet with one click) and Twittfilter (a much faster way to check the profiles of those who follow you). Set limits and make sure you get your other work done.

Some of these have amazing business uses:

TwitterHawk—This marketing app helps you connect with consumers in your area and related to the keywords you choose. TwitterHawk will send Twitter users your custom response when they tweet your keyword in locations that you specify. Say you sell shoes and you want your response to reach anyone within a 20 mile radius of your business. When someone 7 miles away tweets about shoes, your response will automatically be sent to that person.[13]

You can also set up temporary or permanent alerts and Tweet in response. Social media strategist Chris Brogan suggested this example:

> *I just cooked up this Twitter search http://search.twitter.com/ search?q=staying+sxsw+where, which looks at where people are staying for the SXSW conference, and I found several people asking for lodging. If I were an Austin, TX hotel property with open beds, I'd go after each and every one of them with a rate quote and an easy link to make the reservation. You can do this ceaselessly. Twitter offers up all kinds of data from business travelers all the time for free.*[14]

It's also important to use Twitter strategically. You must provide high enough value that others want to follow you, and that means keeping a high signal-to-noise ratio in your Tweets. Mix up comments to others, retweets, useful links, requests for help, and self-promotion. If your profile is too full of either inane chatter or blatant sales, you won't get much of a following. One trick is to send thank-yous or something useful to only one person as a Direct Message and keep it out of your public feed.

Kai Turner outlines five strategic Twitter brand-building objectives (with elaboration and real examples) in his Mashable article, "Finding the Right 'Brand Voice' on Twitter":

1. See it as an exercise in developing your brand personality.
2. Create a unique voice; don't imitate.
3. Acknowledge mistakes—and repair them, publicly.
4. Do more than just stream your RSS feed; let a real person put it in context.
5. Know your goals for using Twitter, and formulate a goal-appropriate voice.[15]

In an article in the marketing publication *B to B,* Paul Gillin attributes some of Twitter's success to its simplicity and ease of use, and contrasts it with the much more complex platform Second Life, which many companies had thought would be the Next Big Thing. Twitter offers a very intuitive interface, doesn't require any special software, and provides immediate and clear business value if you follow the right people. He also notes its growing popularity in the business-to-business sector, with companies like Gartner and McKinsey participating (along with 4 million other people).[16]

All of these tools are fundamentally about building, expanding, and nurturing your community: turning real-life friends and business contacts into online buddies, finding new people who network with your network, and using your own humanity to brand yourself as someone to follow, and ultimately do business with.

And for that reason, not only businesses but also nonprofits and political campaigns have been quick to embrace Twitter (and a number of other social media tools as well). Two months after the election, and without a new post since his victory, Barack Obama still had over 154,262 followers on Twitter on January 4, 2009. During the 2008 presidential campaign, he used it to post his campaign appearances, announce news items, and, most importantly, contribute to that vital sense of belonging that propelled his entire campaign. Unlike many celebrities, he followed back everyone who followed him, and even a few more. On January 4, 2009, he was following 165,973 people. Of course this doesn't mean he was actually reading all those messages—but it surely helped build the feeling that he cared.

After he was inaugurated as President, Obama started Tweeting more actively again, making a few Tweets almost every month. The higher activity has vastly increased his popularity on Twitter; as of August 19, 2009, he has 2,011,305 followers, making him the 10th most popular Tweeter according to Twitterholic. He's following back 762,037 people, making him the only one of the 100 most popular Twitter users to have more than half a million Twitter friends.[17]

Of course, we all know that Obama had to give up his beloved BlackBerry and stop doing his own unofficial e-mail. But the campaign continued to harness the power of social networks. Between the election and the inauguration, the Obama transition team used its numerous web sites to organize issue-focused house parties and discussion groups, and to poll the American public directly on its priorities. This level of transparency and openness may be unprecedented in modern government, and provided Obama with a significant marketing edge—breathing room to try new initiatives—as he took the reins of power.

As for nonprofits, Leslie Poston wrote a great article on Mashable.com, on January 1, 2009, noting that many nonprofit campaigns have begun using Twitter, and that mechanisms even exist to interface between Twitter and PayPal to seamlessly collect donations. She listed eight different payment technologies to get donations, and noted that these methods have raised money for such causes as drinking water wells and school supplies. One of the sites doesn't even require money donations. Donors provide ad space on their own sites, and corporate donors provide the funding.[18]

Given the success of other online political initiatives such as MoveOn.org and the 2004 Howard Dean campaign, this rush to adopt new technologies is not surprising.

■ SOCIAL MEDIA DOS AND DON'TS

Old-style in-your-face marketing simply doesn't work in this new wired world. If you bore or insult or annoy people, they leave. Thus, your marketing can't be intrusive; it has to blend into the culture. And when it does, it can be extremely powerful.

Therefore, use social networking communities not just to shill your own products and services but to build a reputation that is useful, helpful, and intelligent. Join some groups. Answer questions that get asked in these groups (especially on LinkedIn and CollectiveX), as well as some that get posted on the Yahoogroups pages. (Check your Yahoogroups occasionally via the Web, even if you normally get them as e-mail, so you can see and respond to the questions.) Write on people's profile pages (or their Walls on Facebook), but only when you have something useful to say. Pick someone that you've connected with and go through his or her other connections, seeking people you'd like to connect to, and send connection requests to group members whose posts you like. Post links to great content you didn't write. Retweet Twitter tweets you especially like, so your own network gets to see them. Customize any form messages you send, such as LinkedIn networking requests. Say thank you as appropriate, but in general, keep the thank-yous private unless you're sharing a resource or brag. Use a short version of your signature, including a link to your web site, but keep it to just a quick tagline and URL. (In e-mail discussion lists, four to six lines is usually okay.) Don't waste space on Twitter on this, but do provide a custom background on your profile page that highlights your best features, and do take advantage of the ability to post your picture, your URL, and a brief statement about yourself.

Of course, take full advantage of the ability to flesh out your profiles on most social networking sites; that's where you *can* strut your stuff. Even the apparently silly items like favorite books, movies, and television shows can lead to very interesting conversations.

Don't ignore this trend just because you don't understand it. For consumers ages 15 to 25, Facebook is completely incorporated into the culture, and e-mail is not. But older people are rapidly moving in; 12.4 million people between ages 35 and 49 joined Facebook in 2008. Not having a social network presence will rapidly become like not having an e-mail address or web site. Already, according to Neilsen Online, in 2008, more users worldwide accessed a social network (66.8 percent) than used e-mail (65.1 percent).[19]

➤ Should You Develop Your Own Social Network?

Taking it a step farther, some companies have actually created their own interactive communities, filled with user-generated content. A great example is Girlspace®,[20] set up by Kimberly-Clark's Kotex brand to create a safe space for adolescent girls to discuss puberty, sexuality, and other topics they might not want on their Facebook pages or as family dinner conversation. Social workers are on hand to answer questions and guide discussions. The site provides helpful resources—and doubtless builds loyalty in a product choice that can last 40 years.

Nike set up a private community for just one of its sports niches (running) and generated $56 million in revenue in 2008 alone. The company also grew market share from an already impressive 48 percent in 2006 to 61 percent two years later.[21]

Of course, this is much easier for a company with the reach of Kimberly-Clark or Nike. But even a nonprofit with a few hundred members could find benefit in a dedicated community, especially one that can scale as the membership grows. Look at how MoveOn.org used Internet scalability to go from a tiny splinter group opposing the impeachment of President Clinton to a fundraising and issue-selection powerhouse with influence in presidential politics.

As your networks grow, so will your influence.

■ USER-FRIENDLY WEB SITES WITH NEWSLETTERS

Your web site is another necessary (and inexpensive) arrow in your marketing quiver. The site should be quick to load, easy to navigate, and genuinely useful to your prospects and any journalists, investors, and other constituencies that might visit. If they find helpful information and a sense that they can trust you, visitors will buy from you at all hours, whether you're open for business or sitting at your computer.

Because most people will only visit once even if they bookmark your site and intend to come back again, it's crucial to have a way to capture e-mail addresses: newsletter or e-zine subscriptions, notifications of events or of new content (if it's not done too often), free downloads, and so forth. However, if you plan to use these addresses to create a marketing relationship, explicitly ask for permission. And under no circumstances should you allow anyone else access to these addresses. That's a sacred trust, and you will not be forgiven if you betray it.

Also include as many ways as possible to contact you: e-mail, phone, Twitter, social networking profiles, fax, and postal (even your cell phone or pager, if you use them to be accessible to clients).

One of the many two-sided benefits in a good web site is that providing visitors with the information they need reduces the administrative burden on you. If your support staff answers the same questions over and over, put up an FAQ (Frequently Asked Questions) page on your site. If you're in an industry where prices fluctuate, let visitors get price quotes dynamically, right from your web site. If you distribute information, e-mail and download files can automate much of the process while saving you significant printing, mailing, and labor costs. And, of course, if people need to contact you, get your hours, locate your nearest distributor, or find a map to your store, the web site makes it very easy. Even as far back as 1995, Sun Microsystems' Neil Knox estimated that his company saved about $8 million annually by using the Web—not even counting a substantial direct-sales benefit.[22]

All your publicity and marketing should not only list your web address but also provide at least one specific reason to visit. Here's a real-life success story: Shel did a radio interview in Kansas City about his book on Frugal Fun. He always gives reasons to visit the site, such as "I mention a number of great cheap airfare sites in back issues of my Frugal Fun Tips. You'll find them on the archives page at www.frugalfun.com in the travel section." A listener heard the interview, went to the site, ordered both the fun book and one of the marketing books, and then hired him for a few copywriting projects.

It's well worth the effort. On the Web, you have essentially unlimited space to convince prospects to enter into a relationship with you. A well-designed, content-focused web site can become one of the best and most cost-effective marketing tools you can create, and one that can keep evolving as your business and the online culture change over time.[23]

■ APPAREL AND PREMIUMS

Everyone loves a new article of clothing. Why not do something that reinforces your brand? You get exposure for your message, and your prospect, customer, or trade-show visitor gets something spiffy to wear.

But don't just slap your name and logo across a T-shirt. Crystallize your core message into a few words that attract attention and provide a reason why someone viewing the shirt (hat, tote bag, etc.) would want to do business with you—and include your URL, nice and big. For shirts, forget about the golf shirts with a tiny logo under the pocket. The whole idea is to be seen by people encountering the person wearing your shirt. For the same reason, print on the front side. In the winter, the back will be covered up by a warmer layer.

If the clothing is attractive enough, people may want to buy it from you. That's good, because it means they'll actually use the item. You can also give them away as incentives for buying certain quantities and so forth.

As for other advertising specialties, in general, we don't think most of them are all that effective. But if you can come up with something that dovetails well with your products and services that can actually reinforce your brand, it's worth a bit of experimentation. Refrigerator magnets are one possibility; many people use them to hold up all sorts of temporarily important notes. Another would be something so useful that it won't be ignored, and so closely identified with your business that it serves as a constant reminder of what you can do for the client. A coffee roaster could do mugs, or even an imprinted carafe—but wouldn't want to do a calendar. A CPA or a renewable-energy consultant might want to give away solar calculators. An auto parts store could use auto sunshades (printed on both sides, since they're reversible).

■ HIGHLY TARGETED ADVERTISING AND DIRECT MAIL

Though they're relatively expensive compared to the other tools in our toolbox, there is a place for traditional advertising methods, both online and offline and for direct mail. Purchased ad strategies that may make sense over the Internet include advertising in e-zines and newsletters that match your demographic target, purchasing clicks (but *not* exposures) at search engines or social media sites—and perhaps, in very particular circumstances, banners or other types of display ads. Offline, highly targeted ad buys such as trade journals and Yellow Pages, or deeply discounted (but still targeted) ad buys such as remaindered space, may make some sense.

One key is to make sure that you have targeted so carefully that the vast majority of people seeing or hearing the ad, or receiving the letter, will be actual prospects (your own customer list is a very good place to start). Often, classifieds can be a better bet than display ads;

they target even within the publication's readership, and they're a lot cheaper.

And the other key is to provide copy that focuses on what the reader or listener wants, and not on what you want. Solve problems, relieve pain, demonstrate benefits—and reinforce in every part of the ad or letter how your mutual success philosophy is going to create a better situation for the prospect.

These two keys will move your advertising into the everyone-wins mode. The people you talk to will be eager to hear from you, and you'll slash your marketing costs by talking mainly to people who are your prospects.

In any medium, test your ad first online, then offline on a small audience before rolling out a big, expensive campaign.

Finally, remember that unless you've hit the prospect who has an immediate and crucial need, one impression is generally not enough. So consider a telephone follow-up program—but train your telephone sales staff so thoroughly in customer-focused marketing that the calls are actually welcomed. (Quite a bit of detail appears in the telemarketing chapter of *Grassroots Marketing.*)

■ GUERRILLA GIFTING AND SAMPLING

It has long been known that giving something away can be very good for business. Beyond the obvious ways—such as a free gift with purchase or subscription, annual holiday gifts, or giving away obsolete inventory with a marketing piece about the latest version—let's discuss a few unusual, innovative marketing tricks that offer long-term benefit to your business, and to the recipient.

➤ Library Gifts with Bookplate or Stamp

This brilliant idea comes from a reader who prefers to remain anonymous. The beauty of it is that any business can benefit by using books as a guerrilla marketing weapon—whether your business has anything at all to do with books.

Here's the deal: Look for holes in a library's collection. Buy a few books to fill those gaps—and there are a gazillion ways to find cheap books. Now, put a bookplate or rubber stamp on the inside front cover, and perhaps a few other choice locations: "Donated By (your business name, marketing tagline, URL, and contact info)." Obviously, the more closely the books match the interests of your own prospects, the more value you get out of it.

Still, even if it's not such a close match, there can be substantial benefit—especially if there's a strong cross-cultural component, which makes the materials exotic and desirable.

The book donor writes about how he used this to help the owner of a specialized training school.

> *I bought several books when I was in Spain, in Spanish, of direct interest to high school students, put "donated by xxx school" with a rubber stamp at least 10 times per book, on the title page, back page, on blank pages in the text, and sent them to the high school Spanish teacher in the town where my friend lives. Spanish books? For a Spanish teacher? Books that can't be bought at any price in the US, mostly, but which cost me 1–5 Euros in Spain? The teachers will use them until the paper crumbles. Those advertisements will last 20 years at least. Tourist posters are free in Spain—stamp your "donated by . . ." on them, and send them to high school Spanish departments. I assure you your ad will be on the wall until the paper falls apart.*[24]

He also bought a case of Shel's 1993 book *Marketing without Megabucks*, at a deep discount, to distribute them (mailing by ultra-cheap International M-Bag, which has since been discontinued) to libraries in Spain, India, and elsewhere—again, as a gift from a business he wishes to benefit. "Libraries abroad are *desperate* for good books in English. Even if it's an old book, those books will be on the shelf for decades."

He has been using this little trick for a decade now and has noticed definite and positive results.

➤ Work with Your Retailers and Sales Outlets to Broaden the Sale

A retail partner will be very happy with you if you significantly increase the total sale, even if that means plugging products that don't come from you. Kare Anderson, of the always-interesting *Say It Better* e-zine, shows how to make the cash register numbers jump at an author appearance:

> *Gain more in-bookstore visibility by helping bookstore managers increase sales. When seeking book-signing opportunities, offer to provide a 20-minute mini-seminar. Busy people will attend; you inspire them to tarry. In advance, provide a camera-ready*

tip-sheet and seminar announcement that booksellers can print 2-up on an 8 1/2" × 11" sheet. In it include "the companion collection" of three books you recommend reading, in conjunction with yours. If possible, refer to a local author you admire. In the seminar, refer to those books as you discuss yours. Suggest that the bookseller display your book, and "the collection," on a special table, along with a Lucite stand to hold your tip sheets—and build buzz for your event. Also provide 2- to 3-sentence mini-reviews of the books you recommend (include your name and book title at the end) and provide these mini-reviews in printed form for booksellers to tape to the shelves where those books are displayed.[25]

This costs you nothing but a few minutes of your time, yet leaves the retailer with a long-term appreciation that you have his or her needs at heart. That will create word-of-mouth buzz for you long after your celebrity appearance is a distant memory.

A spin on this strategy, for authors particularly, is to review books by others at Amazon.com and other book review sites. Of course, your review will mention that you're the author of such-and-such a book that readers of this book will also enjoy.

There are literally hundreds of ways to bring others along and pump up overall sales. We talked earlier about bundling items from different companies, and about working out partnerships for premiums and incentives, which you can either purchase or obtain for free. Then there are package stuffers, where you find people whose products complement yours, and insert fliers for each other's products into outbound shipments. If utility companies can do it, why can't we?

Many food manufacturers have teams of people who go to supermarkets and do cooking demos and product samplings. It doesn't take a genius to figure out that this will usually create a sharp spike in sales—and, with luck, some long-term converts. Think about how this model can apply to your business, even if you don't sell food.

We've mentioned going after co-op ad programs if you are a retailer. If you're the manufacturer or distributor, consider sponsoring a co-op program. And it doesn't have to be just advertising, either. For instance, offer co-op dollars toward your retailers' direct-mail and Web campaigns, too—but insist on approving the copy before you put your name on the marketing piece or provide any funds. In fact, because so few businesses understand effective marketing, you may want to offer co-op dollars only if you supply the creative elements (copy and design).

➤ Donate Your Product to a Store

Go to the store manager and offer to donate some special, collectible version of your product. Examples would be for authors or musicians, a couple of signed copies of your latest book or CD, for manufacturers, a one-off prototype, for food manufacturers, a low-volume run made with some unusual seasonal ingredient—but get a written agreement to buy more through regular channels if they sell within a certain time. The store then gets more than double its usual share of the price, can place the goods in inventory and track them, and has an incentive to display your wares prominently. By making the store owner, manager, and staff into allies and evangelists, you help them while gaining significant exposure for your merchandise, and they'll likely sell your products with a good deal more enthusiasm.

➤ Donate Your Product as a Premium

Here's another brief excerpt (rewritten slightly, for clarity out of context) from *Grassroots Marketing: Getting Noticed in a Noisy World* about giving away your products and services on radio and TV.

> *Both commercial and noncommercial broadcasters give away amazing numbers of records, concert tickets, retail gift certificates, and other prizes; these are almost invariably donated by publicity-seeking merchants. Prizes may be raffled off in charity auctions, given to random callers or those who can answer trivia questions, or used as incentives for people to subscribe to noncommercial stations. (Charity auction premiums may even yield the added bonus of a line in newspapers or brochures listing your prize and the time it will be auctioned.)*
>
> *If you listen, you'll hear a rap on the order of "I have a hot tub pass for two at Heavenly Heat on Bath Street in Anytown for the third caller who can tell me Ringo Starr's kid brother's name" or, at subscription time, "Jeff Jacobs, who owns the Witty Words bookstore, just called to offer a twenty-dollar gift certificate to the next two people who pledge thirty dollars or more. So if your library's getting kind of run-down, now's the time to call in your subscription."*
>
> *Not only do you get the air time, but when the lucky winner comes to redeem the prize, s/he will have to make the acquaintance of your business or service—and, ideally, be added to your valued regular customers. Meanwhile, the station gets more money. Everyone wins.*

Virtually all prizes and premiums given away by commercial stations are bartered for publicity. Often, it's possible to barter goods and services directly for advertising [discussed in more detail in Grassroots Marketing, *Chapter 13].*

Better yet, get someone else to spring for "your" cost. Jordi Herold of the Iron Horse Music Hall in Northampton, Massachusetts is a master at this.[26] "Whenever possible, you get somebody else to pay for the premium you're using. If we use tapes, CDs, posters, a weekend at an inn, somebody else has paid for all those things." Herold even manages to get subsidized ticket giveaways. "Often, when we use tickets as premiums, we are able to get the record companies to pay for them. They buy a block of tickets." Herold has also taken risks to promote unknown bands; the groups' record companies will buy enough seats to pay the performers, and have Herold give all the rest of the tickets away for free. Free sampling is a time-honored marketing method, and then, of course, a number of the attendees will buy CDs and pay to see future shows.

Here's a variation from Jay: If you advertise on a show that's built around an on-air personality, give the announcer a freebie: lessons, product samples, a dinner in your restaurant, whatever. Then just provide your radio celebrity with an outline of what you want covered in your ad. The radio star may provide you with an eloquent, unsolicited on-air testimonial that may run far longer than the number of seconds you're actually paying for.

Karon Thackston tells of one of her clients who approached magazines to offer a freebie to their readers in exchange for space to sell his own products. While it's common to offer a freebie and then up-sell through your own literature when you fill the order, this is a bit different, because not only did it happen at the same time as the original exposure, but it didn't cost the entrepreneur anything for the space. He ran full-page ads, of which the top fourth was devoted to the freebie; the rest was his to use as he wished.[27]

There are obviously many other ways to benefit by giving products away besides ensuring media coverage. For instance, whenever you go to a Chamber of Commerce networking event, bring something to give away as a door prize. When you attend a conference, ask ahead if you can donate something for the attendee and/or presenter goodie bags (many conferences will not charge for this if you're adding value). If there are 100 people in attendance, 100 people get to see your item waved around and hear your name mentioned. Similarly, donate giveaway items to many charity fundraisers.

> **Achievement, Birthday, and Anniversary Gifts**

Forget drowning in the deluge of holiday gifts and cards; recognize your customers at other times. If you become aware of some significant achievement (or a personal moment such as a new baby or a marriage), send a congratulatory note and perhaps a small gift. If you collect information in a database, send a gift for your client's birthday, or on surpassing a certain purchase level—ideally, a gift that fits in perfectly with the kinds of things that that customer likes to buy. Your more creative approach will be noticed and appreciated. Dave Ratner, who owns several pet food stores, buys Thanksgiving pies for over a thousand of his best customers, whom he tracks with a barcode-scannable club membership, just as many supermarkets do.

Ratner's use of technology to provide personal shopping experiences is only the beginning of what's possible. *National Geographic* asked for reader photo submissions to supplement the professionals for an anthology called *Visions of Paradise*. Those whose photos were chosen got a copy of the book with their own photo on the cover. You can bet those books get shown around a whole lot more often than a mailmerge letter that misspells your name three times while it tells you that you may have won a million dollars—but it's basically the same technology.[28]

■ THE TRIANGLE OF EXPERTISE: GET PAID TO DO YOUR OWN MARKETING

Marketing does *not* have to be a cost. It can be revenue-neutral, or even a profit center.

The Triangle of Expertise consists of three activities that can generate revenue, all of which also serve as marketing channels for you: speaking, consulting, and writing/publishing. When you tap into this triangle, your marketing activities reinforce each other and build the perception that you are *the* expert in your niche.

You can add media visibility for a Rectangle of Expertise, but you don't get paid to be interviewed by a journalist. However, publishing your own articles in various media can be a very definite income stream.

So, when you do a for-pay speaking engagement, first of all, you're getting paid to give the speech. If you have books or other information products, you ought to sell some quantity to attendees, at full price or at a slight discount. A smaller percentage of attendees may want to hire you for some kind of consulting or other professional services—or to give a speech somewhere else. And of course, those people who consume your information products may be moved to hire you, as well (especially if you've made it clear within the content of the info product that you offer these services).

People might buy your book and then hire you to perform services for them, or people hear you speak and then buy your book, or they hire you first and later decide to learn more about your skill area, so they buy the book. Or people who know of you through media exposure (including Internet discussion groups, e-zines, and your own and others' web sites, as well as print, radio, and TV) know and respect your advice, so they buy your information products or hire you to speak so they can gain more of it.

Use your book (audio, video, etc.—some kind of tangible information product) and consulting credentials to get speaking gigs, sell your books before and after the talk, and follow up—as soon as you get back to your office—with the consulting prospects who eagerly and even desperately press their business cards into your hand (annotate them before you stick them in a pocket).

If you build your business as a speaker (paid or volunteer), that opens up many barter possibilities, too. Here are a few examples, and the names of the speakers who suggested them:[29]

➤ When speaking at a conference that also includes a trade show, offer an extra session on a different topic for free, in exchange for booth space. (Elizabeth Fried)

➤ Speaking for free to a local chapter of a national organization? Prepare a contract that clearly states the dollar value of the gift, and trade for a complete list of attendees with contact information and a contact and recommendation to the national association. (Padi Selwyn)

➤ If there's a local nonprofit group related to the topic of your talk, get volunteers from that group to staff your sales table, in exchange for giving the group space to display and sell its own wares. (Bob Ingram)

Sometimes, because of the difference in production cost and market value, barter can help leverage an enormous amount of marketing clout. Here's how it worked for another speaker, Tom Antion, www.GreatInternetMarketingTraining.com:

I was asked to speak at the first Wharton Business School Club e-commerce event in Washington, DC. I provided 100 of my Multimedia Internet Marketing Training CDs as "sign up premiums."

They cost me $2.00 each to duplicate, but at a retail cost of $199.00 it made me a $20,000.00 sponsor. My name was plastered on many of their promotions around the world to both the public and Wharton School Graduates.[30]

Martha Retallick, owner of LRP Designs, a Web design and information publishing firm in Tucson, Arizona, points out that you can draw the triangle differently depending on your own set of skills and interests. In her case, she doesn't make paid speeches, but her design services complete the triangle.

■ LESSONS AND ACTIONS

➤ Market through a wide range of traditional and Internet media, including community-based interactive methods.

➤ Develop creative partnerships with retailers where everyone wins.

➤ As a writer, speaker, and/or consultant, you can even get paid to do your own marketing.

Chapter 16

Give the People What They *Want*

■ WHEN SATISFACTION ISN'T ENOUGH

Years ago, Jimmy Cliff had a song called "Give the People What They Want." He was referring to politics, but it works pretty well for marketing, too. Many companies talk a good line when it comes to customer service, but how many really and truly put it into practice? How many have so thoroughly integrated the policy of delighting customers into their mission that it shapes the way they do business?

And what is the cost of not doing so? Writing on the Marketing-Profs.com web site, Kristine Kirby Webster cites auto-industry statistics that 85 to 95 percent of customers claim to be satisfied, but only 40 percent repurchase. She also notes that up to 80 percent of customers who defect to a competitor, across all industries, expressed satisfaction with their previous vendor even right up to the point where they jump ship.[1] So how do you turn satisfaction first into delighted amazement, and then into loyalty, and finally into ambassadorship for your brand?

Timothy Keiningham and Terry Varva, in *The Customer Delight Principle: Exceeding Customers' Expectations for Bottom-Line Success,*[2] stress that merely satisfying your customers isn't enough to build loyalty, let alone the fervent ardor necessary for customers to recruit more customers on your behalf. You have to delight them. And the bar on delight keeps getting higher, because one of the factors leading to delight is that it's unexpected.

In other words, when a new, delightful practice is successful, it is adopted by the organization, and then becomes an industry best practice. Then it goes from being delightful to merely satisfying, because the customer begins to expect it as part of a minimum service standard. Innovation plays a key role.

161

Want an example? Consider Dell, the computer company. Breaking almost every rule in traditional marketing of computers, Dell has specialized for years in custom-building systems to the exact specifications of its purchasers—and doing it quickly. As Keiningham and Varva might say, Dell added delight, and customization of computers became an industry standard. But then Dell failed to initiate another game-changing innovation to once again turn the PC industry upside down, and its reputation started to slide.

Keiningham and Varva's research also points out the following:

➤ The ROI on improving delight is nonlinear. Certain little improvements may make a huge improvement in profitability, whereas others that cost more may have little effect, and the returns may shrink over time.

➤ Profitable delight initiatives often target high-dollar-value, low-cost clients.

➤ If your customer survey is self-serving and focuses on your wants rather than the customer's, you won't get the data you need to improve.

➤ It's relatively easy to figure out which initiatives will offer the greatest return. Just identify factors in the customer's experience that the customer sees as of critical importance, but where the current satisfaction rating is low.

➤ Not everyone is delighted in the same ways, so segment your markets accordingly.

➤ Multiple touches, when handled correctly, can make a customer feel appreciated and welcomed and special.

➤ To delight customers, you need employees who are at least satisfied.

➤ Marketing's primary role is not to shove products down people's throats, but "to understand the wants, needs, and expectations of current and potential customers, feeding this information into the business organization to help it create and distribute products or services that more closely address and answer these inherent needs," and its secondary role is to form and nurture connections with customers.

➤ Customer delight strategies look at a customer's lifetime value and not so much at the current transaction.

➤ Delighted customers not only proselytize to friends and colleagues on your behalf but they also spend substantially more.

Robert Middleton, of the popular marketing e-zine *More Clients,* prefers the term *inspiration.* When you inspire your clients, he says, great things happen:

> Inspiration has very little to do with "Rah, rah, you can do it!" It's not about a veneer of excitement. It's not about a tone of voice or an inspiring vocabulary. It's not even about being sincere; that's superficial, not true inspiration.
>
> Inspiration comes from an unwavering commitment to make a difference. It's not something you do; it's a place you come from.
>
> When you love and appreciate your clients and stand behind their vision and goals, your clients know it. They can feel it. They know you are on their team and committed to them winning.
>
> Commitment + action = inspiration
>
> And where does that commitment come from? You've just met a prospect or started with a client. How can you be committed so soon, let alone be inspiring? Doesn't that take a long time?
>
> Not at all.
>
> The source of commitment is authentic interest. If you can't get truly interested in your prospects and clients, you'll never get committed to their dreams and projects and never become a source of inspiration to them.
>
> I've often asked my clients how much they've learned about a client in their first interview. How much did they research about this client? Did they really dig in and find out about the business or the person? Did they demonstrate a high level of excited curiosity about this prospect or client?[3]

■ COMPANIES THAT GET IT

➤ Catch a Piece of Maine

Not too many beginning lobstermen can build a $600,000 business in their first three months. But Brendan Ready did so with just one of his multiple product lines. He packaged the experience in terms of belonging to a community, making it very experiential, and also emphasized the exclusivity, the support-local, the personal touch, and the sustainability aspects as included value-adds to differentiate his company, Catch a Piece of Maine—and to charge an astonishing 12,000 percent more than most of his colleagues.

Just 25 years old, Ready turned the commodity-based lobster industry into an exclusive private membership in which each investor gets the entire harvest of one trap. He is seeking 400 memberships in the first year, at $2,995 each, and has already sold half the slots in three months. That's $599,000 not counting the additional revenues from $799 four-meal memberships, $249 full-course dinners, $19.95 calendars, T-shirts, and gift certificates. He's formed partnerships with several lobstermen and has a waiting list for more.

Understanding the experiential nature of his business, Ready piles on the extras. For example, with the $799 membership comes:

➤ A DVD of your lobsterman

➤ Cooking instructions and recipes

➤ A map detailing when and where your dinner was caught

➤ A personal note and picture of your lobsterman

➤ Monthly newsletter from the wharf

➤ An actual phone call from the lobsterman the day your lobsters are delivered

And the site itself is full of down-home videos and blog entries featuring Ready and other lobstermen offering weather reports, discussing lobstering and lobster preparation, and more.

Although targeting the luxury consumer, Catch a Piece of Maine fills its web pages with talk about sustainability and social responsibility, and how their customers are participating in enhancing those values. Here's a little snippet:

> We as lobstermen are all stewards of the sea; always making sure today's catch is available for tomorrow's lobsterman. Our industry exemplifies hard work, tradition, heritage, and sustainability. We pride ourselves on our eco-friendly manner of harvesting, producing little to no by-catch and enforcing strict laws to allow the release of all lobsters too small and too large. Lobstering is hard work and capital intensive, requiring boats that cost as much as a house, on top of equipment, traps and fuel. In the past several years the price of bait and fuel has tripled while we've watched our working waterfront slowly disappear.
>
> According to the Island Institute 2007 Access Report, of the 5,300 miles of the Maine coast, only 20 miles remain as working waterfront. As the next generation of Maine lobstermen it is both

our honor and obligation to preserve and share this heritage. We love the ocean and the way of life it offers. We can't imagine working anywhere else and we want to share our passion with our Catch a Piece of Maine partners while offering fresh caught lobsters that they can ship to themselves, clients or family.

Read more about this venture in Troy White's three-part article at www.makepeacetotalpackage.com/troy-white/frank-talk-about-selling-lobsters-by-the-boatload-part-3.html, and at the company's own site, www.catchapieceofmaine.com.

➤ **Mercedes-Benz USA**

One of the cases Keiningham and Varva cite, Mercedes-Benz USA, is especially interesting, because unlike many of their other examples, this wasn't about fixing a broken system. Rather, the focus was on incorporating delight into the corporate culture with a true focus on serving the customer—and creating an entire business unit, in its own building, to do so.

Among other things, Mercedes integrated 11 different databases, collecting different types of customer data, into a single system that anyone could access before interacting with a client. (The company stopped using the word *customer* and stopped referring to its franchisees as *dealers*.) It also developed a strategic separation between client acquisition and retention functions, something Keiningham and Varva strongly advocate.

The database tracked delight factors far beyond just providing emergency road service to such amenities as pretrip routing services similar to AAA, a line of branded merchandise for sale, and multiple touchpoints including anniversary of vehicle purchase and mileage awards at 100,000, 200,000, and 500,000 miles.

In other words, this wasn't cheap. But it was amazingly effective. After initiating the program, Mercedes was projecting an astonishing 86 percent repurchase rate. Even if their projections turn out to be inflated by 100 percent, a 43 percent repurchase rate on a $50,000 to $100,000 item is going to look mighty good for the bottom line.

➤ **RentQuick**

MarketingSherpa.com profiled a company called RentQuick.com.[4] The company offers business equipment rentals, such as laptops and projectors, to professional speakers and other businesspeople on the go. Although it competes with much larger, more established companies in an industry that requires expensive capital purchases, RentQuick—originally based in owner Brett Hayes's home—has been profitable since its very first month and enjoys one of the highest profit ratios in its field.

And that's because Hayes set out from the start to make his company a place that his customers enjoy doing business with. The web site copy is you-focused (on the customer) rather than we-focused (on the retailer). It asks immediately, "How can we help you?" It uses trust-building techniques (guarantee, testimonial, and product photos) right on the home page, and clearly offers multiple ways to contact the company—on every single page. There is a voice mail tree, but it has only a few levels, and then human beings quickly answer the telephone. Instant messaging and e-mail also get immediate attention. And Hayes encourages his support reps to answer the customer's actual question, in the first e-mail. Hayes uses these electronic communication tools to answer the easy questions, but his reps actually encourage customers with more complex questions to switch over to telephone.

Although RentQuick is a price leader, the site doesn't emphasize low prices. Instead, the company focuses on providing an extremely positive experience at every point of interaction, of which competitive pricing is only one small part. "The mantra around here is 'build trust,'" Hayes says. That means a commitment to supply the right equipment to meet the customer's needs, on time, and in full working order, and being around to support the purchase in every way.

Several of his competitors have recently closed; RentQuick continues to grow. A look at its home page[5] shows why. The eye goes first to the top right, with a 24-hour toll-free number and the slogan just underneath, "Exceeding expectations since 1998." Below that is a seven-item navigation bar including testimonials and live chat help. On the left of this attractive page, there's a one-sentence mission statement followed by "Your satisfaction is guaranteed with every rental."

Next down is a hotlink that says, "Watch the introduction video to see how it all works (Flash in a new window)." How many companies bother to warn people if they're hitting a flash presentation? And below that, a customer testimonial. The middle of the page has an eye-catching layout of product category links with pictures and their lowest prices, above a banner link that says "Videos . . . Watch the boys from RentQuick" (and leads to three short humorous videos).

And on the right, a page-dominating graphic of a man carrying a projector, with the caption, "Our customers are smarter." In short, the site is customer-centric, easy to navigate, and has a light touch. Does yours do as well?

➤ **First Bank of Troy**

Can you imagine a single-location bank that has 12 times as many account holders as residents of the town? That was true for the First Bank of Troy, Idaho, according to Denny Hatch's *Target Marketing* magazine.[6] Troy had 514 residents; the bank had over 6,000 customers. Why? Because for decades, each time a resident's child turned six, that child would receive a personal invitation to come down to the bank, meet the president, and take from his hand a crisp $1 bill. Then the two of them would walk over to a teller and start an account. The child felt a personal connection with the bank president, and remained an account holder long after moving away. This kind of genuine customer relationship management will trump any computerized customer relationship management (CRM) system, Hatch says.

➤ **Swedish Hospital, Issaquah, Washington**

Even as normally cold a place as a hospital emergency room can create a welcoming atmosphere and a customer-service home run.

> We had to take my four year-old daughter to the emergency room yesterday. No, there wasn't an accident—but a really bad cough turned for the worse and we needed medical advice, pronto.
>
> We took her to Swedish Hospital's Issaquah ER and got exactly what we were looking for, and more.
>
> Though we'd never been to this ER before, instead of being handed a stack of forms and sent to the waiting room, we were in a private room in front of a doctor in approximately five minutes.
>
> Seriously.
>
> Along the way, we were helped by at least five people who were friendly, attentive and professional.
>
> We learned my daughter has a viral form of pneumonia, were provided with care instructions and then discharged promptly.
>
> As we left, a woman in reception asked her if she'd like a surprise and showed her a large display of Beanie Babies. With a huge smile, she picked a rainbow-colored bear and was given the chance to pick a Beanie for her brother, as well.
>
> "My brother loves red," was her response as she pointed to "Snort" the bull.
>
> We've never left the ER with a smile on our faces, until yesterday. And with that, Swedish won one family's business for life.[7]

➤ Pandora.com

Roy Williams, author of *The Wizard of Ads* books, praises companies that can anticipate your thoughts and feelings, and not just respond but be there waiting when you're ready. He calls this mind-reading "thought particle technology."[8] He cites Pandora.com, a music database that plays songs by your favorite artists and other musicians it thinks you might like. Pandora turns out to be a remarkably good guesser. Shel has bought several CDs from artists he discovered there.

➤ Experience Engineering

Of course, there are consultants to help you. One company, Experience Engineering (EE), has built its business by helping its clients—some large, familiar companies as well as many smaller firms—determine exactly why customers come to them, and help those companies deliver optimal experiences based on those preferences.

EE believes that a company's brand is not just its marketing, or even its product recognition. Rather, a company brand is built on the total perception of the customer: the way that customer feels when he or she walks in, satisfaction with both the service and the product, and how the total experience is remembered (including post-sale follow-up or troubleshooting). EE attempts to anticipate and understand consumers' rational *and* emotional needs, and to set up experience management systems for its clients that enhance the customer experience—which in turn increase the customer's positive perception of the brand. EE's success is in helping its clients see the experience through their customers' eyes. Sometimes its clients find themselves moving in directions they hadn't even considered.

Many companies claim to be driven by their customers and claim to provide exemplary customer service. And some of them—not nearly as many as those businesses that claim they do—actually follow through and provide customer service that's good enough to produce fan mail and flowers from their customers. But this is something much deeper. This is anticipating the customers' wants and needs and meeting them before they're even expressed. Remember Alexander Hiam's example of the photocopier loaner program in Chapter 5? That's the kind of thing we're talking about here. The experience of doing business with you becomes almost an organic part of the customer's own consciousness. You achieve the result through scientific study, but it feels as if it comes straight from the heart. The thing the customer most wants is there, without being put into words.

In fact, a consistent positive experience may be *the* driving factor in repeat business, and in positive word-of-mouth. As franchise businesses or company-owned locations become an ever bigger part of the retail picture, this concern is spreading to every sector. Whether the store sells books, tires, or winter coats, executives want a customer to have a positive and consistent experience in Albuquerque, Abu Dhabi, or Adelaide.

Let's look at specific examples that will make sense of this rather abstract concept:

➤ A grocery chain observed that many of its customers were pregnant, so it set aside reserved parking spaces just for pregnant women—and made CNN news.

➤ A major office-supply chain discovered that its clients cared even more about being steered to the right technology than about price—and changed its advertising, store signage, and other cues to bring that message forward.

➤ A large car-rental company noticed that its customers had a lot of stress about returning cars in time to get through the longer security lines and reach their departure gates. By halving the return time for preferred customers and establishing experiential clues that their managers were committed and efficient (giving them headsets, for example), the company made it clear to its customers that smoothing the car return was a priority. This company was later named Number 1 in brand loyalty across all industries.

Even complaint resolution—which, for too many companies, is all they think of when they think of customer service—can offer a superior experience, and thus create direct revenue through upsells and saved cancellations. A MarketingExperiments.com study demonstrated additional profits of up to $110,448 per customer service rep.[9]

■ SHOPPING AS EXPERIENCE AND ENTERTAINMENT

Building on EE's philosophy, let's look at the experience of shopping for a moment. In recent years, shopping itself has become a tourist experience.

Consider what's happened to coffee. Just 30 years ago, in 99 percent of U.S. restaurants, coffee was coffee. You had a choice of regular or decaf. And it cost 50 cents a cup, but sometimes the pot hadn't been cleaned in days.

When was the last time you bought a cup of coffee like that? Coffee has been transformed into an experience. You choose among 20 or so different beans and roasts and grinds, sip it slowly in an elegant café, and pay $2 to $5 for the privilege. Even some highway rest stop service stations offer half a dozen gourmet blends.

Ever been to the Vermont Country Store, packed to the rafters with all sorts of exotic local foods? They give out hundreds of dollars worth of food samples every day, their parking lot is packed, and their cash registers are ringing. Their prices are substantially higher than other stores, which more than covers the cost of all that free food. Once again, this is an example of a scenario with a lot of winners. The store wins, of course, because it is constantly busy. The suppliers win because they see substantially increased sales after people sample the merchandise. The local economy, which gets a big shot of tourist dollars and a number of jobs, wins big. And the hungry tourists win because they can actually get lunch walking around sampling the food. By creating a tourist experience instead of just a place to shop, this store has found a formula to set itself apart from other food retailers.

If you create a craft or manufactured good, make your shop into a destination by showing the public exactly how your product is made. Shel still remembers, as a child, touring the Hershey chocolate factory. The image of chocolate flowing from a huge cauldron (and the wonderful smell) is indelibly burned in his brain, even though Hershey has since replaced the real factory tour with a movie. But as customers and as marketers, we still love a good plant or craft studio tour. It builds a palpable connection between the user and the product, and the percentage of tour-takers who purchase something afterward is very high. We've toured cheese plants, wineries, an ice-cream factory, glassblowers, a *damasquiña* (gold inlay) workshop in Spain, the outdoor studio of a Guatemalan man who makes giant rock sculptures, textile studios, and much more.

In Deerfield, Massachusetts, Yankee Candle has made its vast retail complex into the second-largest tourist destination in the state. In addition to an enormous collection of candle shops, it also has an exhibit on the history of candle making, a Bavarian Christmas theme room, model trains running above the heads of tourists in many of the shops, eateries at every price range, and more. This store is part of a corporate headquarters complex that stretches on both sides of a town line. (The company's other outlets are simply candle shops; this one gets busloads of tourists.)

Other chains that blend shopping and entertainment include Disney, Warner Brothers, Hard Rock Café, and—aimed at a very different audience—The Museum Store and Ten Thousand Villages. (The latter has a charitable component that adds another benefit to the mix: helping indigenous craft artists from around the world come up out of poverty.)

■ REPUTATION MANAGEMENT IN THE TWENTY-FIRST CENTURY

Once upon a time, a company's reputation had a lot to do with its advertising and traditional PR efforts; that day is long gone. Today, shortsighted, even boneheaded penny-wise, pound-foolish service experiences probably do more to undermine a brand than anything else.

Worse yet, that unhappy customer is likely to complain to friends and colleagues—and perhaps to 10,000 of your best prospects on an Internet discussion list or social media network.

If you care about your company's reputation, not only do you have to keep your company's actions squeaky-clean but you also need to carefully watch the perceptions of others. A nasty blog entry, a yourcompanysucks.com web site (actual examples include http://disney-sucks.com, www.starbucked.com (dissing Starbucks since 1995), www.allstateinsurancesucks.com, and at least five sites set up either to disparage or organize against Wal-Mart), a post to non-company-specific gripe sites like www.pissedconsumer.com, www.ripoffreport.com, and www.webgripesites.com,[10] or even a conversation on Twitter can badly damage companies that are unethical, clueless, or simply not paying attention. Of course, savvy consumers have known about the Better Business Bureau's complaint logs and *Consumer Reports'* ad-free, unbiased product evaluations for decades, but now it takes only a few seconds to find the dirt.

Here are two extreme examples. The first shows what happens when senior executives are dangerously out of touch. And the second demonstrates that every single employee not only needs to understand the importance of making the customer feel special, valued, and appreciated but also must be empowered and trained with the flexibility and understanding to head off customer service disasters at the pass.

Blogger Jason Calacanis wrote a post with the headline, "CIGNA kills Nataline Sarkisyan." The story described a young woman whose insurance company refused and refused to cover a liver transplant, finally relenting the day she died. As Tom Watson notes in his book

Causewired, Calacanis's outrage included a call to contact top CIGNA executives, with their contact information. The cause went viral and was even picked up by Senator John Edwards, who made it a part of his presidential campaign in 2008.[11]

Bill Glazer came into a national chain food store with a $5 gift certificate. It had no expiration date, but the counter clerk and the store manager not only said they wouldn't honor the certificate because they had switched to electronic gift cards, but they also refused to provide a corporate address so Glazer could send his certificate in for a gift card. Now, this kind of stupidity is completely inexcusable under any circumstances, but in this case, the irritated customer happens to publish a newsletter aimed at very sophisticated persuasive marketers, and he told the story (naming the company) to thousands of the most influential marketers in the country.

As Glazer writes,

> *It has been 6 months since the incident and I haven't (and never will) stepped back into one of their stores because of this totally stupid action. Not to mention that I'm telling this story to tens of thousands of GKIC Members through this newsletter. This also doesn't help them build goodwill with their brand.*[12]

That last sentence is putting it mildly. But even if he weren't a successful publisher with a large platform, it would be easy enough to trash the company online. What a public relations disaster! How many thousands of dollars did that $5 blunder cost?

Here are a few among thousands of other examples:

➤ Blogger and Twitter outrage in November 2008 about an ad by Johnson & Johnson's Motrin brand forced the company to quickly withdraw the spot.[13] (Ironically, *Advertising Age* and other pundits say the original campaign was actually a lot more successful because of the media storm.[14])

➤ When Vincent Ferrari tried to cancel his dad's AOL account and was put through over 20 minutes of clueless behavior from the customer service rep, he posted the entire recording of the call on his blog and other sites, including YouTube—where the call got 62,827 hits in the first two days. A Google search for ["Vincent Ferrari" AOL] brought back 9,590 citations on December 15, 2008—something we're pretty sure AOL is not very thrilled about.

➤ CNN aired a story about Wal-Mart's attempt to grab back the insurance payments for an employee who'd been injured so badly on the job she had to go into a nursing home—an employee for whom the company had actually paid medical bills after the accident—inspiring thousands of bloggers to organize boycotts. The company was forced to relinquish its claim on the money.[15]

Companies that understand the proper use of social media, though, build a lot of trust and are much more easily seen as responsible. Here are some examples of doing right:

➤ The shoe company Zappos, known for being extremely people-centered, was widely praised in November 2008 for the way it went about laying off 8 percent of its employees—never a pleasant undertaking and often one that could result in a lot of negative feeling. CEO Tony Hsieh used his corporate blog[16] to lay bare the facts leading to the decision (pressure from a major investor), demonstrate his concern for the laid-off employees and share the details of a generous severance package, and gather support—and then Tweeted a link to his blog. Several Tweets praised his transparency. Even employees had kind things to say. One wrote to Hsieh's attention, "@zappos decisions like this are tough; I know they weren't made lightly, I don't envy any of the folks who had to make the call."[17] (Amazon.com bought Zappos for $850 million in July 2009, apparently because of its legendary customer focus.)[18]

➤ Rubbermaid added customer reviews to its web site, and yes, some products received negative feedback. But the company used that as an opportunity to find out where communication was breaking down. Rubbermaid discovered that people were using the products improperly because instructions weren't clear, immediately rewrote instructions, incorporated them into the product package, posted to the web site along with an explanatory blog post, and wrote individually to those who had posted the reviews.[19]

➤ In December 2008, Tyson Foods donated 100 pounds of food to food pantries for every person who commented on its blog about the initiative—and responded directly to comments. Tyson built support for the campaign via Twitter, and filled two tractor-trailer loads for the Food Bank of Greater Boston within hours. The company also donated to other food pantries in Austin and San Francisco.[20]

Like Tyson, you can take active steps to build a positive reputation in cyberspace—before problems arise—and then, if issues develop, you'll have a much easier time mobilizing support. In an article on MarketingSherpa.com, Andy Beal, co-author of *Radically Transparent:*

Monitoring and Managing Reputations Online, suggests several steps in online reputation management:[21]

> ➤ Be honest in your self-analysis and really look at the areas that need improvement.

> ➤ Control internal communication. Enforce policies that prohibit dissing customers or other stakeholders.

> ➤ Monitor the conversations taking place about your company and your industry. Cast a wide net for this monitoring, using such tools as Google and Yahoo alerts, Digg, Technorati, and YouTube, as well as the blogs and e-zines of key influencers. (To this list, we'd add Twitter and Facebook at the least, and maybe several others.)

> ➤ React strategically after analyzing the situation. Ignore the problem if it's really small and not likely to grow. For bigger issues, correct rumors and issue public apologies and make-goods with "sincerity, transparency and consistency."

> ➤ Control (or at least take a prominent role in) external discourse, for example, by hosting a forum page to publicly discuss the issue.

> ➤ Stay away from clueless responses such as arrogance, condescension, responding without knowing the facts, or making threats.

As far back as 2005, monitoring helped Dow Jones defuse a tricky situation when a blogger got angry, perceiving a new product as a privacy invasion. Alan Scott, chief marketing officer for Dow Jones, picked up the mention and quickly wrote a personal note explaining the product's purpose. The blogger was mollified, and a potential firestorm never materialized.[22]

■ LESSONS AND ACTIONS

> ➤ You must delight your customers. Satisfaction is not nearly enough.

> ➤ Making the ordinary into something special gets you out of commoditization (with all its profitability problems), and turns customers into fans.

> ➤ In the twenty-first century, reputation management is crucial.

Chapter 17

Marketing as Social Change, and Social Change as Marketing

The man that says a task is impossible should get out of the way of the man doing it.

—CHINESE PROVERB

The merely difficult, we do immediately. The impossible takes a while longer.

—AUTHOR UNKNOWN

Remember the discussion of framing in Chapter 9? One definition of *marketing* is an action or message (or series of actions or messages) that causes someone else to take an action of some kind: to buy a product, try a service, accept a new idea. In short, marketing involves persuasion.

The best persuaders, the best negotiators, have always come from a mindset where both parties win.

They tend to be excellent listeners, able to tune in exactly on the other person's issues, whether or not those issues are verbally expressed. And they are able, time and time again, to figure out how the other person can benefit from what they want to happen and not just benefit, but actually meet—or even exceed—his or her goals. Sometimes this is a matter of persuading, sometimes listening, but always responding with ideas that move everyone forward.

And moving forward isn't always a pure business proposition. Often, it's about changing the world. Shel's earliest training in marketing was in doing volunteer public and media outreach for various social change groups. His desire to heal the earth's damaged environment and the rifts that drive people to war is still a dominant factor in his marketing career, his approach to business, and, he believes, his success. Both of us live our lives around the idea that we *can* make a difference in the world we live in. As Shel puts it, "I have both the skills and the obligation to try to make the world better in some way."

Coming out of the corporate world, Jay reached a similar conclusion. He writes in his recent book *The Guerrilla Entrepreneur:*[1]

> *Guerrilla entrepreneurs know that they are citizens of the earth and of their community...noble causes such as improving the environment, helping the homeless, abetting the U.S. economy, teaching people to read, curing dreaded diseases, and bettering life for children are beneficiaries of their business success as well....*
>
> *Whatever form your altruism takes, the important thing is to nurture that sense of philanthropy, and then activate it with your business.... Whoever heard of creating a small business with the idea of bettering life on earth? Well, you have now, and guerrilla entrepreneurs have been aware of this concept—even acted on it—for several decades. In this new millennium, giving back to your community or environment will prove to be less of a choice for the guerrilla entrepreneur, but a criterion for success.*

And both of us believe there is tremendous synergy between marketing and social change. When a social change message becomes mainstream, that's when the ideas take hold and change begins to occur. Social change and environmental groups that ignore marketing will find themselves unable to reach anything more than a marginal splinter of an audience. Their ideas will never become mainstream because there is no one to interpret their message for the mainstream audience. Social change advocates who make no attempt to reach the everyday world are just spitting in the wind. It may feel good, but it won't accomplish much.

Indeed, some of the most out-there social change folks were marketing geniuses, understanding fully and completely how to play on the edges of mass consciousness and instill radical changes: Abbie Hoffman and Jerry Rubin of the Yippies, Dan and Phil Berrigan and their group of radical Catholic pacifists, Martin Luther King Jr., and Saul Alinsky, to name a few prominent examples from the 1960s. In our own generation, the Adbusters collective clearly understands and uses the medium it attacks.

And it's not just a left-wing thing, either. The rise of the New Right in the 1980s was directly related to its understanding of marketing, from Ronald Reagan's successful presidential campaigns, to televangelists such as Jerry Falwell who understood the enormous power the medium provided, to Rush Limbaugh and other conservative talk-show hosts, to Newt Gingrich's brilliantly crafted message: a Contract with America. The marketing mavens on the Left, incidentally, quickly dubbed that last one the Contract *on* America, in the underworld hit-man sense.

Successful community organizing has to be at least in part about marketing. Examine the people who have changed the direction of an entire society, from the shift against the Vietnam War and the acceptance of the Civil Rights movement to the Reagan-era gutting of the traditional antipoverty safety net in the early 1980s. They did it by combining the persuasive power of top-notch marketing with the ability to organize and energize vast numbers of people. And the best organizers, including Barack Obama and his key advisors, understand that the line between marketing and organizing is blurry, and that they need to walk both sides of it. The 2008 U.S. presidential election was about both. Obama was not going to repeat the mistakes of Dukakis, Gore, and Kerry, all of whom let their opponents back them into a corner over and over again. Obama's flights of oratory, firm understanding of the problems confronting the country, ability to inspire a mass audience (including many who had never voted before), and, crucially, his determination to frame the discourse all contributed heavily to the first election since Jimmy Carter's extremely narrow victory in 1976 in which a nonincumbent Democrat received more than 50 percent of the vote.[2] (Clinton, in 1992, got 43 percent in a three-way contest.)[3]

These skills are learned. Even Martin Luther King, Jr. was not a natural-born marketer; his early sermons were less than thrilling. His biographer, Stephen B. Oates, noted the evolution:[4]

> *His sermons tended to be sober and intellectual, like a classroom lecture. But he came to understand the emotional role of the Negro church, to realize how much black folk needed this precious sanctuary to vent their frustrations and let themselves go. And so he let himself go. The first "Amen!" from his congregation would set him to "whooping" with some old-fashioned fireworks, in which he made his intellectual points with dazzling oratory. For what was good preaching if not "a mixture of emotion and intellect"?*

By the time he made his "I Have a Dream" speech, King had become fully aware of the marketing power of what he did, and of the impact he could have on a national and international audience. Of

86 sentences in the speech, 82 use classic marketing techniques of storytelling, analogy, and metaphor—that works out to 95.35 percent. This was the oration named the best speech of the twentieth century,[5] beating out Roosevelt's "Day of Infamy" and Kennedy's "Ask Not What Your Country Can Do for You," among others. This was the oration that catalyzed a nation to do something about ending segregation once and for all—and ensured King's own place in history—and it was a marketing document.

This chapter focuses more on the marketing of ideas than on the marketing of products or services. Think about how visionary thinking can relate to success with marketing tangible items, or services, in your own business.

■ BARBARA WAUGH, CORPORATE REVOLUTIONARY

Barbara Waugh wrote a book called *The Soul in the Computer: The Story of a Corporate Revolutionary.*[6] She recounts a number of amazing stories in her career at Hewlett-Packard, where time after time, she was able to gain consent from her higher-ups to do socially conscious projects that computer companies don't usually get involved with. And interestingly, not only did she continue to get the company involved, but each time, after the dust settled, she had more responsibility and a bigger paycheck. Her initiatives not only accomplished many of their missions but also kept getting her promoted.

Barbara Waugh epitomizes the power of positive persuasion. In her book's Foreword, Alan Webber of *Fast Company* magazine comments about people who will change your life:

> They do it by rearranging your sense of what is possible...
> convincing you that the only limits to your future are those you...
> impose upon yourself...by expressing the absolute conviction
> that you have within you dreams and aspirations that you've
> never acknowledged—and...the absolute confidence that your
> dreams matter absolutely....It wasn't that Barbara is a great
> talker, and that what she said changed my life—quite the oppo-
> site. It was that Barbara is a great listener, and how she listened
> changed my life.

Coming out of volunteer work in the civil rights and women's movements, Waugh was originally hired by HP in 1984 as a recruiting manager for a manufacturing division, charged with hiring 110 new engineers. And she wasn't there very long before she began to work for small increments of change within the company. Her strategy was to do what's right and stand up for it, move slowly enough to maintain support but quickly enough to galvanize people, find co-conspirators who would support her within the struggle, and then find ways to change enemies into allies within the corporate structure. One of her first victories was in confronting an arrogant, belligerent colleague who didn't even realize he was intimidating most of his coworkers; he not only changed his behavior but became an important ally.

Scaling up these steps, she took on ever-bigger projects. Over time, she initiated a corporationwide sustainability drive, started a focus group of women in technology that evolved into a series of national conferences, and eventually helped create a massive program to bring HP's technology to developing countries where it could play a major role in empowering the local populations. The aim is to serve the world's poorest 4 billion people in ways that can help bring them out of poverty and still turn a profit for the company. These are only a few of her projects over the years.

The whole focus in her odyssey is the idea that doing well is a natural consequence of doing good. Make the world better, and you will be more likely to succeed personally and professionally—and the company you work for will benefit as well.

In fact, the world's most successful entrepreneurs consistently talk about some sort of higher purpose. They didn't generally start their businesses just to make a lot of money—but to accomplish a much larger social goal. Perhaps this is why even some of the corporate giants who came out of the Robber Baron period of the late nineteenth and early twentieth century were driven to massive philanthropy. Even steel magnate Andrew Carnegie funded hundreds of small-town libraries, in villages that had never had a library before.

But Waugh was not a company founder or CEO. In fact, while reviewing a draft of this section, she wrote,

> *I wish we could somehow draw attention to the enormous uncelebrated, unidentified entrepreneurial initiative of the grassroots—it isn't only or even mostly CEOs, but you'd never know it from the literature—perhaps due to the business model of consulting—the function that most amplifies what's going on inside companies—that requires the big bucks that only the top can cough up. I've advocated, with limited success, that a percent of consulting dollars spent by the top on the top be made available to the rest of the organization, as an internal consulting budget for the troops.*

Barbara's book demonstrates her amazing power to persuade others—because she goes about it in a systematic way, seeking alliances and stakeholders, and clearly showing at every corner that all the players come out ahead.

She's also willing to examine herself critically, to push herself past her own prejudices. Many times in her career, she finds that someone she expected to be hostile to her ideas was actually a key ally—but first she had to overcome her initial resistance to even starting the conversation.

Like Barbara Waugh, Shel came up out of various social justice movements and had to learn how to work with mainstream people, how to be open rather than cynically skeptical, and how to accomplish change from within the power structure as well as outside of it. And like Waugh, Shel has had a few important victories. Here's an example that he's particularly proud of.

■ CASE STUDY: SAVE THE MOUNTAIN

In November 1999, a developer announced a plan to desecrate ridgetop land abutting a state park by building 40 trophy homes two miles from Shel's house. The original newspaper article interviewed several local conservationists who expressed variations on "Oh, this is terrible, but there's nothing we can do."

But Shel refused to accept that. Within four days, he had drawn up a petition, posted a web page, called a meeting for two weeks later, and sent out press releases and fliers about the formation of Save the Mountain (STM).

Note that all of these actions are marketing actions. He could have called a meeting and not told the public, and then a few friends would have shown up and realized that they couldn't do very much. But by harnessing the power of the press, the Internet, and the photocopier, and crafting a message that would resonate with his neighbors—that not only was this terrible, but that there *was* something they could do—he was able to spark something that truly had an impact.

Shel and his wife, Dina Friedman, expected 20 or so people to come to the first meeting; they had over 70. From that day until December 2000, the group fought the project on every conceivable level: technical issues such as hydrology, rare species, and slope of the road; organizing and marketing components including a petition drive (over 3,000 signed), turnout of up to 450 at various public hearings, lawn signs, tabling, a big press campaign with over 70 articles;

working with the state Department of Environmental Management to investigate options for saving the land; and more.

Literally hundreds of people got involved with some degree of active participation. Many, many people brought widely varying expertise to the movement, far more than any of them could have had on their own.

By using his own skills in marketing and organizing, Shel was able to convert the outrage and despair and shock felt throughout a three-county area when this project was announced into a powerful—and highly visible—public force. As a group, STM had about 35 core activists, all working on many levels, both public and private. The persuasion in this case was not about the desirability of stopping the project; they had near-consensus on that, community-wide. Rather, it focused on the ability of a committed group of people to make a difference even when the experts said it was impossible.

Within two months, STM had established itself firmly in the public eye—and had actually shifted the discourse from "There's nothing you can do" to "Which strategies will be most effective?" Collectively, the group used its powers of persuasion and its skills at reaching the public with this message, to change the project from inevitable to impossible. The land was permanently preserved in just 13 months—four years ahead of Shel's original five-year estimate for victory.

You probably have victories in your own life as well, where you achieved a marketing success that advanced a social or environmental good (using marketing in a broad sense, not just to sell a product). If you're inspired to share them, we'll put your comments on a web page of reader contributions on persuasive marketing. Please e-mail your success stories to Shel at shel@principledprofit.com with the subject: Persuasive Marketing Success Story.

■ LESSONS AND ACTIONS

➤ Effective social change relies on key marketing principles— whether within a community, a corporation, or a country.

➤ Sometimes it's a matter of changing the discourse; the social or environmental change will follow.

Chapter 18

Community-Focused and Charity / Social Change Marketing

The Save the Mountain story in the last chapter is the perfect segue to one of our favorite parts of the marketing toolbox: affinity marketing that benefits both you *and* a worthy cause.

In our other marketing books, we demonstrate that working with a charity allows you to take advantage of free media publicity and many other marketing opportunities that are denied to strictly-for-profit enterprises. Newspapers promote your event, radio stations have you on the air to talk about it, and store owners let you put posters in their windows. Bloggers and Twitterers spread your message in cyberspace; libraries make space for your flier on their bulletin boards. Lots of people show up, you have a great event, and present the charity with a large check.

The reason why this works so well, of course, is that when you give back to the community, the community is eager to work with you as a partner. You gain valuable credibility and PR as a socially minded company, and attract that segment of the market that puts a high value on social responsibility. Combine this approach with superior products and services, and the combination is almost unbeatable.

Think about companies like Ben & Jerry's. Yes, the ice cream is delicious. But the company's willingness to donate 7.5 percent of pretax profits to social causes, its socially conscious purchasing and employment practices, environmentally friendly manufacturing methods, and counterculture marketing strategies have helped consumers justify its premium prices. Ben & Jerry's has over 40 percent of the superpremium ice-cream market;[1] its plant is Vermont's single largest tourist attraction. Only Häagen-Dazs, with an 17-year head start and the marketing muscle of one of the world's largest food corporations behind it, sells slightly more superpremium ice cream.[2]

Socially responsible investing pioneer Terry Mollner, who coauthored the original criteria for social investing and cofounded the first fully screened social investment fund back in 1982, happens to serve on the Ben & Jerry's board. He sees the future not in the triple bottom line, but in "common good corporations," that explicitly and eagerly put social good ahead of purely profit-based approaches.

Mollner insists on a business climate where human beings make decisions to benefit other human beings, and are accountable to them—following patterns found in nature. Today's laws that force businesses to put shareholder interests above all else, and subsume humanity to what he calls "an immoral contract" between business and government, have to be changed for species survival.

He sees this shift as both a "moral imperative" on par with addressing environmental issues, *and* a path to immense financial returns.

> *28 companies moving in this direction had profits eight times higher than the S&P 500 over a ten year period. . . . Sustained and deepening customer loyalty will naturally gravitate toward common good corporations even more than they have toward socially responsible companies. The environment movement has grown, widened, and deepened over the last 38 years because it spoke to an increasingly obvious truth: if we do not take care of our planet we could all die. The common good corporation also speaks to an increasingly obvious truth: if each individual, group, and company does not freely choose to give priority to the common good, monopolistic behaviors and conflict could also result in us all dying.*[3]

Charity tie-ins are also a great way to change slow times into busy times. An in-store benefit event during a normally slow period can create great foot traffic. During the annual Piece of the Pie Day in Shel's area of western Massachusetts, restaurants donated 10 percent of gross revenues for the day to a local food pantry, and all the participating eateries were mobbed. In the most recent year, 148 restaurants participated and raised $46,087; there were about 40 the first year. More recently, the organization switched to donation checkoffs from individual diners (and grocery shoppers), rather than a percentage of the take. One recent promotion raised over $52,000.[4]

The possibilities range from quick, easy events that raise a small amount of money to elaborate affairs requiring months of planning. Just to provide some idea starters, here are a few possibilities:

➤ Invite cookbook authors or famous restaurant chefs to do dinner fundraisers.

➤ Have local musicians impersonate famous acts and raise money for your local arts council, as Bob Cilman does in Northampton, Massachusetts every year.

➤ Auction or raffle off artwork, memorabilia, or other exotic prizes.

➤ Donate a percentage of sales to a deserving charity.

➤ Volunteer for a dunking booth at the fair, with proceeds going to a local agency.

➤ Organize or participate in a bike-athon, walk-athon, skate-athon, or dance-athon.

➤ Sponsor a Little League team.

➤ Take responsibility for cleaning a section of highway or park (which usually earns you a little sign, too).

Remember: People *want* to do the right thing. If you provide a social benefit and your offerings are otherwise comparable with those that don't offer the same benefit, you will find a niche.

Many, many companies have done extremely well for themselves by being socially responsible, and then telling others about it. Ben & Jerry's may be the most well publicized among companies that act out of social responsibility, but there are hundreds, if not thousands, of others. A few examples: Seventh Generation (environmentally friendly products), Stonyfield Yogurt (supports community-based farming), Green America (worker-owned businesses and consumer co-ops), and ShoreBank (funds businesses started by low-income people). The owner of Malden Mills kept everyone on the payroll after a disastrous fire closed the plant for several months. The national publicity he received propelled him into a professional speaking career, in his 70s.

■ LESSONS AND ACTIONS

➤ CSR can be a key driver of corporate identity and branding—and profitability.

➤ Charity components open up many new doors for marketers.

Chapter

19

Taking the Concept beyond Marketing: Abundance and Sustainability in Businesses and in Society

You may find this chapter a bit off-topic—but to us, it's the most important chapter in the book. Bear with us and read it through, even if you think it doesn't pertain to you. In this chapter you will find some of the most powerful business examples in the entire book.

This is where you may find yourself ready and willing to make an enormous difference in the larger society. By the time you've read this chapter, we hope we will have motivated you to do something to bring these ideas out of the marketing realm and into the world at large.

It's probably worth an entire book, and one of us may write that book sometime down the road—or maybe you will.

■ RECAP OF OUR CORE PRINCIPLES

Time for a quick review: let's remind ourselves of some of the most important principles in this book, all in one place.

➤ Green, ethical marketing—based not only on sustainability but also on quality, integrity, and honesty—not only *feels* better, but *works* better.

➤ The more people who have a vested interest in your success, the more likely that success will come. Thus, marketing that benefits your customers, employees, suppliers, distribution/retail channels, and even competitors is a key to that success.

➤ Cooperation is an extremely effective strategy.

➤ In the abundance paradigm, there's plenty to go around. And in the vast majority of cases, that means market share is irrelevant.

➤ When you've set up the right marketing systems, selling becomes less of a concern. By the time a prospect contacts you, that prospect really *wants* to become your customer.

➤ To achieve your goals, you can follow numerous paths; rarely is there only one way to accomplish your agenda.

Now, let's keep those principles in mind as we start to look at the big picture: the whole huge canvas of Planet Earth.

■ WHAT COULD A SUSTAINABLE FUTURE LOOK LIKE?

What kind of world would we live in if the abundance paradigm were integrated into every aspect of society? There'd be enough to go around, yes—enough food, shelter, energy, drinkable water, medical care, and so forth. But what kinds of changes would that create?

Take a few minutes to think about that, and jot down your answers. (You can e-mail them if you like to shel@principledprofit.com, subject line: Sustainable Future Ideas. We'll consider them for posting on a web page dedicated to this topic and perhaps immortalize you in a future book.)

Here is the short version of our vision (writing from our perspective as residents of the United States):

By eliminating scarcity, we eliminate poverty and famine. Everyone has adequate food and water for survival, and access to quality health care. As that frees up time that had been spent on basic survival, people who never had the luxury of education begin to build new skills and knowledge. A massive but noncoercive educational campaign not only raises the literacy rate but decreases overpopulation worldwide. We're talking about sustainability for future generations, too. The drastic reduction in population growth will actually find support among the affected populations. They will realize that nearly all of their children will live, and therefore, they do not have to have so many babies just to make sure there is someone to take care of them in their old age.

By switching the entire society from nonrenewable to renewable, clean, and abundant energy—solar, hydrogen, wind, water, geothermal, and so on—we eliminate oil, coal, and petroleum as reasons to go to war. We also eliminate the stranglehold that certain foreign governments have on developed societies, so they can be dealt with on the merits of their actions, and not out of a need to appease or overpower them in order to maintain access to their oil. Pollution will be drastically decreased, and as a result, the cost of medical care will go down. Reforestation programs will make sure that we have not only adequate timber resources but adequate oxygen supplies for generations to come.

The energy shift includes switching agriculture from chemically dominated factory farming to methods that not only preserve— even enhance—the soil, but produce significantly healthier and more nutritious food. Over time, this will raise yields, eliminate another source of pollution, and again reduce medical costs. These organic farms will produce in abundance, and the challenge will be distribution: getting food to the parts of the world where, so far, there hasn't been enough to go around. And it won't just be farms. City dwellers will grow food (and collect solar energy) on their rooftops and windowsills. Most families will have access to at least a small garden.

Transportation and housing planning will lead many communities toward a village cluster model, where the buildings are relatively close together and the open space surrounding homes and workplaces is available to all. There will be a movement away from commuting long distances; many more people will either work from home or within bicycling distance.

Throughout every aspect of society, systems will be designed along the lines of John Kremer's biological model. Changes in building and transportation design will allow all of us to live more lightly on the earth, while enjoying greater physical comfort.

The communications revolution will continue; the Internet will reach into the remotest villages. This will open up vast powerhouses of learning, sustainable commerce, and global community building. Every home will become its own university campus. And that, in turn, will eventually lead to locally based, grassroots mass citizen action to bring down dictatorships around the world. And this awesome, globally distributed computer power will be able to automate a lot of the drudge work of managing corporations, schools, hospitals, and factories.

With no need to wage war for resources, and most dictators removed from power by their own citizens, the need for such a vast and powerful military apparatus will be sharply reduced. The enormous resources the military currently consumes can be channeled toward such pursuits as environmental regeneration, research to cure diseases, and perhaps even a nonmilitary exploration of space. Terrorist groups will have far fewer reasons to attack us, as these policy changes shift us away from behaviors they see as oppressive (e.g., consuming far more than our share of resources, propping up vicious dictatorships, and sanctioning exploitative labor practices abroad).

The economy will undergo some major shifts. As some of society's largest entities shrink and retract, the abundance mentality will make sure these people are employed. There will be a movement toward a shorter workweek. Instead of 40 hours on the job (and up to 10 more hours commuting), most people might work 20 hours or so, and would be able to maintain or expand their standard of living at that level, because so much less of their paychecks would be spent on consumption of nonrenewable resources. However, excess compensation packages in the tens or hundreds of millions would no longer be tolerated.

This reduced workweek, in turn, could lead to a major flowering of arts, culture, science, recreation, volunteering at service agencies and schools, and lifelong learning.

This world is possible in our own lifetimes, if we can bring the leverage of a motivated and informed population. If you doubt that this kind of sweeping change is possible, look at just a few of the accomplishments of just the last 50 years:

> ➤ Apartheid was ended in South Africa, Rhodesia/Zimbabwe, and the American South.

> ➤ Peace came to some perpetual trouble spots, such as Northern Ireland.

> ➤ Water and air in much of the world are far cleaner than they were, and pollution is now considered a crime instead of the right of whatever industrialist got there first. Huge strides have been made to develop safe, clean, renewable technologies that will free us from dependence on carbon fuels.

> ➤ Most countries now have a medical system that treats health care as a fundamental right, and several deadly diseases have been largely wiped out.

> ➤ Women, people of color, people with disabilities, and cultural or sexual minorities have been integrated into every level of many societies, and the world has benefited greatly from their contributions.

■ MAKING IT HAPPEN

So, how do we get from where we are to the kind of world you came up with, or the kind that we described?

For starters, we need to recognize that a lot of the ideas and technologies in that vision are already here today. We just need to alter their distribution so they're accessible to all. Here's a quick and easy example: millions of computers are replaced every year, and most of them are in fine working order. A computer that's three years old may not be able to run the latest software, but the word-processing, spreadsheet, Internet, and other applications that it *can* run would make a huge difference in the lives of people who have no computer.

So instead of creating a solid waste disposal problem and adding it to the landfill, you could donate that computer to an inner-city minority youth program, or to a college in a developing country. Years later, when it has truly worn out, materials recycling programs can take it apart and use the raw materials to make new computers. But first, computer repair training programs could use it to provide hands-on experience.

Speaking of water.... Bottled water has enormous environmental consequences. *USA Today* columnist David Grossman reports that in the United States alone, manufacturing our 28 million disposable plastic water bottles each year consumes 17 million barrels of oil and three times as much water as they contain, adds enormously to our landfills and our littered streets, and eventually photodegrades into pieces small enough to harm marine life.[1] So one very easy thing you can do is to switch yourself and your office from throwaway water bottles to filtered tap water. (Some popular brands are only filtered tap water to begin with. If it says PWS on the label, that stands for *public water supply*.)

Here are a few more ideas that have essentially no cost or lifestyle consequences but significant environmental benefits—and give you bragging rights and points of differentiation from your competitors in your marketing (as so many early adaptors have done, and benefited from):

➤ Switch to low-power lightbulbs. LED lights are beginning to come on the market and promise to be much more environmentally friendly, and longer-lasting, than even the compact fluorescent bulbs that have largely supplanted the old incandescents.

➤ Use power strips to completely stop the flow of electricity to office equipment and appliances when not being used (such as overnight).

➤ Turn off unneeded lights, especially when your place of business is closed.

➤ Change your water consumption habits when washing dishes or brushing teeth, so the water is only running when it's actually being used, and not freely running down the drain.

➤ For electrical outlets and phone jacks on exterior walls, amazing amounts of heat and air-conditioning energy can be saved if you install foam outlet insulators behind them (about two minutes per outlet and requiring only a screwdriver) and insert baby outlet protectors into unused sockets.

You'll find many more equally easy tips online in Shel's e-book, "Painless Green: 111 Tips to Help the Environment, Lower Your Carbon Footprint, Cut Your Budget, and Improve Your Quality of Life—With No Negative Impact on Your Lifestyle." Go to www.painlessgreen book.com.

In every aspect of our lives, these changes are possible and practical. Let's conclude this chapter by excerpting two articles from the Sustainable Business section of Shel's webzine, *Down to Business*. Both of these notes were speeches by two of today's greatest practical futurists: Amory Lovins and John Todd.[2] As you read, think not only about how such changes could impact your own business but how this harmonizes so well with John Kremer's concept of biological marketing, which we discussed earlier. Once again, the earth can show us how to do amazing things with minimal resources.

■ AMORY LOVINS: REINVENTING HUMAN ENTERPRISE FOR SUSTAINABILITY

Amory Lovins is a sweeping visionary in the tradition of Leonardo da Vinci, Ben Franklin, and Buckminster Fuller—but his focus is on how humans can fit better into this Earth of ours. Though he lives in the Colorado Rockies, where it often goes well below zero Fahrenheit ($-18°C$) on winter nights, his house has no furnace (or air conditioner, for that matter). It stays so warm inside that he actually grows bananas. He uses about $5 per month in electricity for his home needs (not counting his home office). Whether your company is looking for a huge competitive advantage, a more responsible way to do business, or both, the Lovins approach may be the answer.

Lovins built his luxurious 4,000-square-foot home/office in 1983, to demonstrate that even then, when energy technology was much less evolved, a truly energy-efficient house is no more expensive to build than the traditional energy hog—and far cheaper and healthier to run.

The payback for energy efficiency designs in Lovins's sprawling, superinsulated home was just 10 months. The sun provides 95 percent of the lighting and virtually all the heating and cooling, as part of an ecosystem of plants, water storage devices, and even the radiant heat of the workers in his office.

Noting that energy-efficiency improvements since 1975 are already meeting 40 percent of U.S. power needs, Lovins claims a well-designed office building can save 80 to 90 percent of a traditional office building's energy consumption.

Conventional building logic, says Lovins, says you insulate only enough to pay back the savings in heating costs. But Lovins points out that if you insulate so well that you don't need a furnace or air conditioner, the payback is far greater, "because you also save their capital cost—which conventional engineering design calculations, oddly, don't count."

"Big savings can cost less than small savings," Lovins says—*if* designers learn to think about the overall system, and how different pieces can work together to create something far greater than the sum of its parts. The trick is to look for technologies that provide multiple benefits, rather than merely solving one problem. For instance, a single arch in Lovins's home serves 12 different structural, energy, and aesthetic functions.

He consulted on a 1,656-square-foot tract house in Davis, California, where temperatures can reach 113 degrees Fahrenheit, which does not need any heat or air-conditioning. If the methods used in the house were introduced on a mass scale, construction cost would be $1,800 cheaper than a comparable conventional house, and maintenance costs would be cut by $1,600 per year. While it's easier to achieve these dramatic savings in new construction, even on a retrofit, the savings can self-fund these improvements.

Just by switching an industrial project from long, narrow, turning pipes to short, wide, straight ones, Lovins was able to cut energy costs by 92 percent—and slash construction and maintenance costs and operating noise, too.

Lovins has also looked long and hard at transportation. He and his associates have developed amazing car designs, under the service mark Hypercar.

Again, it's a whole-systems approach. By changing everything from the construction materials to power source to the aerodynamics to the possible uses of a parked car, Lovins's team designed an SUV that not only can hold a whole family (or two people and their kayaks), but weighs 52 percent less than a Lexus SUV, can go 55 miles per hour on the energy the Lexus uses just for air-conditioning, achieves the equivalent of 99 miles per gallon (except that it runs on hydrogen fuel cells—330 miles on 7.5 pounds of hydrogen), offers greater safety than a heavy steel SUV (even if it hits one), is undamaged by a 6-mph collision, emits only water, and is so well made that its designers expect to offer a 200,000-mile warranty.

When parked, the Hypercar "could be designed to become a power plant on wheels." Plug it into the electrical grid and watch your meter spin backwards, eliminating any need for nuclear or coal plants.

Lovins says cars like this could be in production within five years, dominate the market within a decade, and essentially wipe out today's steel-bodied, internal combustion–fired, polluting cars within 20 years. (Hypercar, Inc., spun off from Lovins's Rocky Mountain Institute as a separate business in 1999.)

But for Lovins, even this is not the true big picture. "We still have to look systemically at land use, alternative modes, virtual mobility, and transit; we need to drive less or run out of roads and space." Even a super-advanced car can still get stuck in traffic, after all.

Lovins has developed a few key principles over the years:

➤ Design whole systems for multiple benefits, rather than components for single benefits

➤ Redesign production to close all the loops in a system and eliminate both waste and toxicity

➤ Reward service providers and customers who do more and better, with less, for longer

➤ Reinvest the resulting profits in scarce natural and human capital

The sustainability model can have a huge impact not only in developed countries, but in areas of deep poverty, too.

Lovins described an effort by the Zero Emissions Research Initiative to grow houses out of bamboo, in a developing country with an acute housing shortage. The houses cost only about $1,700 each, can be located where they're most needed, and can finance themselves by selling excess bamboo to carbon brokers for energy or other uses. And of course, if the bamboo is cut back (rather than cut down) to build the houses, the plant can regenerate and maintain an ongoing income stream.

Curitiba, Brazil, was a struggling city with deep-rooted problems. But when city planners began to look at its needs as a system, they were able to shape the agenda and pull the city out of crisis. Rather than building superhighways, they increased road capacity along several parallel routes; this was much less costly and far less destructive to the neighborhoods. Then they provided density bonuses so that the arteries best suited to large traffic volumes could support more residents. And then they reinvented mass transit, with a bus system that moves people as efficiently as a subway, but at a fraction of the cost. The fully integrated approach to changing from a dying to a thriving city is told in Lovins's book *Natural Capitalism*—and can be read online at www.natcap.org/images/other/NCchapter14.pdf.

Using nature as a model and mentor, Lovins encourages companies to rethink their waste streams, too. In many cases, the waste of one system can become a nutrient for another process. Closing these loops is both cleaner and more efficient. (See the next section on John Todd for more on creative reuse.)

One of the great things about the Lovins approach is that it relies on the private sector to do well by doing good, as the Quakers say. Companies that adapt to the systemic approach will be highly profitable key players in the new economy. "Early adopters will enjoy a *huge* competitive advantage," Lovins says.

■ JOHN TODD: WASTE STREAMS INTO FISH FOOD

In downtown Burlington and South Burlington, Vermont, you'll find a very unusual industrial park. This is a place where brewery wastes turn into a growing environment for mushrooms—and in the process create an enjoyable biopark, a green and vibrant ecosystem in the middle of the business district, where downtown workers can enjoy a unique, natural setting.

Welcome to the Intervale, 700 acres of sustainable enterprises and eco-friendly public spaces.

This project is one of many lasting gifts to the earth—*and* to the business world—from John Todd. Todd defines ecological design as "the intelligence of nature applied to human needs": a new partnership between the ecological needs of the planet and the physical and commercial needs of human beings that can "reduce negative human impact by 90 percent."

Todd described a project on Cape Cod to save a pond into which 30 million gallons of toxic landfill waste were being dumped every year. His staff remineralized the pond by adding a rock floor and brought the dead bottom water up to get light with floating windmills. They installed restorers: solar and wind-powered biosystems that process the contaminated water through a series of cells, each with different ecologies—integrated networks of microorganisms, higher plants, snails, and fish. Each of these mini-ecosystems removes specific toxins from the water. Designed to work as a system, the restorers—nine cells in this case—digested 25 inches of sediment within two years—and the water is clean enough to drink now. "This pond was constipated; we uncorked it," says Todd.

In Maryland, Todd worked on a project to clean up waste from a large chicken-processing plant. The highly concentrated waste was being dumped into a lagoon, which flowed directly into Chesapeake Bay. "We planted restorers with 28,000 different species of higher plants and animals. It grew very quickly. Each was designed to break down or sequester different compounds. We reduced the electrical power to convert the waste by 80 percent and cut capital costs in half." This kind of system is "very effective in agriculture, because it's cost-effective enough for farm use."

One of the underlying principles in this work is sharing resources among different pieces of the system and changing the paradigm about what's left over. Instead of disposing of a waste stream, Todd encourages people to think about how to use that material as an input. The goal is zero emissions: no waste generation at all. If wastes are considered as inputs, they can lead to new commercial enterprises—for instance, a mushroom farm. All of a sudden, the cost of waste disposal turns into capital for a new revenue stream.

This is how the natural world works, at least when undisturbed by human pollution. When these systems are integrated, they not only eliminate waste but also provide shared synergy, reduce costs, spread technical and legal expertise, and create both economic and environmental improvements—as occurred at the Intervale, where biowastes feed a commercial fish farm that also cleans the water, and the waste heat from a wood-fired power plant is recaptured to heat the complex.

These concepts can also work easily in developing countries. Todd was working on a water treatment sustainability project in a refugee camp, using a long transparent pipe to expand and contract gases. The range of temperatures and conditions is so great that it kills viruses. "I begin to see a model for college and urban food production. We can begin to think of strengthening our own food security in these troubled times. We're creating a new culture based on earth stewardship."

Todd notes, "The biotech industry looks for magic bullets—single solutions to complex problems. Nature is a symphony"; it doesn't work that way.

■ PROFIT BY THINKING LIKE LOVINS AND TODD

It is interesting to us, though not surprising, that both Lovins and Todd focus their social change work through the business community. Their innovations are not in a vacuum, but designed quite consciously to make a profit. They have found a way to integrate profound social change into a traditional capitalist business—as have Barbara Waugh, John Kremer, Bob Burg, and countless others.

Any kind of verifiably Green enterprise—that holds up to thorough scrutiny and isn't just greenwashing—appeals to a much less price-sensitive, more caring market. When you add innovations that remove the old ways of thinking and the old processes entirely, like building a house that doesn't need a furnace, or purifying water by using nothing more than a pipe running through the desert, you combine higher prices and lower costs, and profits soar. The demand for truly sustainable products is high, and those who can answer that demand by harnessing these sorts of sweeping efficiencies toward a greater social and environmental good will profit handsomely if they choose to.

Here are a few among thousands of examples of both profit-seeking and nonprofit ventures:

➤ The Hungarian firm Rehab Ltd. developed the Kenguru, a tiny electric car, about the size of a Smart or a Mini-Cooper, that can transport a person in his or her wheelchair. Instead of needing a huge van with complex and energy-drinking lift systems, a hatchback and simple ramp allows the driver to roll into place through the back of the car.[3]

➤ The amazing book *Influencers* (see www.guerrillamarketing goesgreen.com/resources) describes how a dreadful parasitic worm was pretty much eliminated just by changing the way water was gathered and stored in a remote African village.

➤ Mr. Ellie Pooh is an innovative venture that produces a toxin-free fine-art/gift paper line made of—are you sitting down?—75 percent elephant poop and 25 percent postconsumer recycled paper! The project accomplishes a number of interlinked objectives: lowering carbon output by reducing the need to produce virgin paper, preserving elephant habitat, and reducing the problem of elephant conflict with agriculture (which has caused the destruction of thousands of elephants).[4]

➤ Interface Carpets is a global company widely recognized as a leader in bringing innovative, Green, sustainable approaches to the floor-covering industry—as well as one of the largest commercial carpet manufacturers in the world. Founder Ray Anderson's vision for the future is to "become the first sustainable corporation in the world, and, following that, the first restorative company . . . to spend the rest of our days harvesting yesteryear's carpets, recycling old petrochemicals into new materials, and converting sunlight into energy. There will be zero crap going into landfills and zero emissions into the biosphere. Literally, our company will grow by cleaning up the world, not by polluting or degrading it."[5]

And this model of sweeping social change within the business context has the power to change the world. If their stories can inspire you to create a business whose ultimate purpose is a significant betterment of the world, then we've done a very good job with this book. I hope that many of you will write to us and tell us how you've put the ideas in this book—not just the last couple of chapters—into practice. Perhaps we'll be able to gather so many success stories that we can write a sequel all together, sharing your successes with the world.

■ A SOCIAL MOVEMENT AROUND BUSINESS ETHICS

Shel would love to be one of those success stories with the Business Ethics Pledge, a campaign to convince 25,000 business leaders to run their businesses according to the ethical principles we've been discussing:

> *I pledge allegiance, in my heart and soul, to the concepts of honesty, integrity, and quality in business. I recognize that the cornerstone of success is treating all stakeholders fairly, with compassion, and with a commitment to service. Working from abundance, I recognize that even my competitors can become important allies. I will not tolerate crooked practices in my business, from co-workers, direct or indirect reports, supervisors, managers, suppliers, or anyone else—and if I encounter such practices, I will refuse to go along with them and report them to appropriate authorities within and outside the company. I pledge to support the "triple bottom line" of environmental, social, and financial responsibility. And I pledge to participate in a serious effort to focus the business community on these principles, by sharing this message with at least 100 other business leaders.*

Signing a pledge like that can not only help shift the world toward values that make sense but can provide powerful marketing advantages to those who sign—as noted on the campaign web site www.business-ethics-pledge.org:

Signing the Pledge Creates Trust. *Every consumer has been ripped off at some point—and we all want to do business with companies we can trust. Your signature on the Pledge shows that you can be trusted. Displaying the Pledge logo helps convince prospects to give you a try, and first-time customers to return (and tell their friends).*

You Get the Benefit of the Doubt. *If there's a problem, your customer is more likely to offer a chance to make it right (a huge favor to you)—and less likely to go out and grumble to the world about the shoddy experience.*

Taking the Pledge is a Commitment. *You're showing your prospects that your company would rather do the right thing (and build customer relationships that last years) than burn people for a quick one-time buck. When you "walk your talk," you'll create fans who will enthusiastically recommend you to others. But if the Pledge raises false expectations and hopes, and the reality is the same old sleazy stuff, it'll backfire.*

You're in the Forefront of a Movement to Make a Better Society. *Why are you in business? Most entrepreneurs answer, "to make a difference." By joining the Pledge campaign,*

➤ *You put your actions in alignment with your beliefs.*

➤ *You participate in change throughout the world.*

➤ *When you hear someone attacking business owners as sleazy and selfish, you can say you're part of a movement to make the entire business culture socially responsible.*

➤ *The link most signers are entitled to from the Pledge website boosts your own ratings in search engine listings (especially Google).*

➤ *If you volunteer for media interviews about the Pledge, you can reach new audiences through the press.*

➤ *When you bring up the Pledge movement when reporters interview you about other matters, you could parlay small stories into larger or more frequent ones—because running an ethical business is newsworthy!*

As of this writing, the campaign is not close to its goal—but even in the early stages, Shel notes that his championing this cause has opened up many doors in his own business. The Law of Attraction, he says, has worked to align this commitment with a healthier, more stable business.

> Since launching the Pledge movement, I've noticed a dramatic shift. This work has directly attracted several large clients who stay with me over a period of time. I no longer have to be in constant marketing mode to attract the next little press release or book cover writing project, because now, I have a steady flow of clients with much larger projects that continue over several months, or even years. My business is much more secure. I still do the smaller projects, but I'm no longer dependent on them—the emphasis on ethics continues to attract the best clients for me.

Having that trust, that reservoir, that benefit of the doubt, has real-world consequences. Kellie McElhaney points out that both Whole Foods and Hewlett-Packard were caught in some pretty nasty scandals, but no long-term damage was done—because both companies had enormous reserves of trust built over the years, and the public gave them a chance to make things right—a chance that was not extended to companies without that stellar reputation, such as Nike.[6]

Why is something like the Business Ethics Pledge even necessary? Because, unfortunately, ethics is not yet ingrained in our culture—yet. Christopher Bauer, the ethicist, laments this:

> *Ethics training is seen as just one more routine organizational obligation rather than representing ethics as integral to the culture of the organization . . . the lack of seeing ethics and values as a part of the core definition of the organization or their individual jobs.*[7]

■ LESSONS AND ACTIONS

➤ Imagine the world we want to create, and take steps to get there.

➤ Learn from Amory Lovins and John Todd to incorporate the Greenest *and* most profitable solutions by thinking holistically.

➤ Build ethics into the core, and join a movement.

Chapter 20

Abundance and Wealth Creation

Although you don't *need* a lot of money in order to embrace abundance, it is nice to have and does make a whole lot of things easier—including the kind of social and environmental change we've been discussing in the last few chapters. As an example, the Save the Mountain success story would have taken years longer to achieve were it not for the philanthropist who funded the state's purchase of the contested land.

Keep in mind, though, that money is not an end but a means. By itself, it's nothing more than a stack of useless paper and coin, or a series of numbers in a computer database. Money gains its power and importance from the things we can buy with it, and money is one among many ways to acquire stuff and help your favorite causes. In other words, money is one more tool, a lever, to convert brain power and work into bettering conditions for yourself, your loved ones, and the world. You can think of it as a form of energy, just like sun, wind, or even your time.

The Internet millionaire Perry Marshall calls business a form of alchemy:

> *Converting worthless things into items necessary and valuable. Moving resources from areas of low return to high return. Harnessing the forces of nature to produce food and wealth for everyone. Politics may be about the endless arguments about how the pie should be sliced—but entrepreneurship is about baking more pies.*
>
> *Take two of the most successful companies of the last decade—Intel and Microsoft. Intel takes desert sand—worth less even than lead—and turns it into Pentium chips—which are worth more than gold.*[1]

■ POWERFUL PRODUCT CREATION

By now, you understand that marketing is a series of conversations: multiple strands of dialogue among you, your customers, clients, prospects, influencers, and followers. So incorporate that attitude into every new product you develop. Find out what your market is looking for, and only then go out and fill the need.

This is an important lesson whether your product launch is enormous or tiny. Coca-Cola and Ford forgot this lesson when they introduced New Coke and the Edsel: utter failures that consumed millions of dollars. New Coke was actually focus-grouped, and the company did a lot of research prior to launch—but didn't know how to correctly evaluate the information it was receiving, just like the old-line companies Timothy Keiningham and Terry Varva write about in *The Customer Delight Principle*. They didn't understand that they were asking the wrong questions about satisfaction instead of delight.

Ford learned from its expensive mistake. The original Taurus, one of the company's top sellers in history, was carefully crafted to reflect feedback from potential users, covering every conceivable detail and yet somehow avoiding the committee-think mentality that can kill a product.

On a much smaller scale, Spanish language and culture entrepreneur Myelita Melton of SpeakEasySpanish.com writes,

> *The manner of teaching was still entrenched in grammar and nonsensical vocabulary no one would ever use. I became discouraged that nothing seemed to have changed about foreign language education in the ten years I had been out of the classroom... except the student.*
>
> *That's when my training in curriculum design kicked in, and I began interviewing people in the classes. Each told me about their jobs, their goals, and more importantly, they told me exactly what they wanted to learn. I went to work. At the end of the first semester, everyone took home several handouts with words and phrases they could actually use on the job. The philosophy I developed then remains with the company today. Communication is more important than conjugation, and what you learn must be relevant to what you do. If you don't use it, you'll lose it!*
>
> *One evening Jenna, an ER nurse in a large metro area hospital, asked me to make a proposal to her facility so I could "go there to offer Spanish programs where they worked." I thought her idea was the best thing since salsa, and it filled me with excitement*

bordering on insanity! Offering customized Spanish courses at business locations where it would be convenient for small groups of employees made perfect sense to me.

Quickly calls started coming in from across the region, and professionals in every job you can imagine began submitting vocabulary they wanted to learn. So, Jenna . . . this was your idea, and I'm giving a special muchas gracias for your spark of genius again this year![2]

Another example: Shel's seventh book, *Grassroots Marketing for Authors and Publishers*, was written in the first place because for 10 years, people had been asking him when he would do a marketing book just about books. When he finally decided that he had enough meaningful advice to grant their requests, he did a two-question survey to a group of independent publishers: what would you most like to see covered in a book about book marketing, and what's your greatest book marketing success story? The final book includes two chapters that Shel never intended to write, but the survey results showed these were areas of keen interest to his market. And it also includes some 40 success stories from other authors and publishers, all of whom feel some sense of ownership in the book and who became voices in the choir of its support.

You'll find our contact information in Chapter 21. Don't hesitate to get in touch.

May you be inspired, ethical, and successful, may you find deep satisfaction in the work you do, and may you never lack for abundance in your life.

■ LESSONS AND ACTIONS

➤ Learn the true meaning of money.

➤ The purpose of business is to create value.

➤ Remember: Effective marketing consists of multiple integrated streams of conversation.

Chapter 21

Resources

■ WEB LINKS

The world of information about marketing, ethics, and sustainability is so abundant, and is growing so rapidly, that it makes sense to keep the information on the Web for easy updating. Please see the latest copy at www.guerrillamarketinggoesgreen.com/resources, where you'll find at least

- ➤ 40 recommended books
- ➤ 26 worthwhile web sites and e-zines
- ➤ 20 clued-in copywriters who can help you create sizzling marketing materials .
- ➤ 10 additional publicity resources
- ➤ The endnotes to the book with all URLs clickable ˙

If you feel this book is a superior offering, and you'd like information on marketing our other products to your own audience through a commission arrangement, please visit

- ➤ www.gmarketing.com for the full line of Guerrilla Marketing materials
- ➤ http://snipurl.com/heqrz **or**
- ➤ www.frugalmarketing.com/affiliate/index.php?req=new account&pid=1 for Shel Horowitz's books, coaching programs, and information products

The official web site for this book is www.guerrillamarketing goesgreen.com. At that site, you will find the complete resources section for this book, updated as we become aware of new materials.

You'll also be able to read additional endorsements that were not received by the time we went to press—or add your own endorsement, if you see fit.

Also, as a purchaser of *Guerrilla Marketing Goes Green,* you're entitled to a complementary 60-day subscription to The Clean and Green Club: Shel's monthly membership program to keep you on the cutting edge of Green and ethical business innovation. You'll get audios, articles, resources, and other goodies. Register at www.guerrillamarketing goesgreen.com/cleanandgreen with the code GMGGBUYER.

■ MORE HELP FROM JAY AND SHEL

Jay Conrad Levinson

Jayview@aol.com

Jay@gmarketing.com

415-453-2162

www.gmarketing.com

www.guerrillamarketingassociation.com

> ➤ To book Jay for a presentation, contact Amy Levinson, 360-791-7479, olympiagal@aol.com.

Shel Horowitz

Accurate Writing & More

shel@principledprofit.com

www.frugalmarketing.com

413-586-2388

Twitter: @shelhorowitz

Country/Time Zone: US/Eastern

> ➤ Strategic marketing planning, with emphasis on ethical, frugal, and effective methods

> ➤ Copywriting: individualized marketing plans, book jacket and cover copy, news releases/press releases, media pitch letters, blogs, newsletters, web pages, direct-mail, print/radio/ online ads (display or classified), brochures, etc., for authors, publishers, small businesses, nonprofits, and community organizations

> ➤ Social media/Web 2.0 marketing: Twitter, Facebook, blogs, and more

➤ Coaching, speeches/presentations, and training on ethics as a success driver, frugal/ethical/Green marketing, and book publishing

➤ Book shepherding: turning you from unpublished writer to published author

➤ Consulting, speaking, and training on how to implement certain Green and ethical business practices

➤ Naming: products, companies, domains, campaigns, and more

The Business Ethics Pledge is located at www.business-ethics-pledge.org.

The Clean and Green Club, monthly resources relating to clean and green business, www.thecleanandgreenclub.com (see page 206 for your 60-day free trial).

Notes

■ CHAPTER 1 BECAUSE PEOPLE MATTER

1. http://www.forbes.com/2002/07/25/accountingtracker.html. (All URLs in this book were live as of when we did our research. Although we cannot guarantee their continued availability, since they're not on our own sites, you can easily find similar data using Google.com or other search engines.)

2. Stephen Apatow of the UK-based Humanitarian Resource Institute, in his "The Golden Rule Principle: Global Religious Leaders Called to Re-Focus on This Universal Objective of the Interfaith Community," cites 13 examples from primary religious texts, from Buddhism to Zoroastrianism. http://www.humanitarian.net/interfaith/goldenrule.html

■ CHAPTER 2 BASIC CONCEPTS

1. Business for Social Responsibility's "Marketplace" White Paper, http://www.bsr.org/BSRResources/WhitePaperDetail.cfm?DocumentID=269. Downloaded Jan. 16, 2003. This source has been taken down, but another study, conducted in 2003, showed that the $230-billion Lifestyles of Health and Sustainability (LOHAS) demographic accounted for nearly 1/3 of all American households even then, and 51% of these 68 million Americans make values-based buying decisions: http://www.npicenter.com/anm/templates/newsATemp.aspx?articleid=4469&zoneid=3, verified July 6, 2009.

2. Natasha Abbas, "Shareholder Action: Victories and Next Steps," *Real Green,* Winter, 2009, 12.

3. "CIS Opposes Election of Exxon Mobil Chief for 'Head in the Sand' Approach to Climate Change," http://www.prnewswire.co.uk/cgi/news/release?id=146589, May 23, 2005.

4. Bill Baue, "Investor Advocacy Networks: Pivot Points for Leveraging Corporate Change," CSRWire News Alert, August 19, 2008, http://www.csrwire.com/News/12897.html855.

5. Business for Social Responsibility's "Marketplace" White Paper, http://www.bsr.org/BSRResources/WhitePaperDetail.cfm? DocumentID=269. Downloaded Jan. 16, 2003. (Referencing a 1997 study by Walker Research.)

6. Jacquelyn Ottman, Green Marketing: Opportunity for Innovation (2d ed.). (New York: J. Ottman Consulting, 1997), 20, citing Keith Baugh, Brian Byrnes, Clive Jones, and Maribeth Rahimzadeh, "Green Pricing: Removing the Guesswork," Public Utilities Fortnightly, August 1995, 27.

7. "Despite Economic Crisis, Consumers Value Brands' Commitment to Social Purpose, Global Study Finds: Strong Personal Beliefs in Making a Difference Signal Opportunity for Marketers," http://www.edelman.com/news/storycrafter/EdelmanNews.aspx?hid=231, November 17, 2008, cited in Tina Stevens, "A Real Swing Shift: Changing Values Require a Change in Marketing Strategies," BusinessWest, February 16, 2009, http://www.businesswest.com/details.asp?id=1914.

8. Christopher Flavelle, "Responsibility Is Still Good for Business," Washington Post, February 15, 2009, http://www.washingtonpost.com/wp-dyn/content/article/2009/02/14/AR2009021400094.html.

9. Searches conducted December 31, 2008.

10. http://www.businessweek.com/smallbiz/content/sep2008/sb2008098_742970.htm.

11. Business for Social Responsibility's "Marketplace" White Paper, http://www.bsr.org/BSRResources/WhitePaperDetail.cfm? DocumentID=269. Downloaded Jan. 16, 2003.

12. "The Gay and Lesbian Market Today," Howard Buford, president, Prime Access, Inc., 2001, http://www.multiculturalmarketingresources.com/experts/art_gaylesbian.html.

13. Neeta Basin, "Meet the South Asians," Diversity Business, November 2008, http://www.diversitybusiness.com/news/supplierdiversity/45200763.asp.

14. Business for Social Responsibility's "Marketplace" White Paper, http://www.bsr.org/BSRResources/WhitePaperDetail.cfm? DocumentID=269. Downloaded Jan. 16, 2003.

15. See, among many examples, "Outlook 2008: Marketers Face Challenges from Economy to Ecology," *BtoB Magazine,* December 10, 2007, and "Wal-Mart Announces New Ethical and Environmental Principles," by Stephanie Rosenbloom, *International Herald-Tribune,* October 22, 2008, http://www.iht.com/articles/2008/ 10/22/business/walmart.php, cited by Chris MacDonald in The Business Ethics Blog, http://www.businessethics.ca/blog/2008/ 10/wal-mart-flexes-its-muscles.html.

16. Ron Robins, "Reminder: Responsible Investing Forum, January 12–13, New York City," e-mail blast from investingforthesoul.com, December 31, 2008.

17. Kellie A. McElhaney, *Just Good Business: The Strategic Guide to Aligning Corporate Responsibility and Brand* (San Francisco: Berrett-Koehler, 2008), ix.

18. Business for Social Responsibility's "Marketplace" White Paper, http://www.bsr.org/BSRResources/WhitePaperDetail.cfm? DocumentID=269. Downloaded Jan. 16, 2003.

19. "Maala Index Indicates a Revolution in Israel's Corporate Philosophy," by J. J. Levine, *Jerusalem Post,* November 19, 2008, http:// www.jpost.com/servlet/Satellite?cid=1226404772569&pagename =JPost%2FJPArticle%2FShowFull.

20. "The financial facts, figures, and bottom line of socially responsible investing," http://www.sristocks.com/Learning/Socially-responsible-investing-facts.html.

21. http://en.wikipedia.org/wiki/Microlending, viewed May 23, 2009.

22. Home page banner at http://www.muhammadyunus.org/, seen May 23, 2009. Text: "We will create a poverty museum by 2030. We will start with Bangladesh."

23. "The financial facts, figures, and bottom line of socially responsible investing," http://www.sristocks.com/Learning/Socially-responsible-investing-facts.html.

24. "New Study Finds Link between Financial Success and Focus on Corporate Values," http://www.csrwire.com/News/3511.html.

25. A. T. Kearney, Inc., "Green Winners: The Performance of Sustainability-Focused Companies in the Financial Crisis,"

February 9, 2009, http://www.atkearney.com/images/global/pdf/Green_winners.pdf.

26. Among the numerous studies and news articles: Darren D. Lee and Robert W. Faff, "Corporate Sustainability Performance and Idiosyncratic Risk: A Global Perspective," and Greg Filbeck, Raymond Gorman, and Xin Zhao, "The 'Best Corporate Citizens': Are They Good for Their Shareholders?," both of which were published in *The Financial Review*, Vol. 44, No. 2, May 2009, and downloaded March 31, 2009, from http://www.thefinancialreview.org/abstracts/Financial-Review-Abstracts-May-2009.html. MSNBC compared Domini's performance against the S&P in "Cause investing: Do-it-yourself giving Shareholder communities reward companies that champion social change," http://www.msnbc.msn.com/id/24863380/, May 28, 2008.

27. Ben Cohen and Mal Warwick, *Values-Driven Business: How to Change the World, Make Money, and Have Fun* (Social Venture Network series). (San Francisco: Berrett-Koehler, 2006), 36–37.

28. Ibid., 34.

29. Ibid., 41, 111.

30. Laury Hammel and Gun Dehnhart, *Growing Local Value: How to Build Business Partnerships that Strengthen Your Community* (Social Venture Network series). (San Francisco: Berrett-Koehler, 2007), 64–67.

31. http://www.ibtimes.com/prnews/20081120/oxbridge-students-choose-work-life-balance-and-ethics-over-a-graduate-career-path.htm.

32. Katherine Mangan, "Business Students Say Their Idealism Is Blunted by Corporate Recruiters," *Chronicle of Higher Education,* April 21, 2008, http://chronicle.com/daily/2008/04/2570n.htm.

33. Thomas Kostigan, "MBA students see green as the way to go," http://www.marketwatch.com/news/story/mba-students-see-green-way/story.aspx?guid={50A42E30-51E3-4C7C-BB32-CBF3BF A38060}&dist=msr_1.

34. "Should Managers Have a Green Hippocratic Oath?" Harvard Business Review's HBR Green e-zine, April 4, 2008. Full HBR article is available for purchase at http://hbr.harvardbusiness.org/2008/10/its-time-to-make-management-a-true-profession/ar/1.

■ CHAPTER 3   ADVANTAGES OF DOING
THE RIGHT THING

1. Frank C. Bucaro, "Beyond the Bottom Line! What REALLY Matters Most?" The Ethics Update monthly e-newsletter, May 21, 2008. Bucaro's web site is http://www.frankbucaro.com.

2. http://www.totalmerrill.com/TotalMerrill/pages/ArticleViewer.aspx?TITLE=higherdividendsandlowervolatilityinvaluebased investing-smartsolutions&referrer=rss.

3. "How Green Is the Deal? The Growing Role of Sustainability in M&A," November 3, 2008, downloaded from http://www.greenbiz.com/resources/resource/green-deal.

4. "The Low Trust Epidemic: Why It Matters and What Communicators Can Do About It," December 2008 White Paper issued by Bon Mot Communications, LLC, http://wwww.bonmotcomms.com (available for download on both the Home and Resources pages as of February 23, 2009).

5. Ibid.

6. Angelique Rewers, "Drop in Trust Leads to Call for Greater Government Regulation of Business," The Corporate Communicator e-newsletter, February 23, 2009, published by bonmotcomms.com; Edelman Trust Barometer 2008, January 2008, http://www.edelman.com/TRUST/2008/TrustBarometer08_FINAL.pdf.

7. "New Data: How to Maximize Impact of Email Newsletter Ads—4 Takeaways on Ad Recall, Forwards & More," MarketingSherpa.com, March 19, 2008, http://www.marketingsherpa.com/article.php?ident=30391.

8. "The Low Trust Epidemic: Why It Matters and What Communicators Can Do About It," December 2008 White Paper issued by Bon Mot Communications, LLC, http://wwww.bonmotcomms.com (available for download on both the Home and Resources pages as of February 23, 2009).

9. Dave Pollard, Finding the Sweet Spot: The Natural Entrepreneur's Guide to Responsible, Sustainable, Joyful Work (White River Junction, VT: Chelsea Green, 2008), 174–175.

10. "How to Practice Defensive Branding: 6 Key Factors to Build Credibility, Swat Bad Buzz." http://www.marketingsherpa.com/article.php?ident=30850.

11. http://www.hyundaiusa.com/financing/HyundaiAssurance/HyundaiAssurance.aspx, as of January 21, 2009.

12. http://responsiblemarketing.com/blog/?p=876.

13. "GM, Ford offer Hyundai-style job-loss protection," http://www.autonews.com/article/20090331/ANA08/903319986/1018.

14. Read a detailed description of the case, the company's response, and its rapid recovery at http://www.aerobiologicalengineering.com/wxk116/TylenolMurders/crisis.html.

15. The full credo can be found at http://www.jnj.com/our_company/our_credo/index.htm.

16. Ford officials discussed the problem even as far back as May 1, 1987, while the Explorer was still in the design phase. The story reached the U.S. press in a report by CBS affiliate KHOU of Houston—long after Ford had already recalled tires in Malaysia, Saudi Arabia, and elsewhere. Public Citizen, a watchdog group founded by Ralph Nader, prepared a detailed chronology at http://www.fordexplorerrollover.com/history/Default.cfm (downloaded January 16, 2003).

17. "Maala Index Indicates a Revolution in Israel's Corporate Philosophy," by JJ Levine, *Jerusalem Post,* November 19, 2008, http://www.jpost.com/servlet/Satellite?cid=1226404772569&pagename=JPost%2FJPArticle%2FShowFull.

18. Kellie A. McElhaney, *Just Good Business: The Strategic Guide to Aligning Corporate Responsibility and Brand* (San Francisco: Berrett-Koehler, 2008), 20.

19. Ibid., 53–55.

20. Christopher Bauer, "Taking Responsibility for Taking Responsibility—Part 2," Weekly Ethics Thought e-mail newsletter, September 1, 2008.

21. http://www.upstatetoday.com/news/2008/nov/21/ethics-plays-major-role-business-collapse/.

22. Ibid.

23. Hazel Henderson, "Changing Games in the Global Casino," e-mail newsletter from www.ethicalmarkets.com, June 25, 2008.

24. http://www.azcentral.com/arizonarepublic/business/articles/2008/11/11/20081111biz-aigresort1111.html, http://www.cnn.com/2008/POLITICS/10/08/politicians.meltdown.aig.ap/.

25. http://www.cnn.com/2008/US/11/19/autos.ceo.jets/.

26. http://www.washingtonpost.com/wp-dyn/content/article/2008/11/14/AR2008111403789_pf.html.

27. http://ethisphere.com/bela/.

28. Chris MacDonald, "'Business Ethics Leadership Alliance: What's in a Promise?," December 12, 2008, http://www.businessethics .ca/blog/2008/12/business-ethics-leadership-alliance.html.

■ CHAPTER 4   MARKETING VERSUS ADVERSARIAL SALES

1. Mollie Neal, "Thank You, Come Again!" http://www.giftshopmag .com/2006/fall/gift_retail_management/develop_a_loyalty _program_and_get_repeat_customers.

2. "Yes, Make the Case for a Loyalty Scheme—But Do It for the Data!" *The Wise Marketer* e-zine, May 26, 2005.

3. "CRM: Pay Attention to Retention," Adrian Mello, ZDNet, Aug. 22, 2002. http://www.zdnetindia.com/biztech/ebusiness/crm/ stories/64691.html.

4. Shel Horowitz, *Grassroots Marketing: Getting Noticed in a Noisy World* (White River Junction, VT: Chelsea Green, 2000).

5. "Overview of Customer Acquisition Costs," Howard Seibel, managing director of Wharton Strategic Services, Target Marketing of Santa Barbara's E-Metrics, July 5, 2002, http://www. targetingemetrics.com/articles/acquisition.shtml.

6. "What's Wrong with the Net?" Harry Tennant, Harry Tennant and Associates, March 25, 2001, http://www.htennant.com/ hta1/askus/wrong.cfm.

7. "Dealership Group Tests the CRM Waters...Cautiously," Cliff Banks, *Ward's Dealer Business,* Aug. 1, 2002, http://wdb.wardsauto .com/ar/auto_dealership_group_tests/.

8. *Un-Marketing* e-zine, January 16, 2004.

9. *I-Sales Digest*, Sept. 27, 2002, quoted with the writer's permission.

10. Joe Mandese, "Tech Chief to AAAA Media Crowd: Stop Being Nudnicks," *Media Post News,* March 7, 2005, http://www. mediapost.com/publications/?fa=Articles.showArticle&art_aid= 27910.

11. Stuart Elliott, "A survey of consumer attitudes reveals the depth of the challenge that the agencies face," http://www. nytimes.com/2004/04/14/business/media-business-advertising- survey-consumer-attitudes-reveals-depth-challenge.html.

12. http://mashable.com/2009/03/09/social-networking-more- popular-than-email/.

■ CHAPTER 5   SALES THE RIGHT WAY

1. Jacques Werth and Nicholas E. Ruben, *High Probability Selling: Re-Invents the Selling Process* (3rd. ed.). (Fort Washington, PA: Abba Publishing Company, 2000).

2. Shel Horowitz, "A Sales Trainer Who Guarantees 'Bulletproof' Results," *Related Matters*, UMass Amherst Family Business Center, Fall 2001, p. 3. The complete article is available at http://www.umass.edu/fambiz/articles/selling_your_business/sales_trainer.html.

3. Shel Horowitz, "Creating a Sales Revolution," *Related Matters*, UMass Amherst Family Business Center, Spring 1999, p. 7, http://www.umass.edu/fambiz/articles/just_business/creating_sales.html.

4. Shel Horowitz, *Related Matters*, UMass Amherst Family Business Center, Fall 1998, p. 7, http://www.umass.edu/fambiz/articles/just_business/marketing_business.html.

5. Craig Garber, "Critical Lesson on Much-Needed Positioning: Don't Bid, Instead.... Audit," http://blog.kingofcopy.com/2008/11/critical-lesson-on-much-needed.html.

6. This story is widely quoted; see, for instance, the *Chicago Tribune* of September 1, 2002, http://www.chicagotribune.com/news/chi-0209010315sep01,0,538751.story. We first found it in a book called *Reclaiming the Ethical High Ground*, by John Di Frances (Wales, WI: Reliance Books, 2002).

■ CHAPTER 6   EXPAND THE MODEL
  EXPONENTIALLY—BY MAKING IT PERSONAL

1. The next four excerpts are from Kremer's speech at the Third Annual Infinity Publishing "Express Yourself" Conference, Valley Forge, PA, October 3, 2002.

2. Bauer's Weekly Ethics Thought is available by e-mail subscription at http://www.bauerethicsseminars.com.

3. All of Burg's programs as well as his current blog articles are available directly from him, at http://www.burg.com.

■ CHAPTER 7   THE NEW MARKETING MATRIX

1. Roy Williams, *Secret Formulas of the Wizard of Ads* (Austin, TX: Wizard Academy Press, 1998), Ch. 47.

2. Visit http://www.freerice.com to see how one entrepreneur combines an ever-changing trivia contest with charitable causes to raise money for world hunger.

3. David Wood, "Pricing and Negotiating Fees," Solution Box e-newsletter, January 7, 2009, http://life-coaching-resource.com/blog/2005/11/mm-50-clever-strategy/.

■ CHAPTER 8 ABUNDANCE VERSUS SCARCITY

1. Scottie Claiborne, "Links Are Good for Business," *High Rankings Advisor*, November 20, 2002, http://www.highrankings.com/advisor.htm.

■ CHAPTER 9 BUILD POWERFUL ALLIANCES—WITH COMPETITORS, TOO

1. William Pride and O. C. Ferrell, *Marketing Concepts and Strategies* (12th ed.). (Boston: Houghton Mifflin, 2003), 56.

2. Assuming, of course, that paying for referrals is legal in your industry, within its code of ethics, and is properly disclosed.

3. *I-PR Digest*, Oct. 22, 2002, http://www.adventive.com.

4. Dave Pollard, *Finding the Sweet Spot: The Natural Entrepreneur's Guide to Responsible, Sustainable, Joyful Work* (White River Junction, VT: Chelsea Green, 2008), 184.

5. http://www.alexmandossian.com/2008/11/13/the-3-marketing-paradoxes-explained-part-3/.

6. Bob Bly, "Playing the Slots," *Early to Rise* e-zine, July 30, 2008, http://www.earlytorise.com/2008/07/30/playing-the-slots.html.

7. Electronic edition, September 2002. Published by the Cooperative Development Institute, Greenfield, MA. http://www.cdi.coop.

8. http://www.activewin.com/articles/general/article_10.shtml.

9. "Viral Marketing" by Steve Jurvetson and Tim Draper, January 1, 1997, http://www.dfj.com/news/article_26.shtml.

10. "6 Steps: Simple Referral Process Keeps Surge in Registrations Coming for UGC Site," January 22, 2009, http://www.marketingsherpa.com/article.php?ident=31011.

11. Reported in Yudkin's e-mail newsletter, "The Marketing Minute," September 25, 2002.

12. Marketing Sherpa, "Viral Email Nets 100% Response from Brand Champs: 3 Simple Steps," http://www.marketingsherpa.com/article.php?ident=30752&pop=no, August 5, 2008.

13. E-mail from Common Cause, January 5, 2009.

14. "Green America Victories: Thought and Action Leadership for a Green Economy," *Real Green,* Winter 2009, 8.

15. http://www.facebook.com/search/?q=whole+foods+boycott& init=quick.

16. Brian Clark, "How to Change the World Using Social Media," November 6, 2008, http://www.copyblogger.com/social-media-change/.

17. "Monday Morning Memo from the Wizard of Ads," December 12, 2004, http://www.mondaymorningmemo.com/?ShowMe= ThisMemo&MemoID=1534.

■ CHAPTER 10 HOW THE ABUNDANCE PARADIGM ELIMINATES THE NEED TO DOMINATE A MARKET AND ALLOWS YOU TO BETTER SERVE YOUR CUSTOMERS

1. Yes, we know that technically, Windows is not an operating system—but it functions as if it is one.

2. See, for instance, "Bill Gates' Secret? Better Products," by Stan Liebowitz in the *Wall Street Journal,* October 20, 1998: "In 1989, Microsoft Excel had a 90 percent share of the Macintosh spreadsheet market, but only a 10 percent share of the PC market. That same year Microsoft Word had a 51 percent share of the Macintosh word-processing market, but only 15 percent of the PC market." http://wwwpub.utdallas.edu/~liebowit/oped.html.

3. Jim Dalrymple, Jonathan Seff, and Philip Michaels, "Apple reports record profit for first quarter," *Macworld,* January 21, 2009, http://www.macworld.com/article/138362/2009/01/earnings.html.

4. Ian Fried, "New iMacs lift Apple's quarter," *CNet,* April 17, 2002, http://news.cnet.com/2100-1040-885301.html.

5. This conclusion is based on years of listening to complaints by software developers on various mailing lists. Eric Anderson of FutureThru group and Alan Canton of Pub 1-2-3 are two among many who have said it's too much bother to develop for the Mac.

6. Kevin and Jackie Freiberg, *Nuts! Southwest Airlines' Crazy Recipe for Business and Personal Success* (New York: Broadway Books, 1998).

7. E-mail communication, October 13, 2002.

■ CHAPTER 11 EXCEPTIONS: ARE THERE CASES WHEN
MARKET SHARE REALLY DOES MATTER?

1. http://www.entrepreneur.com/marketing/publicrelations/
prcolumnist/article172276.html.

2. This chapter owes much to the creative thinking of Patrick and
Jennifer Bishop's *Money Tree Marketing*, a book that we recommend highly for its ideas on how to create mutual benefit scenarios
in which you get paid to market your business by forming co-ops
and resale deals of various sorts. Not all their strategies are in the
mutual success/mutual assistance mode—in fact, there are quite
a number with which we strongly disagree—but enough are that
we're happy to recommend it. See www.guerrillamarketinggoes
green.com/resources for more on this book.

3. http://www.ducttapemarketing.com/sethgodin.pdf, downloaded
February 17, 2009.

4. *How Wal∗Mart Is Destroying America (and the World) and What You
Can Do about It*, by Bill Quinn (Berkeley, CA: Ten Speed Press, 2005)
and *Up Against the Wal-Marts*, by Don Taylor and Jeanne Smalling
Archer (New York: AMACOM, 2005).

■ CHAPTER 12 SOME *REAL* LOYALTY PROGAMS FROM
BIG COMPANIES

1. In fairness to the old paradigm, auto industry analyst Jim Ziegler
told Shel in a telephone interview on December 11, 2002, that although the no-negotiation rule makes the dealerships very profitable, GM has heavily subsidized the division, driving down the
price of the cars and taking a loss of about a billion dollars per
year.

2. "Saturn Honors 11 Retailers for Exceptional Performance," August 21, 2002, http://www.saturnfans.com/Company/2002/2002
summitaward.shtml.

3. "G.M. in Deal to Sell Saturn to Penske," http://www.jdpower.com/
corporate/news/releases/pressrelease.aspx?ID=2008250.

4. "G.M. in Deal to Sell Saturn to Penske," http://money.cnn
.com/2009/09/30/news/companies/penske_saturn/index.htm.

5. http://www.jdpower.com/autos/articles/Vehicle-Sales-
Satisfaction-Improves-For-Third-Straight-Year.

6. http://www.jdpower.com/autos/ratings/quality-ratings-by-brand.

■ CHAPTER 13 MARKETING GREEN

1. http://www.plentymag.com/features/2008/09/plenty_20.php.

2. Alan Greene, MD, "When Your Baby Comes Home: Choosing a Green Pediatrician," November 12, 2008, http://www.healthy wealthynwise.com/article.asp?Article=5565.

3. See, for example, this interview with Chelsea Green's publisher Margo Baldwin, which focuses on the environmental reasons, http://www.bookbusinessmag.com/article/working-toward-point-no-returns-chelsea-green-publisher-president-margo-baldwin-companys-green-partners-program-401270.html, as well as the story in the *Wall Street Journal* about Harper Collins' imprint HarperStudio's nonreturnable deal with Borders: http://online.wsj.com/article/SB122939936289409805.html.

4. Joel Makower *Strategies for the Green Economy* (New York: Macmillan, 2008). Excerpted at http://www.greenbiz.com/feature/2008/11/24/the-four-simple-steps-pitch-perfect-green-marketing.

5. Melissa Chungfat, "Junxion Strategy: Green marketing grows up," http://ecopreneurist.com/2009/03/18/junxion-strategy-green-marketing-grows-up/.

6. Based on information found at the company's web site. The site is another missed opportunity; as of December 22, 2008; nothing on either the Home or About page indicated any of the environmental sustainability pieces highlighted in the ad, which had run almost three months earlier.

7. http://beapreview.bookbusinessmag.com/publication/?m=5790 &l=1, page 13, downloaded May 22, 2009.

8. Fidlar-Doubleday E-Gram, September 18, 2008, prepared by Great Reach Communications.

9. Marcia Yudkin, "Show Your Heart," *Marketing Minute* e-zine, August 13, 2008.

10. http://www1.tide.com/en_US/tidecoldwater/energysavingstips .jsp.

11. Jacquelyn Ottman, "The Five Simple Rules of Green Marketing," http://www.greenmarketing.com/index.php/articles/.

12. http://www.clickz.com/3464211.

13. "What Sustainable Design Means to the Bottom Line: Autodesk: Designing a Greener Future for Businesses," http://www.bnet .com/2422-19726_23-283016.html?tag=content;col1.

14. Martijn Van Dam, Ship Environmental Officer, "Custodians of the Sea," lecture aboard the Holland America *MS Veendam,* January 17, 2009.

15. Sarah Fister Gale, "Eat, Drink and Be Greener," *GreenBiz,* December 8, 2008, http://www.greenbiz.com/feature/2008/12/08/eat-drink-and-get-greener.

16. "8 Steps to Roll Out a Successful Employee Relations Campaign + 2 Pitfalls to Avoid," MarketingSherpa.com, December 5, 2008, https://www.marketingsherpa.com/barrier.html?ident=30952#.

17. E. F. Schumacher Society, "Co-producers of Our Own Economies," e-mail blast, September 1, 2008.

18. BerkShares, "Local Shoppers take BerkShares to 2 Million Mark," e-mail, November 29, 2008.

19. Richie Davis, "U.S. agriculture census sees rise in area farming," *Daily Hampshire Gazette,* Northampton, MA, February 19, 2009, A1, B6.

20. Dan Barber, "Change We Can Stomach," *New York Times,* May 11, 2008, http://www.nytimes.com/2008/05/11/opinion/11barber.html?_r=2&oref=slogin&oref=slogin.

21. http://www.democracynow.org/2009/2/24/us_lags_behind_europe_in_regulating.

22. "Words That Sell," Futerra Sustainability Communications, as reported in Melissa Chungfat's article, "Words that 'Work': What to Write When Marketing Green," http://ecopreneurist.com/2008/12/10/words-that-work-what-to-write-when-marketing-green/. Futerra's full report can be downloaded from that link.

23. http://www.tomsofmaine.com/products/default.aspx.

24. Jacquelyn Ottman, "The Five Simple Rules of Green Marketing," http://www.greenmarketing.com/index.php/articles/.

25. Chris Brogan, "It's All About You," February 18, 2009, http://www.chrisbrogan.com/its-all-about-you/.

26. http://workcabin.ca/index.php?option=com_content&task=view&id=698&Itemid=34, December 1, 2008.

27. See, for example, Corporate Accountability International's "Think Outside the Bottle" campaign, http://www.stopcorporateabusenow.org/campaign/think_outside_the_bottleb_pledge.

28. Even watering down the claims may not have been enough. Many environmental activists have been arguing that bottled water has serious negative environmental consequences, and that

at least where tap water is safe, the environmental costs are unacceptable. See, for instance, http://www.allaboutwater.org/environment.html, among 99,600 citations returned in a Google search for ["bottled water" impact environment], April 12, 2009.

29. James Kanter, "Utilities Offer 'Green' Nuclear Plans to Customers," http://greeninc.blogs.nytimes.com/2009/01/01/utilities-offer-green-nuclear-plans-to-customers/.

30. By Shel, whose first book, *Nuclear Lessons* (Harrisburg, PA: Stackpole, 1980), was all about why nuclear power is a completely inappropriate way to generate electricity. But many others also raise this concern. Google returned 74,000 hits for "nuclear greenwashing" (no quotes) on January 1, 2009, including such respected sites as the San Francisco Bay Guardian, PR Watch, Greenpeace, and Fairness and Accuracy In Reporting (FAIR).

31. http://storywelch.wordpress.com/2008/11/09/the-growing-greenwash-backlash/.

32. http://sinsofgreenwashing.org.

■ CHAPTER 14   GETTING NOTICED IN THE NOISE AND CLUTTER: A BRIEF INTRODUCTION TO EFFECTIVE MARKETING TECHNIQUES

1. As quoted in Adventive's *I-Copywriting Digest,* No. 075, November 11, 2002.

2. Judith Sherven, Ph.D., and Jim Sniechowski, Ph.D., *The Heart of Marketing: Love Your Customers and They Will Love You Back* (Garden City, NY: Morgan James Publishing, 2009).

3. Ibid.

4. "Designing Truly Irresistible Offers: Simple, Quick and Easy Ways to Boost Sales Without Spending a Dime—Day Six," e-mail received December 23, 2008.

■ CHAPTER 15   PRACTICAL TOOLS FOR EFFECTIVE MARKETING

1. Price is current as of March 2009.

2. "How to Get Bloggers' Attention with Personalized Landing Pages & Videos," http://www.marketingsherpa.com/article.php?ident=30540.

3. Paul Krupin, of the media distribution service Direct Contact PR, put up a nice list of 22 media-attention triggers that can help bridge your story to the real news: http://blog.directcontactpr .com/public/getting-more-publicity-getting-more-sales-how-to-be-galvanizing.

4. *Grassroots Marketing* has 39 chapters and over 300 pages. It totals over 150,000 words—more than twice as much information as the roughly 65,000 words in this book.

5. As of November 22, 2008.

6. http://mashable.com/2008/10/31/great-twitter-moments/.

7. http://www.internetnews.com/webcontent/article.php/3790161/ What%20Keeps%20Twitter%20Chirping%20Along.htm.

8. http://www.google.com/search?q=comcast+repairman+sleep& ie=utf-8&oe=utf-8&aq=t&rls=org.mozilla:en-US:official& client=firefox-a.

9. All quoted Tweets in this section were found within the first two pages on profile pages, March 24, 2009.

10. http://www.thinking-outside-of-the-square.com/blog/2009/03/ 25-powerful-ways-and-more-twitter-can-improve-your-customer-service/.

11. HARO began as a Facebook group in November, 2007, and rapidly outgrew Facebook's then–group limit of 1200 members. Shankman set up http://www.helpareporter.com in March 2008 and began accepting advertising some months later. He now has several full-time staff, over 100,000 subscribers, and by April 2009, according to an article in Entrepreneur (http://www. entrepreneur.com/startingabusiness/youngentrepreneurscolumn istscottgerber/article201364.html) was projecting 2009 revenues above $1 million.

12. See, for instance, http://www.observer.com/2009/media/can-social-media-social-change-reinvent-charity-work-maybe (charity) or http://search.twitter.com/search?q=%23changetheweb (discussion).

13. Amanda Stillwagon, "27 Twitter Applications Your Small Business Can Use Today," http://www.smbceo.com/2009/03/top-27-twitter-applications/, March 25, 2009.

14. Chris Brogan, "How Hotels Can Win More Business Travel," March 13, 2009, http://www.chrisbrogan.com/how-hotels-can-win-more-business-travel/.

15. http://mashable.com/2009/03/09/twitter-brand-voice/.

16. Paul Gillis, "Why Twitter Beat Second Life," *B to B,* February 9, 2009, 9.

17. Obama's follower/following numbers as posted on his Twitter profile. Ranking and number of people being followed were found at http://twitterholic.com/top100/followers/, which seems to be a few days behind Twitter in its recordkeeping.

18. http://mashable.com/2009/01/01/social-microfunding/.

19. As reported at http://mashable.com/2009/03/09/social-network ing-more-popular-than-email/.

20. http://girlspace.kotex.com/index.jspa. Thanks to George Tran of i360connect.com, a provider of membership site software, for telling us about this site in his excellent e-book, "The Social Marketing Manifesto: How to Create Your Own Private Social Network to Grow Your Business." Available at http://snipurl.com/ socialmarketingmanifesto λ.

21. Ted Mininni, "Is Some of Nike's Current Success Due to Its 'Running' Social Network?" Marketing Profs, December 11, 2008, http://www.mpdailyfix.com/2008/12/is_some_of_nikes_current_ succe.html.

22. *WebMaster,* November/December 1995.

23. It doesn't have to be difficult, either. See www.guerrillamarket inggoesgreen.com/resources for a tool that inexpensively creates and hosts clued-in web sites that generate significant traffic.

24. Personal e-mail to Shel (October 31, 2002). Used with permission.

25. Kare Anderson, writing in *SpeakerNet News,* November 1, 2002. Used with permission.

26. The Iron Horse is a long-established concert venue in Northampton, Massachusetts; Herold, the founding owner and a very savvy marketer, is cited as a source in many sections of *Grassroots Marketing.*

27. http://www.marketingwords.com/blog/?p=455.

28. "23 Tips for a Successful Book Launch," *Book Business,* December 2008, 10.

29. All of these examples are taken from *Speaking Successfully: 1001 Tips for Thriving in the Speaking Business,* 1999 edition, edited by Ken Braly and Rebecca Morgan from tips that originally appeared in their *SpeakerNet News* e-zine. Order online at http://www. speakernetnews.com.

30. Personal e-mail to Shel from Tom Antion (December 8, 2002). Used with permission.

■ CHAPTER 16   GIVE THE PEOPLE WHAT THEY *WANT*

1. "Actions Speak Louder Than Words," MarketingProfs.com, November 4, 2003.

2. New York: McGraw-Hill/American Marketing Association, 2001.

3. Robert Middleton, "The Key to Inspiration," *More Clients* e-zine, February 4, 2008, http://actionplan.blogs.com/weblog/2008/02/the-key-to-insp.html. His main site is http://www.actionplan.com.

4. "Can Adding Instant Messaging Improve Your Site's Profits? One B-to-B Site's Story," August 6, 2002, https://www.marketingsherpa.com/barrier.html?ident=23047.

5. As of December 20, 2008.

6. http://www.targetmarketingmag.com/article/the-worlds-greatest-marketer-kids-start-em-young-you-got-em-life-32997.html.

7. Patrick Byers, "No bull: Marketing lessons from the ER," The Responsible Marketing Blog, December 15, 2008, http://responsiblemarketing.com/blog/?p=755.

8. Roy Williams, "Monday Morning Memo from the Wizard of Ads," 3/27/2006.

9. "Profit from Inbound Customer Service Tested," http://www.marketingexperiments.com/improving-website-conversion/profit-inbound-customer-service.html, November 28, 2005.

10. The Disney and Allstate sites were current as of February 19, 2009. The five anti-Wal-Mart, starbucked, and two general consumer sites are listed in Dr. Toni Cascio's article, "Have You Been Starbucked? (Part 1)," in *The Corporate Communicator* e-newsletter, February 23, 2009, http://www.bonmotcomms.com/newsletter/10.html.

11. Tom Watson, *Causewired: Plugging In, Getting Involved, Changing the World* (New York: Wiley, 2009), 124–127.

12. Bill Glazer. "The Sales PREVENTION Department," Bill Glazer & Dan Kennedy's No BS Marketing Letter, January 2009, 10.

13. http://strongrhetoric.blogspot.com/2008/11/case-study-dont-make-mommy-mad.html.

14. http://adage.com/article?article_id=132787.

15. "The Low Trust Epidemic: Why It Matters and What Communicators Can Do About It," December 2008 White Paper issued by

Bon Mot Communications, LLC, http://www.bonmotcomms.com (available for download on both the Home and Resources pages as of February 23, 2009).

16. http://blogs.zappos.com/blogs/ceo-and-coo-blog/2008/11/06/update, November 6, 2008.

17. http://twitter.zappos.com/employee_tweets/2008/11/6/11.

18. "Here's Why Amazon Bought Zappos," http://mashable.com/2009/07/22/amazon-bought-zappos/.

19. Meghan Meehan, "Rubbermaid Improves Customer Experience through Ratings & Reviews," http://www.bazaarblog.com/2009/03/09/rubbermaid-improves-customer-experience-through-ratings-reviews/, March 9, 2009.

20. http://frugalmarketing.com/newsletters/2008/12/16/positive-power-spotlight-tyson-foods/.

21. "Protect Your Image on the Digital Highway: 7 Tips & No-Cost Tools to Prevent a PR Nightmare," http://www.marketingsherpa.com/article.php?ident=30793&pop=no, August 26, 2008.

22. MarketingSherpa.com, "Dow Jones Steers Marketing with Plenty of Social Media Data: 7 Key Strategies," December 9, 2008, https://www.marketingsherpa.com/barrier.html?ident=30954.

■ CHAPTER 17 MARKETING AS SOCIAL CHANGE, AND SOCIAL CHANGE AS MARKETING

1. Jay Conrad Levinson, *The Guerrilla Entrepreneur* (Garden City, NY: Morgan James Publishing, 2007), 113.

2. http://www.britannica.com/EBchecked/topic/97239/Jimmy-Carter, viewed November 25, 2008.

3. http://query.nytimes.com/gst/fullpage.html?res=9F0CE3DE153E F936A2575BC0A965958260, viewed November 25, 2008.

4. Stephen B. Oates, *Let the Trumpet Sound: The Life of Martin Luther King, Jr.* (New York: Plume, 1983), 56.

5. *Baltimore Sun* article, quoted in the *Daily Hampshire Gazette* (Northampton, MA, January 15, 2001), 1.

6. Barbara Waugh, *The Soul in the Computer: The Story of a Corporate Revolutionary* (Makawa, Hawaii: Inner Ocean Publishing, 2001).

■ CHAPTER 18 COMMUNITY-FOCUSED AND CHARITY/SOCIAL CHANGE MARKETING

1. B&J's board member Terry Mollner, interviewed by Shel, April 13, 2009. While B&J's is now owned by the multinational food conglomerate Unilever, its popularity and market share long predated its acquisition.

2. The company was founded under the Häagen-Dazs name in 1961; its origins trace back to a family-owned ice-cream wagon in the 1920s (Ben & Jerry's was founded in 1978). Pillsbury bought Häagen-Dazs in 1983; Nestlé owns it as of this writing—and the two brands together account for 87 percent of the superpremium category, according to B&J's board member Terry Mollner in an interview conducted April 13, 2009.

3. Terry Mollner, "Common Good Investing: The Next Stage in the Evolution of Socially Responsible Investing," unpublished paper, slightly repunctuated for clarity. The 28-company study Mollner cites is found in *Firms of Endearment: How World-Class Companies Profit from Passion and Purpose*, by Rajendra S. Sisodia, David B. Wolfe, and Jagdish N. Sheth (Philadelphia: Wharton School Publishing, 2007).

4. Telephone interview with Meagan Finnegan, Development and Marketing Coordinator, Food Bank of Western Massachusetts, March 31, 2009.

■ CHAPTER 19 TAKING THE CONCEPT BEYOND MARKETING: ABUNDANCE AND SUSTAINABILITY IN BUSINESSES AND IN SOCIETY

1. http://www.usatoday.com/travel/columnist/grossman/2008-09-19-bottled-water_N.htm, September 19, 2008.

2. Both speeches were given to the E. F. Schumacher Society, http://www.smallisbeautiful.org, in Amherst, Massachusetts, October 27, 2001. You'll find the complete articles, along with several other good pieces, in the Sustainable Business section of *Down to Business* magazine, http://www.frugalmarketing.com/dtb/dtb.shtml, as well as hundreds of articles on smart marketing and entrepreneurship in other sections of the magazine.

3. "Four Wheelin'," *Utne Reader*, November–December 2008, 17.

4. Information on the home page of http://www.mrelliepooh.com as of February 7, 2009: "According to 'The State of the Paper Industry (2007),' a report by the Environmental Paper Network, 50% of the world's forests have been cleared or burned, and 80% of what's left has been seriously degraded. If the United States cut office paper use by just 10%, it would prevent the emission of 1.6 million tons of greenhouse gases—the equivalent of taking 280,000 cars off the road. http://www.greenpressinitiative.org/documents/StateOfPaperInd.pdf.

   "Compared to using virgin wood, paper made with 100% recycled content uses 44% less energy, produces 38% less greenhouse gas emissions, 41% less particulate emissions, 50% less wastewater, 49% less solid waste and—of course—100% less wood." [Another source for this is http://www.copperwiki.org/index.php/Recycled_paper].

   Information regarding the interactions of elephants and agriculture, and how this project turns elephants from a pest into a resource, is located at http://www.mrelliepooh.com/aboutus.html.

5. As quoted in Dave Pollard, *Finding the Sweet Spot: The Natural Entrepreneur's Guide to Responsible, Sustainable, Joyful Work* (White River Junction, VT: Chelsea Green, 2008), 148.

6. Kellie A. McElhaney, *Just Good Business: The Strategic Guide to Aligning Corporate Responsibility and Brand* (San Francisco: Berrett-Koehler, 2008), 57–58.

7. Christopher Bauer, "An Ethics Thought—More On Why Aren't Ethics Problems Reported," *Weekly Ethics Thought* e-zine, November 17, 2008.

■ CHAPTER 20   ABUNDANCE AND WEALTH CREATION

1. Perry Marshall, "Business = Alchemy," September 30, 2008, http://perrymarshall.wordpress.com/2008/09/30/business-alchemy/. His main web site is http://www.perrymarshall.com.

2. Myelita Melton, "Muchas Gracias to All of You!," e-mail newsletter, November 20, 2008.

Index